Dining with Pioneers

Volume Three

CHAPTER 21

First Printing 2005 15,000 copies
Printed in the United States of America

Manufactured by
Favorite Recipes® Press
an imprint of

FRP™

P.O. Box 305142
Nashville, Tennessee 37230
1-800-358-0560

Table of Contents

In Appreciation

Dining With Pioneers, Volume III, was made possible by the efforts of dedicated individuals who took on the task of beating the bushes for recipes, and the employees and retirees who shared their favorite recipes with us. How could we top Volumes I and II? I think we have a winner. We are especially grateful to Terry Wright, Annie Jane Hayes, and Carol Conley, who did the lion's share of the work compiling the book.

Our deepest thanks to you for your purchase of this book. Funds raised are used by BellSouth employees and retirees engaged in community service projects and education initiatives. They are enthusiastic, tireless, and committed to making our communities a better place. For more information on our projects, see our website: www.bellsouth.com/community.

An attempt was made to use all recipes submitted, and we regret if there are errors or omissions.

Benny Carrell

Benny Carrell, President
BellSouth Volunteer Board of Directors
Tennessee Chapter 21, TelecomPioneers

APPETIZERS AND BEVERAGES

EASY SHRIMP QUICHES

1 (8-count) can refrigerator crescent rolls
3/4 cup finely chopped cooked fresh or frozen shrimp
1/2 cup heavy cream
1 egg, beaten
1/4 teaspoon salt
1/8 teaspoon cayenne pepper, or to taste
1/2 cup (2 ounces) shredded Swiss cheese

Unroll the dough, pressing the perforations to seal. Cut into 24 squares. Press each square over the bottom and 2/3 up the side of a greased muffin cup. Spoon about 2 teaspoons of the shrimp into each cup. Combine the heavy cream, egg, salt and cayenne pepper in a small bowl and mix well. Pour about 2 teaspoons of the mixture into each muffin cup. Sprinkle with equal portions of the cheese. Bake at 375 degrees for 18 to 20 minutes or until golden brown. Serves 12.

Sonya Van Cleave
Memphis, Tennessee

PECAN CHICKEN FINGERS

6 boneless skinless chicken breasts
1 cup all-purpose flour
1 cup pecans, toasted and ground
1/4 cup sesame seeds
1 tablespoon paprika
3/4 teaspoon salt
1/8 teaspoon pepper
1 egg, lightly beaten
1 cup buttermilk
1/3 cup butter, melted

Cut each chicken breast into 4 strips. Combine the flour, pecans, sesame seeds, paprika, salt and pepper and mix well. Combine the egg and buttermilk in a small bowl and mix well. Dip the chicken into the egg mixture. Coat with the flour mixture. Pour the butter into a 10x15-inch baking pan. Add the chicken, turning to coat. Bake at 375 degrees for 30 minutes or until the chicken is cooked through. Remove to a serving plate using a slotted spoon. Garnish with lettuce leaves and lemon slices. Serves 24.

Peggy Burr
Nashville, Tennessee

SHERRIED MUSHROOM EMPANADAS

2 onions, finely chopped
6 tablespoons unsalted butter
1 1/2 pounds mushrooms, finely chopped
2 small red bell peppers, finely chopped
1 (6-ounce) piece serrano ham or prosciutto, finely chopped
1/3 cup cream sherry
1/2 cup packed minced fresh parsley leaves
3 tablespoons dry bread crumbs
Salt and pepper to taste
1 egg
1 teaspoon water
1 (17-ounce) package frozen puff pastry, thawed

Cook the onions in the butter in a 12-inch skillet over medium-low heat until tender, stirring occasionally. Stir in the mushrooms and bell peppers. Cook over medium heat until the liquid from the mushrooms has evaporated and the mixture begins to brown, stirring occasionally. Add the ham and sherry and cook until the liquid has evaporated, stirring occasionally. Combine the mushroom mixture, parsley and bread crumbs in a bowl and mix well. Season with salt and pepper. Let stand until cool. Beat the egg and water in a cup. Place 1 pastry sheet on a lightly floured surface. Roll pastry into a 10×14-inch rectangle. Cut lengthwise into halves using a long sharp knife. Spread 1/2 of 1 pastry sheet with 1/2 the mushroom mixture, leaving a 1-inch border. Brush some of the egg mixture over the pastry border. Place the remaining pastry sheet 1/2 on top, crimping the edges with a fork to seal. Cut several slits in the top using a small sharp knife. Repeat the procedure using the remaining pastry sheet, mushroom mixture and egg mixture. Remove the empanadas to a baking sheet using 2 spatulas. Brush with the remaining egg mixture. Bake on the center oven rack at 375 degrees for 35 minutes or until golden brown. Remove to a serving platter. Cut into 3/4-inch slices. Serves 8 to 10.

Linda Giles
Knoxville, Tennessee

SAUSAGE RO-TEL SQUARES

1 pound bulk pork sausage
1 can Ro-Tel
8 ounces cream cheese
2 (8-count) cans refrigerator crescent rolls

Brown the sausage with the Ro-Tel in a skillet over medium-high heat, stirring until crumbly; drain. Stir in the cream cheese. Unroll 1 can of dough, pressing the perforations to seal. Press over the bottom of a 9×13-inch baking dish sprayed with nonstick cooking spray. Spread evenly with the sausage mixture. Unroll the remaining can of dough, pressing the perforations to seal. Place on top of the sausage mixture. Bake until golden brown using the crescent roll package directions. Let stand for 10 minutes. Cut into squares and serve. Serves 24.

Catherine Brooks
Memphis, Tennessee

HAM AND CHEESE SQUARES

2 cups baking mix
3/4 cup chopped ham
1 cup (4 ounces) shredded cheese
1/2 cup (2 ounces) grated Parmesan cheese
1/2 cup chopped onion
1/4 cup sour cream
2 teaspoons parsley
1/2 teaspoon salt
2 garlic cloves, crushed
2/3 cup milk
1 egg

Combine the baking mix, ham, cheeses, onion, sour cream, parsley, salt, garlic, milk and egg in a bowl and mix well. Spoon into a greased 9x13-inch baking pan. Bake at 350 degrees for 30 to 35 minutes or until brown. Serves 18.

Cathy Funderburk
Knoxville, Tennessee

HAM AND CHEESE ROLLS

2 packages dinner party rolls
1 cup (2 sticks) margarine, melted
3 tablespoons prepared mustard
2 tablespoons Worcestershire sauce
1 onion, finely chopped
3 tablespoons poppy seeds
1 pound cooked canned ham, thinly sliced
1 package sliced Swiss cheese

Remove the rolls from the aluminum pan and cut horizontally into halves. Combine the margarine, mustard, Worcestershire sauce, onion and poppy seeds in a bowl and mix well. Spread over cut sides of the rolls. Layer the ham and cheese on the bottom halves of the rolls. Replace the top halves of the rolls and wrap in foil. Bake at 350 degrees for 20 to 25 minutes or until the cheese is melted. Serves 12 to 16.

Dawn Grant
Nashville, Tennessee

PIGS IN A BLANKET

1 (8-count) can refrigerator crescent rolls
16 cocktail franks

Unroll the dough and separate into triangles. Cut each triangle lengthwise into halves. Place a frank on the long side of each triangle half and roll up. Arrange on an ungreased 9x12-inch baking sheet. Bake at 375 degrees for 12 to 15 minutes or until golden brown. You may add a strip of cheese around each frank for added flavor. Serves 8.

Katherine Williams
Talbott, Tennessee

SWEET AND TANGY COCKTAIL FRANKS

1/2 cup apple jelly or grape jelly
1/4 cup barbecue sauce
1/4 cup ketchup
1/2 cup water
1 package cocktail franks

Mix the jelly, barbecue sauce, ketchup and water in a saucepan. Add the franks and cook over medium heat for 20 to 25 minutes or until heated through. Serves 10 to 12.

Marie Guy
Clinton, Tennessee

SMOKY BACON WRAPS

2 pounds center-cut bacon
1 (1-pound) package cocktail franks
1 cup packed brown sugar

Wrap 1 bacon slice around each frank. Arrange in a foil-lined 10x15-inch baking pan. Sprinkle with the brown sugar. Bake at 400 degrees for 30 to 40 minutes or until the bacon is crisp and the sausage is heated through. Serve warm.
Serves 10 to 12.

Ann Montgomery
Sevierville, Tennessee

PARTY MEATBALLS

1 1/2 pounds ground beef
1/2 cup dry bread crumbs
1/2 cup milk
1 egg, beaten
1/4 cup chopped onion
1 1/2 teaspoons salt
1/4 teaspoon pepper
1/4 teaspoon garlic salt
2 cups spaghetti sauce

Mix the first 8 ingredients in a bowl. Shape into balls and arrange in a baking pan. Bake at 325 degrees for 30 minutes or until brown; drain. Top with the spaghetti sauce and bake for 30 minutes longer. Makes (about) 35 meatballs.

Cathy Funderburk
Knoxville, Tennessee

COCKTAIL MEATBALLS

2 pounds ground round
1 cup cornflake crumbs
1/3 cup dried parsley
2 eggs
2 tablespoons soy sauce
1 teaspoon pepper
1 teaspoon garlic powder
2 tablespoons minced onion
1/3 cup ketchup
1 (16-ounce) can cranberry sauce
1 (12-ounce) bottle chili sauce
2 tablespoons dark brown sugar
1 tablespoon lemon juice

Combine the first 9 ingredients in a bowl and mix well. Shape into 1 1/2-inch meatballs and arrange in a 9x12-inch baking dish. Bake at 350 degrees for 20 minutes; drain. Combine the cranberry sauce, chili sauce, brown sugar and lemon juice in a saucepan over medium heat. Cook until the cranberry sauce is melted, stirring frequently. Pour over the meatballs and bake for 20 minutes longer. Makes (about) 50 meatballs.

Katherine Williams
Talbott, Tennessee

CHILE AND CHEESE SPIRALS

4 ounces cream cheese, softened
1 cup (4 ounces) shredded Cheddar cheese
1 (4-ounce) can chopped green chiles
3 green onions, sliced
1/2 cup chopped red bell pepper
1 (2-ounce) can chopped black olives
4 (8-inch) flour tortillas
1 cup salsa

Combine the cream cheese, Cheddar cheese, green chiles, green onions, bell pepper and black olives in a bowl and mix well. Spread 1/2 cup of the mixture over each tortilla and roll to enclose. Wrap each roll in plastic wrap and chill for 1 hour. Cut each roll into six 3/4-inch slices. Serve with the salsa.
Serves 24.

Barbara Kirby
Jackson, Tennessee

SPINACH BACON MYSTERIES

$1/2$ cup (1 stick) butter
$1/3$ cup water
8 ounces bulk pork hot sausage
2 (10-ounce) packages frozen spinach, thawed and drained
2 cups seasoned stuffing mix
1 cup (4 ounces) grated Parmesan cheese
2 eggs, lightly beaten
2 pounds bacon

Melt the butter in the water in a saucepan. Add the sausage, spinach, stuffing mix, cheese and eggs and mix well. Cut each bacon slice into 3 pieces. Shape the sausage mixture into $1/2$-inch balls. Wrap a piece of bacon around each ball and secure with a wooden pick. Arrange on a broiler pan. Bake at 375 degrees until cooked through, about 10 to 15 minutes. The balls may be frozen and reheated.

Makes (about) 85 balls.

Addie Downs
Antioch, Tennessee

SPINACH ROLL-UPS

1 cup mayonnaise
1 cup sour cream
3 green onions, chopped
1 envelope ranch salad dressing mix
1 (3-ounce) jar bacon bits
1 (10-ounce) package frozen chopped spinach, thawed and drained
9 (10-inch) flour tortillas

Combine the mayonnaise, sour cream, green onions, salad dressing mix and bacon bits in a bowl and mix well. Fold in the spinach. Chill, covered, for 1 hour. Warm the tortillas using the package directions. Spread 2 tablespoons spinach mixture over each warm tortilla. Roll to enclose the filling and press the edges to seal. Arrange on a plate and chill, covered, for 4 to 6 hours. Cut the roll-ups into $1/2$-inch or larger slices. The filling may also be used as a dip for crackers. Serves 48.

Jane Burchfield
Knoxville, Tennessee

STUFFED CELERY

8 ounces cream cheese, softened
1/4 cup mayonnaise
1 cup chopped pecans
3/4 to 1 teaspoon Beau Monde seasoning
1 garlic clove, crushed
1/4 cup chopped fresh parsley
10 ribs celery, cut into 3-inch pieces
Paprika

Combine the cream cheese, mayonnaise, pecans, Beau Monde seasoning, garlic and parsley in a bowl and mix well. Fill each piece of celery with cream cheese mixture. Arrange on a serving plate and sprinkle with paprika. Chill, covered, for 8 to 10 hours. Makes 2 1/2 dozen appetizers.

Peggy Burr
Nashville, Tennessee

VEGGIE PIZZA

2 (8-count) cans refrigerator crescent rolls
16 ounces cream cheese, softened
1 cup mayonnaise
1 envelope ranch salad dressing mix
Broccoli, chopped
Cauliflower, chopped
Green or red bell pepper, chopped
Carrots, shredded
1 cup (4 ounces) shredded Cheddar cheese
1 cup (4 ounces) shredded mozzarella cheese

Unroll the dough and arrange on a baking sheet to form a large rectangle, pressing the perforations to seal. Bake at 375 degrees for 12 minutes. Let stand until completely cool. Cream the cream cheese, mayonnaise and salad dressing mix in a mixing bowl. Spread over the cooled crust. Layer with the broccoli, cauliflower, bell pepper and carrots. Sprinkle with the Cheddar cheese and mozzarella cheese. Chill, covered, until serving time. Cut into squares to serve.
Makes 3 to 4 dozen squares.

Barbara Griffin and JoAnne Rudd
Knoxville, Tennessee

VEGGIE PATCHES

2 (8-count) cans refrigerator crescent rolls
1 egg, beaten
16 ounces cream cheese, softened
1 cup mayonnaise
1 envelope ranch salad dressing mix
1/2 cup each finely chopped broccoli, cauliflower, mushrooms, green bell pepper, tomato and black olives
3/4 cup (3 ounces) shredded Cheddar cheese

Unroll the dough and press over the bottom of a 10x15-inch baking pan, pressing the perforations to seal. Brush with the egg. Bake at 375 degrees for 11 to 13 minutes. Let stand on a wire rack until completely cool. Beat the cream cheese, mayonnaise and salad dressing mix in a mixing bowl until smooth. Spread over the cooled crust. Sprinkle evenly with the broccoli, cauliflower, mushrooms, bell pepper, tomato, black olives and Cheddar cheese. Cut into small squares to serve. Recipe may be halved. Makes 3 to 4 dozen squares.

Barbara Duncan
Hernando, Mississippi

FAVORITE DEVILED EGGS

6 eggs, hard-cooked and finely chopped
1 teaspoon minced onion
3 slices bacon, crisp-cooked and crumbled
1/2 teaspoon salt (optional)
1/2 teaspoon pepper
1/4 teaspoon prepared mustard
1/4 cup mayonnaise
1 cup (4 ounces) shredded Cheddar cheese

Combine the eggs, onion, bacon, salt, pepper, mustard and mayonnaise in a bowl and mix well. Shape into 1-inch balls and coat with cheese. Arrange on a plate. Chill, covered, until serving time. Makes 25 appetizers.

Addie Downs
Antioch, Tennessee

PICKLED FIGS

6 quarts water
1 cup baking soda
7 pounds figs with stems
1 quart vinegar
7 cups sugar
3 tablespoons pickling spices

Bring 6 quarts water to a boil in a stockpot. Add the baking soda gradually to prevent the mixture from boiling over, stirring constantly. Remove from the heat. Add the figs and let stand for 10 minutes; drain. Rinse the figs twice under cold water. Place in a stockpot. Add the vinegar, sugar and pickling spices. Bring to a boil. Reduce the heat and simmer for 30 minutes. Ladle into hot sterilized jars, leaving 1-inch headspace; seal with 2-piece lids. Process in a boiling water bath for 10 minutes. Makes 6 pints.

Hazel Peeples
Southhaven, Mississippi

PICKLES

4 cups sugar
1/2 cup canning salt
1 quart vinegar
1/2 teaspoon turmeric
1/2 teaspoon mustard seeds
1/2 teaspoon celery seeds
1 gallon cucumbers, sliced
3 onions, chopped
1 large bell pepper, chopped

Combine the sugar, canning salt, vinegar, turmeric, mustard seeds and celery seeds in a bowl and mix well. Combine the cucumbers, onions and bell pepper in a gallon jar. Pour the sugar mixture over the cucumber mixture. Chill, covered, for up to 1 year. Serves 20.

Janice Gibson
Trenton, Tennessee

14-DAY SWEET PICKLES

2 gallons cucumbers, sliced
2 cups non-iodized salt
4 tablespoons alum
6 cups sugar
5 cups apple cider vinegar
2 cups sugar
1/3 cup pickling spices, tied in a bag
1 cup sugar
1 tablespoon celery seeds

Place the cucumbers in a crock jar. Bring 1 gallon of water to a boil in a saucepan. Add the non-iodized salt and stir to dissolve. Pour over the cucumbers. Let stand, covered, for 7 days. Drain the cucumbers on day 8. Bring 1 gallon of water and 1 tablespoon alum to a boil in a saucepan. Pour over the cucumbers in the crock jar. Let stand, covered, for 1 day. Drain the cucumbers. Repeat boiling alum water, soaking and draining 3 times. Drain the cucumbers on day 12. Bring 6 cups sugar and vinegar to a boil in a saucepan. Pour over the cucumbers. Let stand, covered, for 1 day. Drain the cucumbers, reserving the liquid in a saucepan. Add 2 cups sugar to the reserved liquid and bring to a boil, stirring to dissolve the sugar. Pour over the cucumbers. Let stand, covered, for 1 day. Drain the cucumbers, reserving the liquid in a saucepan. Add the pickling spices and 1 cup sugar to the reserved liquid and bring to a boil, stirring to dissolve the sugar. Simmer until the syrup is seasoned to taste. Remove the spice bag. Stir in the celery seeds. Pack the cucumbers into hot sterilized 1-pint jars. Add the syrup, leaving 1/2 inch headspace; seal with 2-piece lids. Process in a boiling water bath for 10 minutes. Makes 12 pints.

Glenda Buchanan
College Grove, Tennessee

HOT PICKLES

1 gallon kosher dill pickles
1 (16-ounce) jar jalapeño chiles
5 cups sugar
1 garlic clove

Drain the pickles and jalapeño chiles. Slice the pickles. Layer the pickles, jalapeño chiles, sugar and garlic in a 1-gallon jar until all of the ingredients are used. Cover with plastic wrap, then with the lid. Let stand for 3 to 5 days or until the sugar is dissolved, turning the jar over frequently. Makes 1 gallon.

Doris Volz
Memphis, Tennessee

MARINATED ROASTED PEPPERS

2 large red bell peppers
2 large green bell peppers
1/4 cup olive oil
2 tablespoons chopped fresh parsley
1 1/2 tablespoons white wine vinegar
1 garlic clove, minced
1/4 teaspoon salt
1/4 teaspoon pepper

Arrange the bell peppers on a piece of foil. Bake at 500 degrees for 25 minutes. Place in an airtight container. Let stand, covered, for 10 minutes to loosen the skins. Remove the skins. Cut the bell peppers into halves and remove the seeds. Cut into strips and place in a shallow bowl. Combine the olive oil, parsley, vinegar, garlic, salt and pepper in a bowl and mix well. Pour over the bell peppers. Chill, covered, for 8 hours. Serve on ham or turkey sandwiches or as desired. Serves 8.

Nina and Melba Morris
Carthage, Tennessee

CARAMEL POPCORN

4 cups popped popcorn
1 cup nuts (optional)
1/2 cup (1 stick) butter or margarine
1/4 cup light corn syrup
1 cup packed light brown sugar
1/2 teaspoon salt
1/2 teaspoon baking soda

Combine the popcorn and nuts in a bowl and toss to mix. Melt the butter in a saucepan over medium-high heat. Stir in the corn syrup, brown sugar and salt. Cook until bubbly around the edge. Continue to cook for 4 minutes, stirring constantly. Remove from the heat and stir in the baking soda until foamy. Pour over the popcorn mixture and stir to coat. Spread on a buttered baking sheet. Bake at 200 degrees for 1 hour, stirring every 15 minutes. Makes 6 to 8 servings.

Kathy Duncan
Memphis, Tennessee

PUPPY CHOW PARTY MIX

12 ounces semisweet chocolate chips
1 (10-ounce) jar peanut butter
1/2 cup (1 stick) butter
Peanuts or pecans (optional)
1 (18-ounce) package Golden Honey Grahams cereal
1 (1-pound) package confectioners' sugar

Melt the chocolate chips, peanut butter and butter in a saucepan over medium heat, stirring constantly. Combine the peanuts and cereal in a bowl and mix well. Pour the chocolate mixture over the cereal and stir to coat. Place in a clean paper bag. Add the confectioners' sugar and shake to coat.
Serves 18 to 20.

Barbara Johnson
Collierville, Tennessee

ANGEL WINGS

1 package 7- to 8-inch tortillas
Vegetable oil for frying
2 cups sugar
2 teaspoons ground cinnamon

Cut each tortilla into quarters. Cook in the oil in a deep skillet for 1 minute or until light brown and crispy; drain on paper towels. Combine the sugar and cinnamon in a large sealable plastic bag and shake to mix. Add the tortilla chips in batches, shaking to coat. Serves 12 to 15.

Nancy Bassett
Nashville, Tennessee

CANDIED CITRUS PECANS

2 cups sugar
1 teaspoon lemon juice
2/3 cup frozen orange juice concentrate, thawed
1 tablespoon grated orange zest
3 cups pecan halves

Combine the sugar, lemon juice and orange juice concentrate in a 2-quart saucepan. Bring to a boil over medium heat, stirring constantly. Reduce the heat to low. Cook for 15 to 20 minutes or to 234 to 240 degrees on a candy thermometer, soft-ball stage; do not overcook. Remove from the heat. Add the orange zest and pecans and stir for 7 to 10 minutes or until the mixture is cream colored. Spoon onto waxed paper. Let stand until completely cool. Break into small clusters. Store in an airtight container. Serves 12.

Nancy Bassett
Nashville, Tennessee

SPICED PECANS

1 3/4 cups sugar
2 teaspoons ground cinnamon
1/4 teaspoon ground allspice
1/2 teaspoon ginger
1/4 teaspoon ground cloves
1/4 teaspoon salt
1/4 teaspoon cream of tartar
8 tablespoons water
4 cups pecan halves, at room temperature

Combine the sugar, cinnamon, allspice, ginger, cloves, salt, cream of tartar and water in a large saucepan. Bring to a boil, stirring constantly. Cook over medium heat until the mixture forms a ball when dropped in cold water, stirring constantly. Stir in the pecans. Remove from the heat. Stir until the pecans are well coated; the glaze will change from shiny to dull when the pecans are well coated. Spread in a single layer on a piece of foil, separating the pecans using a fork. Let stand until cool. Serve with plain candy-coated chocolate candies. Serves 16.

Mackie Jernigan
Memphis, Tennessee

COFFEE AND SPICE PECANS

1 tablespoon instant coffee granules
1/2 cup sugar
1/2 teaspoon ground cinnamon
Dash of salt
1/4 cup water
3 cups pecan halves, toasted

Combine the coffee granules, sugar, cinnamon, salt and water in a saucepan. Cook until the sugar is dissolved, stirring constantly. Add the pecans and bring to a boil. Cook for 3 minutes, stirring constantly. Spread in a single layer on waxed paper, separating the pecans using a fork. Let stand until completely cool. Store in an airtight container. Makes 3 cups.

Sue Tronnes
Woodlawn, Tennessee

CHEESE LOAF

16 ounces Velveeta cheese
8 ounces bulk pork sausage
Ground red pepper
Chili powder

Melt the cheese in a saucepan over medium heat, stirring constantly. Brown the sausage in a skillet, stirring until crumbly; drain. Stir the sausage into the cheese. Grease 2 small aluminum loaf pans with butter. Sprinkle with red pepper and chili powder. Pour equal portions of the cheese mixture into each pan. Chill, covered, until set. Serve at room temperature with assorted crackers. Serves 24.

Gwen Spalding
Hermitage, Tennessee

CHOPPED BEEF CHEESE BALL

2 packages sliced roast beef
1 green onion, minced
16 ounces cream cheese, softened
1/2 teaspoon MSG

Chop the roast beef in a food processor. Mix the green onion, cream cheese, MSG and 1/2 of the roast beef in a bowl. Shape into a ball. Coat with the remaining roast beef. Chill, covered, for 1 hour or longer. Serve with crackers. Serves 24.

Allison Turner
Memphis, Tennessee

CHEESE BALL

16 ounces cream cheese, softened
1 tablespoon seasoned salt
1 teaspoon chopped onion
1/4 cup chopped green bell pepper
1 (8-ounce) can crushed pineapple, drained

Mix all the ingredients in a bowl. Shape into a ball. Chill, covered, for 8 hours. Serve with crackers. Serves 16 to 20.

Elaine Huff
Harrison, Tennessee

CHEESE BALL

2 cups (8 ounces) shredded sharp Cheddar cheese
2 cups (8 ounces) shredded mild Cheddar cheese
16 ounces cream cheese, softened
1 cup finely chopped pecans
1 pound bacon, crisp-cooked and crumbled
1 envelope onion soup mix
1/4 cup paprika
1/4 cup chili powder

Combine the Cheddar cheeses, cream cheese, pecans, bacon and soup mix in a bowl and mix well. Shape into a ball and coat with the paprika and chili powder. Chill, covered, until serving time. Serves 32.

Bonnie Chadwell
Nashville, Tennessee

CHEESE ROLL

4 cups (16 ounces) shredded sharp Cheddar cheese
8 ounces cream cheese, softened
1/2 cup chopped pecans
1/2 teaspoon salt
1 teaspoon garlic powder
1/2 teaspoon Worcestershire sauce
1/2 teaspoon Tabasco sauce
1/2 teaspoon red pepper
1/2 teaspoon paprika

Combine the Cheddar cheese and cream cheese in a bowl and mix well. Add the pecans, salt, garlic powder, Worcestershire sauce and Tabasco sauce and mix well. Divide into 2 rolls and coat with red pepper and paprika. Chill, covered, until set. Serves 24.

Colleen Ferguson
Loudon, Tennessee

CANNED PIMENTO SPREAD

25 pimentos
1 1/2 cups vinegar
1 quart mayonnaise-style salad dressing
1 1/2 cups sugar
2 tablespoons salt, or to taste
2 pounds Velveeta cheese or American cheese, shredded

Cut the pimentos into halves and remove the seeds. Grind the pimentos; drain. Combine the pimentos and vinegar in a saucepan and cook over medium heat until tender, stirring occasionally. Add the salad dressing, sugar and salt and mix well. Cook until thickened, stirring constantly. Ladle into hot sterilized pint jars, leaving 1/2 inch headspace; seal with 2-piece lids. Process in a boiling water bath for 10 minutes. To serve, mix the cheese with 1 pint pimento spread in a bowl and serve as desired. You may chill the cheese mixture, covered, for up to 2 weeks. Makes 16 pints.

Janice Gibson
Trenton, Tennessee

GARLIC SPREAD

1 garlic bulb
Olive oil
Salt and pepper to taste

Cut the top off the garlic bulb to expose the cloves. Place cut side up on a baking sheet. Coat with olive oil and season with salt and pepper. Broil for 10 minutes or until tender. Squeeze the cloves into a bowl and mash with a fork. Serve with toasted French baguette slices, any firm bread slices or crackers. Serves 12 to 16.

Jesse Johnson
Knoxville, Tennessee

TOASTED ALMOND PARTY SPREAD

8 ounces cream cheese, softened
1 to 1 1/2 cups (4 to 6 ounces) shredded Swiss cheese
1/3 cup mayonnaise-style salad dressing
2 tablespoons chopped green onions
1/8 teaspoon nutmeg
1/8 teaspoon pepper
1/4 cup sliced or slivered almonds, toasted

Combine the cream cheese, Swiss cheese, salad dressing, green onions, nutmeg, pepper and almonds in a bowl and mix well. Spread in a 9-inch pie plate. Bake at 350 degrees for 8 minutes. Stir the mixture and continue to bake for 7 minutes. Garnish with additional toasted almonds. Serve with bread cubes, crackers, corn chips or Triscuits. You may prepare the spread a day or two ahead and chill, covered, until ready to bake. Makes 1 1/2 cups.

Glenda Buchanan
College Grove, Tennessee

COLD "PIZZA"

8 ounces cream cheese, softened
1 bottle cocktail sauce
1 small can lump crab meat, drained
1 bunch green onions, chopped
1 green bell pepper, chopped
1 large tomato, chopped
2 cups (8 ounces) shredded mozzarella cheese

Spread the cream cheese over the bottom of a serving platter. Layer with the cocktail sauce, crab meat, green onions, bell pepper, tomato and mozzarella cheese. Chill, covered, until serving time. Serve with corn chips or tortilla chips.
Serves 18 to 20.

Sandra McCord
Chattanooga, Tennessee

CHICKEN DIP

1 large can, plus 1 small can chicken breast chunks
2 (8-ounce) packages cream cheese, softened
2 envelopes ranch salad dressing mix

Combine the chicken, cream cheese and salad dressing mix in a bowl and mix well. Chill, covered, until serving time. Serve with crackers. Serves 18 to 20.

Kathy Duncan
Memphis, Tennessee

PIZZA DIP

8 ounces cream cheese, softened
1 (14-ounce) jar pizza sauce
1/3 cup minced onions
1 1/2 cups (6 ounces) shredded mozzarella cheese
1 (6-ounce) can chopped black olives, drained
2 ounces sliced pepperoni, chopped

Spread the cream cheese over the bottom of a 9-inch glass pie plate. Spread with the pizza sauce. Layer with the onions, mozzarella cheese, black olives and pepperoni. Bake at 350 degrees for 25 minutes. Serve with corn chips.
Serves 8 to 10.

Mary Jo Henderson
Rogersville, Tennessee

CHEESE DIP

8 ounces bulk pork sausage
2 pounds Velveeta cheese
1 (10-ounce) can tomatoes with green chiles

Brown the sausage in a skillet, stirring until crumbly; drain. Combine the sausage, cheese and tomatoes with green chiles in a slow cooker. Cook on High until the cheese is melted, stirring every 5 minutes. Cook on Low until serving time. Serve as a dip or over chips as nachos. Serves 10.

Olivia Murley
Jackson, Tennessee

BEAN DIP

1 pound ground beef
1 onion, chopped
1 envelope taco seasoning mix
1 pound Velveeta cheese
1 (10-ounce) can tomatoes with green chiles
1 (15-ounce) can pinto beans, mashed

Brown the ground beef with the onion in a skillet, stirring until crumbly; drain. Add the seasoning mix and water using the package directions. Stir in the cheese, tomatoes with green chiles and pinto beans. Cook until heated through, stirring frequently. Serve with tortilla chips. For a vegetarian dip, use 2 cans pinto beans and omit the ground beef.
Serves 16 to 18.

Rubye Morrison
Shelbyville, Tennessee

THE BIG DIPPER

1 (15-ounce) can chili without beans
1 (10-ounce) can tomatoes with green chiles
1/2 cup sliced green onions
1 1/2 cups (about 8 ounces) processed pasteurized cheese spread, cubed
1/2 teaspoon cayenne pepper

Combine the chili, tomatoes with green chiles, green onions, cheese and cayenne pepper in a saucepan. Cook over medium heat until the cheese is melted, stirring frequently. Spoon into a serving dish. Serve with assorted fresh vegetables, French bread slices or chips. You may serve the dip in a fondue pot. Serves 16 to 18.

Ann Montgomery
Sevierville, Tennessee

SOUTHWESTERN CHILE DIP

2 cups (8 ounces) shredded sharp Cheddar cheese
1 cup mayonnaise
1 small can green chiles
1/4 teaspoon garlic powder
1 small can chopped black olives
1 tomato, chopped
1/4 cup sliced green onions

Combine the cheese, mayonnaise, green chiles, garlic powder and half the black olives in a bowl and mix well. Spread in a 9-inch pie plate. Bake at 350 degrees for 20 minutes. Let stand to cool for 5 minutes. Sprinkle with the tomato, green onions and remaining black olives. Serve with corn chips. Serves 10.

Kathy Duncan
Memphis, Tennessee

CHEESE DIP

1 (10-ounce) can tomatoes with green chiles
5 ounces water
1 teaspoon cumin
1 teaspoon pepper
1 teaspoon garlic powder
16 ounces American cheese, cubed

Combine the tomatoes with green chiles, water, cumin, pepper and garlic powder in a saucepan and mix well. Bring to a boil. Place the cheese in a food processor. Add the tomato mixture and process until well blended.
Serves 10 to 12.

Mark Priest
Olive Branch, Mississippi

TEX-MEX DIP

1 cup mayonnaise
1 cup sour cream
1/4 to 1/2 envelope taco seasoning mix
2 cans jalapeño bean dip
1 jar picante sauce or salsa
2 to 3 cups (8 to 12 ounces) mixed shredded mozzarella cheese and Cheddar cheese
1 bunch green onions, chopped
1 to 2 tomatoes, chopped
1 can sliced black olives

Combine the mayonnaise, sour cream and taco seasoning mix in a bowl and mix well. Layer the mayonnaise mixture, bean dip, picante sauce, cheese, green onions, tomatoes and black olives in a 9x13-inch dish. Chill, covered, until serving time. Serve with chips or crackers. Serves 12 to 16.

Ruby Rigsby
Soddy-Daisy, Tennessee

TEXAS CAVIAR

2 cans Shoe Peg corn, rinsed and drained
2 cans black-eyed peas
2 cans diced tomatoes
1/2 onion, chopped
1/2 green bell pepper, chopped
1 (16-ounce) bottle fat-free Italian salad dressing

Combine the corn, black-eyed peas, tomatoes, onion, bell pepper and salad dressing in a bowl and mix well. Let stand, covered, for 8 to 10 hours. Serve with tortilla scoops or serve as a side dish. Serves 20 to 25.

Vavial Jamison
Shelbyville, Tennessee

MEXICAN DIP

2 cups sour cream
2 envelopes taco seasoning mix
1 large jar chunky salsa
2 cups (8 ounces) shredded Colby Jack cheese
Chopped black olives
Chopped green onions

Combine the sour cream and taco seasoning mix in a bowl and mix well. Chill, covered, for 8 to 10 hours. Layer the sour cream mixture, salsa, cheese, black olives and green onions in a serving dish just before serving. Serve with bite-size tortilla chips. Serves 16 to 18.

Janice Cude
Franklin, Tennessee

BLACK BEAN SALSA

1 envelope zesty Italian salad dressing mix
2 cans black beans, drained
1 can Mexicorn or Shoe Peg corn, drained
1 (10-ounce) can tomatoes with green chiles, drained
1 cucumber, chopped
1 tomato, chopped
1/2 red onion, chopped

Prepare the salad dressing mix using the package directions. Combine the prepared salad dressing, black beans, Mexicorn, tomatoes with green chiles, cucumber, tomato and onion in a bowl and mix well. Chill, covered, until serving time. Serve with tortilla scoops or other chips. Serves 6.

Mary Roberts
Maryville, Tennessee

SALSA

8 tomatoes
1/2 green bell pepper, chopped
2 jalapeño chiles
1/4 cup chopped onion
1 tablespoon garlic powder
1 tablespoon oregano
3 teaspoons salt
1/2 tablespoon basil
1 tablespoon lemon juice
1 tablespoon vegetable oil
1/2 cup apple cider vinegar

Bring enough water to cover the tomatoes to a boil in a saucepan. Add the tomatoes and cook until the peelings begin to pucker; drain. Peel the tomatoes and squeeze to remove excess juice. You may mix the tomato juice with a small amount of salt and reserve for future use. Chop the tomatoes. Combine the tomatoes, bell pepper, jalapeño chiles, onion, garlic powder, oregano, salt, basil, lemon juice, oil and vinegar in a stockpot. Bring to a boil. Simmer for 20 minutes or until thickened. Serve immediately. You may ladle the salsa into hot sterilized jars, leaving 1/2-inch headspace, seal with 2-piece lids and process in a boiling water bath for 10 minutes.
Makes (about) 4 pints.

Jesse Johnson
Knoxville, Tennessee

SALSA

1 bunch cilantro
2 cans stewed tomatoes
2 bunches green onions, chopped
4 ribs celery, finely chopped
1 can chopped green chiles
1 teaspoon chopped jalapeño chiles
1 teaspoon chopped garlic, or to taste
Juice of 1 lime
Salt and pepper to taste
1 can black beans, rinsed and drained (optional)
1 can whole kernel corn, rinsed and drained (optional)

Remove the cilantro leaves from the stems, discarding the stems. Combine the cilantro leaves, tomatoes, green onions, celery, green chiles, jalapeño chiles, garlic, lime juice, salt, pepper, black beans and corn in a bowl and mix well.
Serves 16 to 20.

Allison Turner
Memphis, Tennessee

RIPE TOMATO RELISH

2 quarts tomatoes, peeled and chopped
1/3 cup salt
1 tablespoon pickling spices
1 cup vinegar
1 cup sugar
1 onion, chopped
1 green bell pepper, chopped

Combine the tomatoes and salt in a colander. Let stand over a bowl to drain for 3 hours. Tie the pickling spices in cheesecloth and place in a saucepan. Add the vinegar and sugar and bring to a boil. Remove from heat and let stand until cool. Discard the spice bag. Combine the tomatoes, onion and bell pepper in a bowl and mix well. Add the vinegar mixture and mix well. Chill, covered, until serving time.
Serves 32.

Bob McKnight
Union City, Tennessee

HOT SAUCE

3 large tomatoes
2 or 3 jalapeño chiles
3 cups water
1 onion, cut into quarters
2 garlic cloves
3/4 teaspoon salt
3 tablespoons chopped fresh cilantro

Bring the tomatoes, jalapeño chiles, water, onion and garlic to a boil in a saucepan. Boil for 10 minutes. Remove from heat and let stand until cool; drain. Remove and discard the tomato stems and jalapeño chile stems. Place the tomatoes, jalapeño chiles, onion, garlic, salt and cilantro in a food processor or blender and process until coarsely chopped. Serve with tortilla chips or corn chips. Serves 6.

Olivia Murley
Jackson, Tennessee

BAKED ARTICHOKE DIP

2 cans artichoke hearts, drained and chopped
2 garlic cloves, minced
3 tablespoons fresh lemon juice
1/2 cup bread crumbs
3/4 cup mayonnaise
1 1/4 cups freshly grated Parmesan cheese

Combine the artichoke hearts, garlic, lemon juice, bread crumbs, mayonnaise and 1 cup of the cheese in a bowl and mix well. Spoon into a lightly greased 1-quart baking dish. Sprinkle with the remaining 1/4 cup cheese. Bake at 350 degrees for 30 minutes or until hot and bubbly. Serve warm with gourmet crackers. Serves 8.

Sonya Van Cleave
Memphis, Tennessee

GUACAMOLE

1 avocado
1/4 cup minced onion
1/4 jalapeño chile, seeded, or to taste
1 teaspoon sour cream
Salt and pepper to taste
Drained chopped tomato (optional)

Cut the avocado in half and remove and reserve the pit. Scoop the pulp into a bowl and mash with a fork. Add the remaining ingredients and mix well. Place the pit in the center of the avocado mixture to prevent browning. Serves 4.

Jesse Johnson
Knoxville, Tennessee

ONION SOUFFLÉ

1/2 cup mayonnaise
1 (10- to 12-ounce) package frozen chopped onions, thawed, drained and patted dry
24 ounces cream cheese, softened
2 cups (8 ounces) grated Parmesan cheese

Mix all the ingredients in a bowl. Spoon into a baking dish. Bake at 350 degrees for 20 to 25 minutes or until golden brown. Serve with corn scoops, tortilla chips or crackers. Serves 16 to 18.

Lynn Reynolds
Memphis, Tennessee

FABULOUS DIP

1 cup (4 ounces) shredded Cheddar cheese
1/4 cup chopped cooked bacon or bacon bits
2 cups sour cream
1 envelope ranch salad dressing mix

Combine the cheese, bacon, sour cream and salad dressing mix in a bowl and mix well. Chill, covered, for several hours. Serve with corn chips. Serves 10.

Sonya Van Cleave
Memphis, Tennessee

SPINACH DIP

1 (10-ounce) package frozen chopped spinach, thawed and drained
2 cups sour cream
1 cup mayonnaise
1 envelope vegetable soup mix
1 (8-ounce) can water chestnuts, drained and chopped
3 green onions, chopped (optional)

Squeeze the spinach to remove any excess moisture. Combine the spinach, sour cream, mayonnaise, soup mix, water chestnuts and green onions in a bowl and mix well. Chill, covered, for 2 hours. Stir the spinach mixture just before serving. Serve with fresh vegetables or chips. You may serve the dip in a bread bowl. Makes 4 cups.

Louise Stuart
White Bluff, Tennessee

CURRY DIP

1 cup mayonnaise
1 teaspoon grated onion
1 teaspoon prepared horseradish
1 tablespoon apple cider vinegar
1 tablespoon (or more) curry powder
1 tablespoon garlic salt

Combine the mayonnaise, onion, horseradish, vinegar, curry powder and garlic salt in a bowl and mix well. Chill, covered, for 8 to 10 hours. Serve with fresh vegetables.
Makes (about) 1 cup.

Janice Cude
Franklin, Tennessee

DILL AND ONION DIP

2/3 cup mayonnaise
8 ounces cream cheese, softened
1 tablespoon onion flakes
1 teaspoon parsley
1 teaspoon dillweed
1 teaspoon seasoned salt

Combine the mayonnaise, cream cheese, onion flakes, parsley, dillweed and seasoned salt in a bowl and mix well. Chill, covered, for 8 to 10 hours. Serve with fresh vegetables. Serves 10 to 12.

Elaine Huff
Harrison, Tennessee

VEGETABLE DIP

2 cups mayonnaise
2 cups (8 ounces) shredded mozzarella cheese
2 tablespoons grated Parmesan cheese
1 teaspoon MSG
1 teaspoon sugar
1 tablespoon parsley
2 tablespoons onion flakes
1 cup sour cream
Salt and pepper to taste

Combine all the ingredients in a bowl and mix well. Chill, covered, for 8 to 10 hours. Serve with fresh vegetables. Makes (about) 4 cups.

Janice Cude
Franklin, Tennessee

VEGGIE DIP

2 cups sour cream
1 envelope vegetable soup mix
1/2 envelope taco seasoning mix, or to taste

Combine the sour cream, soup mix and taco seasoning mix in a bowl and mix well. Chill, covered, for 8 to 10 hours. Serve with fresh vegetables or chips. Serves 12 to 16.

Anna Joyner
Knoxville, Tennessee

FRUIT DIP

1 cup pineapple juice
3/4 cup sugar
1 tablespoon all-purpose flour
1 egg, beaten
1 (12-ounce) container whipped topping

Cook the pineapple juice in a saucepan over medium heat until heated through. Stir in the sugar, flour and egg. Cook until thickened, stirring constantly. Remove from the heat and let stand until completely cool. Fold in the whipped topping just before serving. Serve with fresh fruit. Serves 10 to 12.

Zoerita Proctor
McEwen, Tennessee

FRUIT DIP

16 ounces cream cheese, softened
1 cup confectioners' sugar
2 tablespoons amaretto
1/2 teaspoon almond extract
Food coloring (optional)

Combine the cream cheese, confectioners' sugar, amaretto, almond extract and food coloring in a mixing bowl and beat until smooth. Serve with fresh fruit. Serves 16.

Kathy Duncan
Memphis, Tennessee

CITRUS ADE

1 cup lemonade mix
2/3 to 1 cup sugar
Juice of 1 lemon
Juice of 1 lime
Juice of 1 orange
Lemon slices
Lime slices
Orange slices

Combine the lemonade mix, sugar, lemon juice, lime juice, orange juice and enough water to fill a 2-quart pitcher and mix well. Stir in the lemon slices, lime slices and orange slices. Serve over ice in glasses. Serves 8.

Vicki Evitts
Nashville, Tennessee

BANANA PUNCH

4 cups sugar
6 cups water
1 (6-ounce) can frozen orange juice concentrate, thawed
1 (46-ounce) can pineapple juice
Juice of 2 lemons
5 bananas, mashed
1 (2-liter) bottle lemon-lime soda or ginger ale

Combine the sugar and water in a saucepan. Bring to a boil. Boil until the sugar is dissolved. Remove from the heat and let stand until completely cool. Add the orange juice concentrate, pineapple juice, lemon juice and bananas and mix well. Pour into a freezer container and freeze until serving time. To serve, let the mixture stand at room temperature just until slightly thawed. Spoon into a punch bowl. Add the lemon-lime soda and stir. Serves 20 to 25.

Jan Moore
Henderson, Tennessee

BANANA PUNCH

2 cups sugar
1 quart hot water
1 (12-ounce) can frozen orange juice concentrate, thawed
1 large can pineapple juice
4 large bananas
1 cup lemon juice
1 (2-liter) bottle lemon-lime soda

Dissolve the sugar in the hot water in a bowl. Prepare the orange juice concentrate in a 1-gallon pitcher using the package directions. Add the pineapple juice and mix well. Combine the bananas and lemon juice in a blender and process until the bananas are mashed. Add the banana mixture to the pineapple juice mixture and mix well. Stir in the lemon-lime soda. Freeze, covered, until firm. Remove from the freezer. Let stand for 4 to 8 hours or just until slushy. Serves 50.

Mary Perry
Joelton, Tennessee

QUICK FRUIT TEA

2 cups hot water
1/4 cup instant tea granules
2 cups sugar
1 cup orange juice
1/2 cup lemon juice

Combine the hot water, tea granules and sugar in a 1-gallon pitcher and stir until the tea granules and sugar are dissolved. Add the orange juice and lemon juice and mix well. Add enough water to fill the pitcher and mix well. Serve over ice cubes in glasses. Makes 1 gallon.

Carolyn Carter
Antioch, Tennessee

TEA PUNCH

3 tea bags
Sugar or artificial sweetener to taste
Juice from 3 lemons
Juice from 1 (15-ounce) can sliced pineapple
2 to 3 cups orange juice
1 (1-liter) bottle ginger ale

Prepare the tea bags in a 1-gallon pitcher using the package directions for 1 quart of tea. Add the sugar and stir until dissolved. Add the lemon juice, pineapple juice and orange juice and mix well. Chill, covered, until serving time. Stir in the ginger ale just before serving. Serves 16.

Carolyn Carter
Antioch, Tennessee

SALADS AND SOUPS

MARINATED CRAB SALAD

1 pint crab meat, shells removed and flaked
1 small onion, finely chopped
5 tablespoons white vinegar
Juice of 2 lemons
Salt and pepper to taste
1 teaspoon dry mustard
Basil and thyme to taste
Lettuce leaves

Combine the crab meat, onion, vinegar, lemon juice, salt, pepper, dry mustard, basil and thyme in a bowl and mix well. Chill, covered, for 8 to 10 hours. Spoon onto a lettuce-lined serving plate. Garnish with fresh parsley and lemon wedges. Serve with crackers. Serves 8.

Sonya Van Cleave
Memphis, Tennessee

NO-GREEN SALAD

1 small can crab meat, drained
1/4 cup minced celery
1/4 cup mayonnaise
2 eggs, hard-cooked and chopped
1/2 cup chopped mushrooms
1/2 cup water chestnuts, drained
1/2 cup chopped purple onion
1/2 cup (2 ounces) shredded Cheddar cheese
1/4 cup black olives
1/4 cup sunflower seeds
Ranch salad dressing

Combine the crab meat, celery and mayonnaise in a bowl and mix well. Add the eggs, mushrooms, water chestnuts, onion, cheese, black olives and sunflower seeds and mix well. Add the desired amount of salad dressing and toss to mix. You may substitute any type of salad dressing for the ranch salad dressing. Serves 4.

Nancy Wallis
Clinton, Tennessee

SMOKED CHICKEN SALAD

8 ounces chopped smoked chicken
2 cups drained artichoke hearts, cut into quarters
12 cherry tomatoes, cut into halves
1 cup chopped yellow bell pepper
1/2 cup chopped red onion
1/2 cup packed fresh basil leaves, slivered
2 tablespoons lemon juice
1 tablespoon olive oil
1/4 teaspoon pepper
1/4 teaspoon prepared mustard
Pinch of salt
8 leaves radicchio

Combine the chicken, artichoke hearts, tomatoes, bell pepper, onion and basil in a bowl and mix well. Combine the lemon juice, olive oil, pepper, mustard and salt in a bowl and whisk to mix. Pour over the chicken mixture and toss to coat. Chill, covered, until serving time. Line a serving platter with the radicchio. Top with the chicken mixture. Serves 4.

Betty Shields
Morristown, Tennessee

CHICKEN SALAD

2 large chicken breasts
1 cup red grapes, cut into halves
1/4 cup broccoli florets
2 tablespoons sweet pickle relish
1 celery rib, chopped
Mayonnaise to taste
Chopped pecans or almonds (optional)

Combine the chicken and enough water to cover in a saucepan. Bring to a boil. Cook until cooked through. Chop the chicken, discarding the skin and bones. Combine the chicken, grapes, broccoli, pickle relish, celery, mayonnaise and pecans in a bowl and mix well. Chill, covered, until serving time. Serves 4 to 6.

Rubye Hahn
Bridgeport, Alabama

CHICKEN SALAD

1 large apple, cored and chopped
1 tablespoon lemon juice
2 chicken breasts, cooked and chopped
1 small can pineapple tidbits, drained
2 celery ribs, chopped
1/2 cup chopped grapes
1/2 cup chopped pecans
1 tablespoon honey
Salt to taste
3/4 cup mayonnaise
Lettuce

Toss the apple and lemon juice in a bowl. Add the next 8 ingredients and mix well. Serve on lettuce-lined plates with crackers or croissants. Serves 4 to 6.

Vera Raines
Lake City, Tennessee

MEXICAN BLACK BEAN SALAD

1 1/2 cups water
1 cup whole wheat couscous
3 tablespoons white wine vinegar
1 teaspoon cumin
3 tablespoons thyme
Dash of pepper
4 ounces each Monterey Jack cheese and pepper Jack cheese, chopped
2 (15-ounce) cans black beans, rinsed and drained
1 (4-ounce) can chopped green chiles
4 to 6 roma tomatoes, chopped
2 celery ribs, chopped
2 cups chopped fresh parsley
1/4 cup olive oil

Bring the water to a boil in a saucepan. Stir in the couscous and boil for 2 minutes. Remove from the heat. Let stand, covered, for 5 minutes. Spoon the couscous into a bowl and fluff with a fork. Stir in the next 8 ingredients. Combine the tomatoes, celery and parsley in a bowl. Add the olive oil and toss to coat. Chill, covered, until serving time. Garnish with sliced black olives, sliced banana chiles, unsalted dry-roasted peanuts and oyster crackers. Serves 8 to 10.

Bob Tickle
Morristown, Tennessee

SEVEN-LAYER SALAD

1 large head lettuce, torn
1 small onion, chopped
1 green bell pepper, chopped
2 (8-ounce) cans water chestnuts, chopped
2 (15-ounce) cans green peas
5 tablespoons mayonnaise-style salad dressing
10 eggs, hard-cooked and chopped
Salt and pepper to taste
2 packages fully cooked bacon, crumbled
2 cups (8 ounces) shredded Cheddar cheese

Layer the lettuce, onion, bell pepper, water chestnuts, peas, salad dressing and eggs in a salad bowl. Sprinkle with salt, pepper, bacon and cheese. Chill, covered, until serving time. Serves 8 to 10.

Wilma Kelly
Knoxville, Tennessee

TACO SALAD

1 pound ground beef
1 pound sharp cheese, shredded
1 (15-ounce) can ranch-style beans, drained, or chili with beans
1 large head lettuce, torn
1 (5-ounce) jar olives, sliced
1 large onion, chopped
2 large tomatoes, chopped
1 (13-ounce) package taco-flavor tortilla chips
1 (16-ounce) bottle Catalina salad dressing

Brown the ground beef in a skillet, stirring until crumbly; drain. Combine the ground beef, cheese, beans, lettuce, olives, onion and tomatoes in a bowl and toss to mix. Add the tortilla chips and salad dressing just before serving and toss gently. Serves 6 to 8.

Wilma Kelly
Knoxville, Tennessee

BROCCOLI SALAD

1 1/2 to 2 pounds broccoli florets
1/4 cup chopped green onions
6 slices bacon, crisp-cooked and crumbled
1/2 cup golden raisins
1/4 cup sunflower seeds
3/4 cup mayonnaise
1/4 cup sugar
2 tablespoons red wine vinegar

Combine the broccoli, green onions, bacon, raisins, and sunflower seeds in a bowl and mix well. Combine the mayonnaise, sugar and vinegar in a bowl and mix well. Pour over the broccoli mixture and toss to coat. Serve immediately. Serves 6 to 8.

Bernice Curtis
Knoxville, Tennessee

BROCCOLI SALAD

1 large bunch broccoli, chopped
1 head cauliflower, chopped
4 to 6 eggs, hard-cooked and finely chopped
1 onion, finely chopped
1 green bell pepper, finely chopped
1 can water chestnuts, finely chopped
Green olives to taste, finely chopped
1/4 teaspoon garlic salt
1/2 teaspoon salt
1/4 teaspoon pepper
Mayonnaise

Combine the broccoli, cauliflower, eggs, onion, bell pepper, water chestnuts, olives, garlic salt, salt and pepper in a bowl and toss to mix. Stir in just enough mayonnaise to moisten. Chill, covered, for 8 to 10 hours. Serves 8 to 10.

Sadie Tipton
Lafollette, Tennessee

BROCCOLI AND CAULIFLOWER SALAD

1 bunch broccoli, chopped
1 large head cauliflower, chopped
1 red onion, finely chopped
3/4 cup mayonnaise or mayonnaise-style salad dressing
1/2 cup vegetable oil
1/3 cup white vinegar
1 teaspoon prepared mustard
3/4 cup sugar
1 (2-ounce) jar chopped pimento, drained
Salt and pepper to taste

Combine the broccoli, cauliflower and onion in a bowl and mix well. Combine the mayonnaise, oil, vinegar, mustard, sugar, pimento, salt and pepper in a bowl and mix well. Pour over the broccoli mixture and mix well. Chill, covered, for 8 to 10 hours. Serves 10.

Doris Jones
Lexington, Tennessee

RAMEN CRUNCH SLAW

2 packages pork or oriental ramen noodles
1 (16-ounce) package coleslaw mix
Chopped green onions to taste
1 (3-ounce) package salted sunflower seeds
2 ounces slivered almonds, toasted
3/4 cup vegetable oil
1/3 cup sugar
1/3 cup white vinegar

Crumble the ramen noodles, reserving the seasoning packets. Combine the ramen noodles, coleslaw mix, green onions, sunflower seeds and almonds in a bowl and mix well. Combine the oil, sugar, vinegar and reserved seasoning in a bowl and mix well. Add the dressing to the coleslaw mixture and mix well. Serve immediately. You may make the dressing ahead of time and let stand at room temperature until serving time. Serves 8 to 10.

Ann Howell Tickle
Morristown, Tennessee

SWEET-AND-SOUR SLAW

1/2 cup white vinegar
1/2 teaspoon salt
1/2 teaspoon dry mustard
1/2 teaspoon celery seeds
1/3 cup vegetable oil
1/2 cup sugar
1 (16-ounce) package coleslaw mix
1 red onion, chopped

Combine the vinegar, salt, dry mustard, celery seeds, oil and sugar in a saucepan. Bring to a boil. Boil for 1 minute, stirring constantly. Remove from the heat. Let the dressing stand until cool. Combine the coleslaw mix and onion in a bowl and toss to mix. Pour the dressing over the coleslaw mixture and mix well. Chill, covered, until serving time. You may substitute one 1-pound cabbage, coarsely grated, plus 2 medium carrots, grated, for the coleslaw mix. Serves 6 to 8.

Faye Richardson
Memphis, Tennessee

COLESLAW

1 small head cabbage, chopped
1 green bell pepper, chopped
1 (2-ounce) jar chopped pimento, drained
1 onion, chopped
1 cup sugar
1 cup vinegar
1/2 cup vegetable oil
2 teaspoons salt

Combine the cabbage, bell pepper, pimento and onion in a bowl and mix well. Combine the sugar, vinegar, oil and salt in a saucepan. Bring to a boil. Pour over the cabbage mixture; do not stir. Chill, covered, for 8 to 10 hours. Serves 20.

Linda Brumley
Oakfield, Tennessee

FREEZER SLAW

1 head cabbage
1 green bell pepper
1 red bell pepper
1 carrot
1/2 cup vinegar
1/2 cup water
2 cups sugar
2 teaspoons salt
1 teaspoon celery seeds

Grate the cabbage, bell peppers and carrot and place in a colander. Let stand to drain over a bowl for 1 hour. Combine the vinegar, water, sugar, salt and celery seeds in a saucepan. Bring to a boil. Remove from heat and let stand until cool. Pour over the cabbage mixture and mix well. Spoon into rigid freezer containers and freeze, covered, until serving time. Let stand at room temperature to thaw before serving. Serves 18 to 20.

Bob McKnight
Union City, Tennessee

CARROT SALAD

2 pounds carrots
1 onion, chopped
1 green bell pepper, chopped
1 can tomato soup
1/2 cup vegetable oil
1/2 cup vinegar
1/2 cup sugar

Combine the carrots with enough salted water to cover in a saucepan. Cook over medium heat until tender; drain. Let stand until cool. Cut into slices and place in a bowl. Add the onion and bell pepper and mix well. Combine the soup, oil, vinegar and sugar in a saucepan. Cook until the sugar is dissolved, stirring constantly. Pour over the carrot mixture and mix well. Chill, covered, until serving time. You may serve the salad warm. Serves 6.

Rosalie Williams
Chattanooga, Tennessee

UN-POTATO SALAD

1 large head cauliflower, chopped
2 cups chopped celery
1 cup chopped red onion
2 cups light mayonnaise
1/4 cup cider vinegar
2 teaspoons salt
2 teaspoons artificial sweetener
1/2 teaspoon pepper
4 eggs, hard-cooked and chopped

Combine the cauliflower and 1 tablespoon water in a microwave-safe bowl. Microwave, covered, on High for 7 minutes. Let stand for 3 to 5 minutes; drain. Add the celery and onion. Combine the mayonnaise, vinegar, salt, sweetener and pepper in a bowl and mix well. Pour over the cauliflower mixture and mix well. Stir in the eggs. Chill, covered, until serving time. Serves 12.

Marie Guy
Clinton, Tennessee

CORN SALAD

2 cans white corn, drained
1 tomato, chopped
1 green bell pepper, chopped
1 cucumber, chopped
1 red onion, chopped
1/2 cup sour cream
1/4 cup mayonnaise
2 tablespoons white vinegar
1/2 teaspoon dry mustard
1/2 teaspoon celery seeds
Salt and pepper to taste

Combine the corn, tomato, bell pepper, cucumber, onion, sour cream, mayonnaise, vinegar, dry mustard, celery seeds, salt and pepper in a bowl and mix well. Chill, covered, until serving time. Serves 8.

Betty Gainous
Tullahoma, Tennessee

SHOE PEG CORN SALAD

1 (14-ounce) can French-style green beans, drained
1 can Shoe Peg corn, drained
1 can green peas, drained
1 medium can chopped pimento, drained
1 cup chopped celery
1 cup chopped green onions with tops
1 green bell pepper, chopped
1 cup cauliflower florets (optional)
Dressing (below)

Combine the green beans, corn, green peas, pimento, celery, green onions, bell pepper and cauliflower in a bowl and mix well. Pour the hot dressing over the mixture and mix well. Let stand, covered, for 8 to 10 hours. You may use yellow corn in place of the Shoe Peg corn. Serves 6 to 8.

Sweet-and-Sour Dressing

1/2 cup vegetable oil
1 cup sugar
3/4 cup white vinegar
1 tablespoon water
1 teaspoon salt
1 teaspoon pepper

Combine the oil, sugar, vinegar, water, salt and pepper in a saucepan. Bring to a boil.

Pauline NeSmith
Morristown, Tennessee

CUCUMBER SALAD

3 or 4 cucumbers, peeled and sliced
1 Vidalia onion, sliced
1 tablespoon salt
1/2 cup sugar
1/2 cup vinegar
1/2 cup heavy cream

Mix the cucumbers, onion and salt in a bowl. Chill, covered, for 6 hours or longer; drain. Add the sugar, vinegar and heavy cream and mix well. Chill, covered, until serving time or for up to 3 days. Serves 6 to 8.

Wilma Kelly
Knoxville, Tennessee

BLACK-EYED PEA SALAD

3 (16-ounce) cans black-eyed peas, drained
1 (2-ounce) can chopped pimento, drained
1 large red or purple onion, thinly sliced
1 large red or green bell pepper, thinly sliced
1 garlic clove, minced, or 1 teaspoon minced garlic
1/4 cup white vinegar
6 tablespoons red wine vinegar
6 tablespoons sugar
6 tablespoons vegetable oil
1/2 teaspoon salt
1/8 teaspoon pepper
6 drops of Tabasco sauce

Combine the black-eyed peas, pimento, onion and bell pepper in a bowl and mix well. Combine the garlic, white vinegar, red wine vinegar, sugar, oil, salt, pepper and Tabasco sauce in a bowl and mix well. Pour over the black-eyed pea mixture. Chill, covered, for 8 to 10 hours. Serves 8 to 10.

Ruby Rigsby
Soddy-Daisy, Tennessee

IRISH POTATO SALAD

6 potatoes, scrubbed
4 eggs, hard-cooked and chopped
1/4 cup canola oil
3 celery ribs, chopped
1 green bell pepper, chopped
1 large onion, chopped
3 ounces pimentos, drained and chopped
2 tablespoons vinegar
Salt and pepper to taste
Celery salt to taste
Mayonnaise

Combine the potatoes with enough water to cover in a saucepan. Bring to a boil. Boil until tender; drain. Let stand until cool. Peel and chop the potatoes. Combine the potatoes, eggs and canola oil in a bowl and stir to coat. Add the next 8 ingredients and mix well. Stir in just enough mayonnaise to moisten. Serve immediately or chill, covered, until serving time. Serves 6 to 8.

Ella Mae Hasty
Memphis, Tennessee

CAJUN POTATO SALAD

5 pounds Yukon gold potatoes or red potatoes, peeled and chopped
2 tablespoons Cajun seasoning
Salt to taste
8 eggs, hard-cooked
5 small sweet pickles, finely chopped
1/4 cup prepared mustard
2 dashes of Tabasco sauce
1 teaspoon Cajun seasoning
1 (16-ounce) jar mayonnaise

Combine the potatoes, 2 tablespoons Cajun seasoning and enough water to cover in a saucepan. Cook over medium-high heat until tender; drain. Sprinkle with salt and let stand until cool. Chop the egg whites, reserving the egg yolks. Mash the reserved egg yolks in a bowl. Add the pickles, mustard, Tabasco sauce, 1 teaspoon Cajun seasoning and half the mayonnaise and mix well. Stir in the egg whites. Chill, covered, until serving time. Combine the potato mixture and egg mixture in a bowl and mix gently. Fold in the remaining mayonnaise. Serve immediately. Serves 8.

Linda DeSoto
Murfreesboro, Tennessee

POTATO SALAD

20 ounces potatoes, scrubbed
2 tomatoes, sliced
1 cup thinly sliced radishes
2 red onions, thinly sliced
1 tablespoon plus 1 teaspoon olive oil
1 tablespoon vinegar
Pinch of salt

Combine the potatoes and enough water to cover in a saucepan. Bring to a boil and cook until tender; drain. Let stand until cool. Cut the potatoes into quarters and place in a bowl. Add the tomatoes, radishes, onions, olive oil, vinegar and salt and toss to mix. Divide among 4 salad plates and garnish with endive leaves and minced chives. Serves 4.

Betty Shields
Morristown, Tennessee

ITALIAN MACARONI SALAD

16 ounces shell pasta or veggie rotini
2 tomatoes, chopped
2 celery ribs, chopped
1 green bell pepper, chopped
1 purple onion, chopped
4 ounces pepperoni, chopped
4 ounces hard salami, chopped
1 can black olives
8 ounces mozzarella cheese, shredded
Chopped broccoli (optional)
1 jar chopped pimento, drained (optional)
Dressing (below)

Cook the pasta using the package directions; drain. Combine the pasta, tomatoes, celery, bell pepper, onion, pepperoni, salami, black olives, cheese, broccoli and pimento in a bowl and toss to mix. Pour the dressing over the pasta mixture and toss to coat. Chill, covered, until serving time. Serves 10 to 15.

Herbed Dressing

1 teaspoon oregano
1/2 teaspoon basil
1 teaspoon garlic salt
1/4 cup vinegar
2/3 cup vegetable oil

Combine the oregano, basil, garlic salt, vinegar and oil in a bowl and mix well.

Barbara Johnson
Collierville, Tennessee

ITALIAN PASTA SALAD

1 green bell pepper, chopped
1 (2-ounce) can sliced black olives
3/4 cup sliced green olives
3/4 cup (3 ounces) shredded Colby Jack cheese, or 1 1/2 cups cubed
1 cucumber, sliced and quartered
1/2 onion, chopped
12 ounces rotini, cooked and drained
1 (16-ounce) bottle Italian salad dressing
4 teaspoons Salad Supreme seasoning

Combine the first 6 ingredients in a bowl and mix well. Add the pasta and salad dressing and mix well. Sprinkle with the seasoning and mix well. Chill, covered, for 2 hours or longer before serving. Serves 6.

Angel Harris
Memphis, Tennessee

PASTA SALAD

16 ounces rotelle
1 1/2 cups sugar
1 cup apple cider vinegar
1/2 cup vegetable oil
2 teaspoons prepared mustard
1 garlic clove, minced
2 teaspoons salt
1 teaspoon pepper
1 cup peeled and sliced cucumber
1 cup chopped red onion
2 tablespoons minced fresh parsley
2 tomatoes, chopped
1 green bell pepper, chopped

Cook the pasta using the package directions; drain. Combine the sugar, vinegar and oil in a saucepan. Cook over low heat until the sugar is dissolved, stirring constantly. Remove from the heat. Stir in the next 4 ingredients. Pour over the pasta in a bowl. Fold in the cucumber, onion and parsley. Chill, covered, for 8 to 10 hours. Mix in the tomatoes and bell pepper just before serving. Serves 6 to 8.

Glenda Buchanan
College Grove, Tennessee

PASTA SALAD

1 package tricolor rotini
4 carrots, peeled and sliced
4 ribs celery, sliced
Florets of 1 bunch broccoli
8 green onions, sliced
Salt and pepper to taste
Italian salad dressing

Cook the pasta using the package directions. Remove the pasta with a slotted spoon to a bowl of cold water; drain. Combine the carrots and enough water to cover in a saucepan. Bring to a boil. Cook for 5 minutes. Add the celery and cook for 5 minutes. Remove the carrots and celery with a slotted spoon to a bowl of cold water to stop the cooking process. Add the broccoli to the boiling water. Cook for 3 to 5 minutes and remove with a slotted spoon to the cold water. Let stand until completely cool; drain over a bowl for 15 minutes. Combine the carrots, celery, broccoli and pasta in a bowl and mix well. Chill, covered, until serving time. Add the green onions, salt, pepper and the desired amount of salad dressing and toss to mix. Serve immediately or chill, covered, for up to 3 days. Serves 6 to 8.

Cynthia Collins
Clarksville, Tennessee

CORN BREAD SALAD

1 skillet corn bread, crumbled
1/2 cup chopped red onion
1 can whole kernel corn, drained
1 green bell pepper, chopped
1 can pinto beans, drained and rinsed
1 cup (4 ounces) shredded Cheddar cheese
1 bottle ranch salad dressing

Layer the corn bread, onion, corn, bell pepper, pinto beans and cheese in the order listed in a bowl. Pour the salad dressing over the top. Garnish with crumbled crisp-cooked bacon and 1 chopped tomato. Serves 6 to 8.

Vavial Jamison
Shelbyville, Tennessee

CORN BREAD SALAD

1 package corn muffin mix
1 green bell pepper, chopped
1 small bunch green onions, chopped
Butter
1 (15-ounce) can pinto beans
1 large tomato, chopped
8 ounces cream cheese, softened
2/3 cup mayonnaise
1/3 cup sweet pickle juice
3 or 4 slices bacon, crisp-cooked and crumbled

Prepare the corn muffin mix and bake in a 9-inch skillet using the package directions. Let stand until cool. Sauté the bell pepper and green onions in a small amount of butter in a skillet. Crumble the corn bread and place in a dish. Spoon the undrained beans over the corn bread. Layer with the bell pepper mixture and tomato. Combine the cream cheese, mayonnaise and pickle juice in a bowl and mix well. Spread over the layers in the dish. Sprinkle with the bacon. Chill, covered, until serving time. Serves 6 to 8.

Marie Guy
Clinton, Tennessee

TABBOULEH

1/2 cup couscous
1 cup tomato juice
4 bunches parsley, minced
1 onion, finely chopped
1 cucumber, seeded and finely chopped
4 garlic cloves, crushed with salt
1/2 cup lemon juice
2 cups olive oil
1 teaspoon sugar
1/2 teaspoon dry mustard
Pepper to taste
Fresh mint, finely chopped
Honey (optional)

Cook the couscous using the package directions. Combine the couscous, tomato juice, parsley, onion, cucumber, garlic, lemon juice, olive oil, sugar, dry mustard, pepper, mint and honey in a bowl and mix well. Serves 30.

Nina Morris and Michele Duchastel
Carthage, Tennessee

RICE SALAD

3 cups cooked rice, rinsed and drained
1 (8-ounce) can green peas, drained
1/2 cup chopped onion
1/2 cup chopped celery
1 (2-ounce) jar chopped pimento, drained
1 teaspoon salt
1/4 teaspoon pepper
1/2 cup mayonnaise-type salad dressing
1 cup cubed Cheddar cheese

Combine the rice, peas, onion, celery, pimento, salt, pepper, salad dressing and cheese in a bowl and toss to mix. Instant rice is not recommended. Serves 10 to 12.

Willie White
Germantown, Tennessee

RASPBERRY SALAD DRESSING

1/4 cup sugar
1 tablespoon minced dried onion
1/2 teaspoon dry mustard
1/2 teaspoon pepper
3 tablespoons raspberry-flavor vinegar
1/2 cup vegetable oil
1 tablespoon poppy seeds

Combine the sugar, onion, dry mustard, pepper and vinegar in a blender and process until blended. Add the oil and process until blended. Add the poppy seeds and mix well. Serve over a mixture of salad greens, grapes, blue cheese chunks and toasted walnuts. Makes (about) 1 cup.

Sandra McCord
Chattanooga, Tennessee

CARAMEL APPLE SALAD

1 (8-ounce) can crushed pineapple
2 tablespoons all-purpose flour
2 tablespoons vinegar
$^1/_2$ cup sugar
4 Granny Smith apples
1 small package salted peanuts
16 ounces whipped topping

Combine the pineapple, flour, vinegar and sugar in a heavy saucepan. Bring to a boil, stirring constantly. Boil over medium heat for 2 minutes, stirring constantly. Remove to a large bowl. Let stand until completely cool. Cut the apples into small pieces and crush the peanuts. Fold the apples, peanuts and whipped topping into the pineapple mixture. Chill, covered, until serving time or for up to 3 days. Serves 12.

Sondra Wright
Mt. Pleasant, Tennessee

FRUIT SALAD

3 egg yolks
$^1/_3$ cup sugar
Pinch of salt
12 ounces whipped topping
3 apples, chopped
4 bananas, sliced
36 miniature marshmallows

Combine the egg yolks, sugar and salt in a saucepan. Cook over low heat until thickened, stirring constantly. Remove from heat and let the dressing stand until completely cool. Fold in the whipped topping. Combine the apples, bananas and marshmallows in a bowl and mix well. Pour the dressing over the fruit and mix well. Serves 8.

Bobbie Latta
Columbia, Tennessee

FALL FRUIT SALAD

2 Granny Smith apples, chopped
1 (11-ounce) can mandarin oranges, drained
1 cup seedless red grape halves
1 1/2 cups miniature marshmallows
8 ounces low-fat vanilla yogurt
3 tablespoons chopped nuts

Combine the apples, mandarin oranges and grapes in a bowl and mix well. Add the marshmallows and yogurt and mix gently. Chill, covered, until serving time. Spoon into a salad bowl. Sprinkle the nuts over the top. Serve immediately. Serves 12.

Trilby Williams
Morristown, Tennessee

TUTTI-FRUTTI

1 cup grapefruit or orange sections
1 cup sliced strawberries
1 small Granny Smith apple, chopped
1 cup chopped cantaloupe
1/2 banana, sliced
1 tablespoon orange juice
1 teaspoon sugar

Combine the grapefruit, strawberries, apple, cantaloupe, banana, orange juice and sugar in a bowl and toss to mix. Chill, covered, until serving time. Toss before serving. Serves 4.

Betty Shields
Morristown, Tennessee

FROZEN FRUIT SALAD

1 cup sugar
1 (8-ounce) container whipped topping
1 cup sour cream
1 small can crushed pineapple
1 cup chopped pecans
2 bananas, mashed
1 small jar maraschino cherries, drained and chopped

Combine the sugar, whipped topping, sour cream, pineapple, pecans, bananas and maraschino cherries in a bowl and mix well. Spoon into a square or rectangular dish. Freeze, covered, for 8 to 10 hours. Cut into squares to serve. Serves 6 to 8.

Kaye Lewis
Joelton, Tennessee

FRUIT SALAD

1 (15-ounce) can pineapple tidbits in syrup
1/2 cup sugar
1 tablespoon all-purpose flour
1 egg, beaten
2 (15-ounce) cans fruit cocktail, drained
2 bananas, sliced
1 cup miniature marshmallows

Drain the pineapple, reserving 1/2 cup syrup. Combine the sugar and flour in a saucepan. Add the egg and mix well. Stir in the reserved syrup. Bring to a boil. Cook until of the consistency of pudding, stirring constantly. Pour into a bowl. Chill the dressing and the fruit separately, covered, for 8 to 10 hours. Combine the dressing, pineapple, fruit cocktail, bananas and marshmallows in a bowl and mix well. Serve immediately. Serves 6.

Carolyn Carter
Antioch, Tennessee

24-HOUR SALAD

1 large can juice-pack pineapple chunks
1/2 cup chopped celery (optional)
Shredded cheese
3 cups miniature marshmallows
1 1/2 cups chopped pecans
3 tablespoons all-purpose flour
Pinch of salt
2 tablespoons vinegar
1 egg
Whipped cream

Drain the pineapple, reserving the juice. Combine the pineapple, celery, cheese, marshmallows and pecans in a bowl and mix well. Combine the flour, salt, vinegar, egg and reserved juice in a saucepan. Cook over medium-low heat until thickened, stirring constantly. Remove from heat and let stand until cool. Pour over the pineapple mixture and mix well. Fold in the whipped cream. Chill, covered, for 8 to 10 hours. Serves 6 to 8.

Ethel Ann Burson
Dickson, Tennessee

DUMP SALAD

1 can cherry pie filling
1 can crushed pineapple
1 (16-ounce) container whipped topping
1 can sweetened condensed milk
1 cup chopped nuts

Combine the pie filling, pineapple, whipped topping, condensed milk and nuts in a bowl and mix well. Spoon into a freezer-proof dish. Freeze, covered, until firm. Cut into squares to serve. Serves 4 to 6.

Zoerita Proctor
McEwen, Tennessee

FROZEN CRANBERRY SALAD

1 (16-ounce) can cranberry sauce
1 (20-ounce) can crushed pineapple, drained
1/4 cup lemon juice
1 (14-ounce) can low-fat sweetened condensed milk
8 ounces whipped topping
3/4 cup crushed pecans

Combine the cranberry sauce, pineapple, lemon juice, condensed milk and whipped topping in a bowl and beat vigorously for 40 strokes or until well mixed. Spread in a 9x13-inch or 8x8-inch dish. Sprinkle with the pecans. Freeze, covered, until firm. Let stand at room temperature for 20 minutes before serving. Cut into squares. Serves 12.

Bob Jeffries
Southaven, Mississippi

GRAPE SALAD

16 ounces sour cream
8 ounces cream cheese, softened
1/4 cup granulated sugar
1 teaspoon vanilla extract
3 pounds seedless grapes
1 cup chopped pecans
1 cup packed brown sugar

Cream the sour cream, cream cheese, granulated sugar and vanilla in a mixing bowl. Add the grapes and mix gently. Spoon into a serving dish. Sprinkle with the pecans and brown sugar. Serves 10 to 12.

Elaine Roberts
Jackson, Tennessee

GRAPE SALAD

8 ounces cream cheese, softened
1 cup sour cream
1/2 cup granulated sugar
1 cup packed brown sugar
1 cup chopped pecans
1 cup (4 ounces) shredded Cheddar cheese
1 1/2 bunches white and red seedless grapes

Cream the cream cheese, sour cream and granulated sugar in a mixing bowl. Combine the brown sugar, pecans and Cheddar cheese in a bowl and mix well. Place the grapes in a 9x13-inch or larger dish. Pour the cream cheese mixture over the grapes. Sprinkle with the brown sugar mixture. Chill, covered, for 8 to 10 hours. Serves 6 to 8.

Janis Barker
Chattanooga, Tennessee

BLUEBERRY SALAD

1 (6-ounce) package black cherry gelatin
1 cup boiling water
1/2 cup cold water
1 can blueberry pie filling
1 small can crushed pineapple
1 cup sour cream
6 ounces cream cheese, softened
1/2 cup sugar
1/2 teaspoon vanilla extract
1/2 cup chopped pecans or walnuts

Dissolve the gelatin in the boiling water in a bowl. Stir in the cold water. Add the pie filling and pineapple and mix well. Pour into a dish and chill until set. Combine the sour cream, cream cheese and sugar in a mixing bowl and beat until well blended. Stir in the vanilla and pecans. Spread over the gelatin layer. Chill, covered, until serving time. Serves 12.

Cathy Funderburk
Knoxville, Tennessee

CRANBERRY SALAD

1 (6-ounce) package cherry gelatin
2 cups boiling water
1 envelope unflavored gelatin
1/4 cup water
2 cans whole cranberry sauce
1/4 cup lemon juice
Topping (below)
1 cup chopped pecans

Dissolve the cherry gelatin in the boiling water in a bowl. Soften the unflavored gelatin in 1/4 cup water in a cup. Stir into the cherry gelatin mixture. Add the cranberry sauce and mix well. Stir in the lemon juice. Pour into a 9x13-inch dish. Chill, covered, until set. Spread with the topping and sprinkle with the pecans. Chill, covered, until serving time. Serves 8 to 10.

Topping

8 ounces cream cheese, softened
1 cup whipped topping
1 (8-ounce) can crushed pineapple

Combine the cream cheese, whipped topping and pineapple in a mixing bowl and beat until fluffy.

Jeana Pesch
Wartrace, Tennessee

CRANBERRY SALAD

1 (6-ounce) package strawberry gelatin
1 cup boiling water
1 cup chopped pecans
1 large can crushed pineapple
1 can whole cranberry sauce

Dissolve the gelatin in the boiling water in a bowl. Add the pecans, pineapple and cranberry sauce and mix well. Pour into a 10x12-inch dish. Chill, covered, until set. Serves 6 to 8.

Barbara Sneathern
Marion, Arkansas

CRANBERRY SALAD

2 (3-ounce) packages orange gelatin
1 (3-ounce) package cherry gelatin
2 1/2 cups boiling water
4 oranges
1 quart cranberries
2 cups sugar
1 cup chopped pecans

Dissolve the orange gelatin and cherry gelatin in the boiling water in a bowl. Peel the oranges and discard the seeds, reserving the peel of 2 oranges. Combine the cranberries, oranges and reserved orange peel in a food chopper and process until ground. Combine the cranberry mixture, sugar, pecans and gelatin mixture in a bowl and mix well. Pour into a mold or rectangular dish. Chill, covered, until set. Serve with chicken and dressing or turkey and dressing. Serves 8 to 10.

Nancy Bassett
Nashville, Tennessee

LIME SEVEN-UP SALAD

3 ounces cream cheese, softened
1 (3-ounce) package lime gelatin
1/2 cup hot water
1/2 cup Seven-Up
1 small can crushed pineapple, drained
1/2 cup chopped pecans
1/2 cup chopped drained maraschino cherries

Combine the cream cheese and gelatin in a bowl and mix well. Add the hot water, Seven-Up and pineapple and mix well. Spoon into a serving dish. Chill, covered, until partially set. Fold in the pecans and maraschino cherries. Chill, covered, until set. Be sure the gelatin mixture is partially set and the maraschino cherries are drained before adding to the gelatin mixture to assure a green color. Serves 6.

Pat Breeden
Rossville, Georgia

LIME SALAD

- 1 (6-ounce) package lime gelatin
- 2 cups boiling water
- 2 cups miniature marshmallows
- 8 ounces cottage cheese
- 1 cup mayonnaise
- 1 (14-ounce) can sweetened condensed milk
- 1 (20-ounce) can crushed pineapple

Combine the gelatin and boiling water in a bowl and stir until the gelatin is dissolved. Add the marshmallows, cottage cheese, mayonnaise, condensed milk and pineapple and mix well. Pour into a 9x13-inch dish. Chill, covered, for 8 to 10 hours. Serves 8 to 10.

Opal Midgett
Lebanon, Tennessee

MANDARIN ORANGE SALAD

- 1 small package sugar-free orange gelatin
- 2 cups low-fat cottage cheese
- 1 small can crushed pineapple, drained
- 1 can mandarin oranges, drained
- 8 ounces light whipped topping

Combine the gelatin and cottage cheese in a bowl and mix well. Add the pineapple and mandarin oranges and mix well. Stir in the whipped topping. Spoon into an 8x8-inch glass dish. Chill, covered, for 1 hour before serving. Serve with crackers. Serves 4.

Rebecca Cook
Mt. Pleasant, Tennessee

PEACH SALAD

1 (29-ounce) can peaches
1 (3-ounce) package peach gelatin
8 ounces cream cheese, softened
12 ounces whipped topping

Drain the peaches, reserving 1 cup juice. Bring the reserved juice to a boil in a saucepan. Remove from the heat. Dissolve the gelatin in the juice. Combine the gelatin mixture, peaches, cream cheese and whipped topping in a blender and process until blended, or mix with a hand mixer. Pour into a bowl or mold. Chill, covered, until set. Serves 6 to 8.

Peggy Burr
Nashville, Tennessee

PEACH SALAD

1 medium container whipped topping, thawed
1 package peach gelatin
16 ounces cottage cheese
1 can peaches, drained and chopped

Combine the whipped topping and gelatin in a bowl and mix well. Add the cottage cheese and mix well. Stir in the peaches. Chill, covered, for 8 to 10 hours. Serves 4 to 6.

Anna Joyner
Knoxville, Tennessee

WATERGATE SALAD

1 (20-ounce) can crushed pineapple
1 (3-ounce) package pistachio instant pudding mix
9 ounces whipped topping
1 cup chopped pecans
1 cup miniature marshmallows

Combine the pineapple and pudding mix in a bowl and mix well. Stir in the whipped topping, pecans and marshmallows. Chill, covered, for 8 to 10 hours. Serves 6 to 8.

Wilma Kelly
Knoxville, Tennessee

TROPICAL FRUIT SALAD

16 ounces low-fat cottage cheese
8 ounces light whipped topping
1 (3-ounce) package orange gelatin
1 (20-ounce) can pineapple chunks, drained
1 (15-ounce) can mandarin oranges, drained
1 (15-ounce) can apricots, drained and chopped
2 bananas, sliced
1/2 cup shredded coconut
1/2 cup chopped pecans, toasted

Combine the cottage cheese and whipped topping in a bowl and mix well. Sprinkle with the gelatin and mix well. Fold in the pineapple, mandarin oranges, apricots and bananas. Stir in the coconut and pecans. Chill, covered, until serving time. You may use different fruit and gelatin flavors. Serves 6 to 8.

Billie Pruitt
Nashville, Tennessee

PINK PARTY SALAD

No. 2 can pineapple
24 large marshmallows
1 package strawberry gelatin
1 cup heavy whipping cream
2 cups small curd cottage cheese
1 cup chopped nuts

Drain the pineapple, reserving the juice. Combine the marshmallows, reserved juice and gelatin in a saucepan. Cook until the marshmallows are melted, stirring constantly. Remove from heat and let stand until completely cool. Beat the whipping cream in a mixing bowl until stiff peaks form. Fold in the pineapple, cottage cheese and nuts. Fold in the marshmallow mixture. Spoon into a 9x12-inch dish. Chill, covered, for 8 to 10 hours. Serves 12.

Patricia Hanna
Selmer, Tennessee

CLAM STEW

4 (4-ounce) hot Italian sausages
48 littleneck clams, scrubbed
4 onions, cut into halves and thinly sliced
2 heads Belgian endive, coarsely chopped
2 tablespoons minced fresh garlic
1 jalapeño chile, seeded and chopped
1 or 2 Scotch bonnet chiles, seeded and chopped (optional)
1/2 teaspoon red pepper flakes (optional)
3/4 cup dry white wine
1 1/2 cups chopped canned tomatoes in purée
1/2 cup (1 stick) unsalted butter, cut into 1/2-inch slices

Remove sausage casings. Add the sausages to 6 cups boiling water in a saucepan. Boil for 8 minutes; drain. Let stand for 10 minutes or until cool. Cut diagonally into 1/2-inch slices. Arrange the clams in a single layer in a roasting pan. Layer with the sausages and remaining ingredients. Bring to a boil on the stovetop. Bake at 500 degrees for 8 minutes and stir to mix. Bake for 5 to 10 minutes longer or until the clams have opened. Spoon 12 clams into each of 4 heated soup bowls. Add equal portions of the sausage mixture. Garnish with julienned scallions and lemon quarters. Serves 4.

Peggy McCanless
Nashville, Tennessee

CHICKEN, SAUSAGE AND SHRIMP GUMBO

3 tablespoons vegetable oil
3 tablespoons all-purpose flour
1 (2 1/2- to 3-pound) chicken
2 quarts water
2 large onions, chopped
1/2 cup chopped green onions
2 pounds shrimp, peeled, deveined and cooked
2 pounds smoked sausage, chopped
Salt and pepper to taste
2 tablespoons chopped fresh parsley
Filé powder to taste
Hot cooked rice

Heat the oil in a large heavy stockpot over medium-high heat. Stir in the flour. Cook until dark brown, stirring constantly. Add the chicken and cook for 3 to 4 minutes, turning occasionally. Add the water, onions and green onions. Bring to a simmer. Cook for 1 hour or until the chicken is cooked through. Chop the chicken, discarding the skin and bones. Return the chicken to the stockpot. Stir in the shrimp, sausage, salt and pepper. Remove from the heat and stir in the parsley and filé powder. Serve over rice in soup bowls. Serves 8 to 10.

Melvin Gauthia
Jackson, Tennessee

HOT AND SOUR SOUP

6 dried black mushrooms
4 ounces pork, cut into thin strips
1/2 teaspoon cornstarch
1/2 teaspoon salt
1/2 teaspoon soy sauce
6 cups chicken broth
4 to 8 ounces firm tofu, cut into thin strips
8 ounces bean sprouts
1/2 cup bamboo shoots, cut into thin strips
3 tablespoons white vinegar
1/2 teaspoon sesame oil
1/4 teaspoon white pepper
Soy sauce to taste
2 eggs
2 teaspoons cold water
2 teaspoons cornstarch
6 green onions, sliced

Combine the mushrooms with enough water to cover in a bowl. Let stand for 20 minutes; drain. Cut into thin strips. Combine the pork, 1/2 teaspoon cornstarch, salt and 1/2 teaspoon soy sauce in a bowl and mix well; cover and chill. Bring the chicken broth to a boil in a large saucepan. Add the mushrooms, tofu and the next 5 ingredients and mix well. Stir in the pork mixture and soy sauce to taste. Cook until the pork is cooked through, stirring frequently. Add the eggs 1 at a time, stirring constantly. Mix the cold water and 2 teaspoons cornstarch in a bowl and stir into the soup. Cook until thickened, stirring constantly. Stir in the green onions. Ladle into soup bowls. Serves 6.

Peggy McCanless
Nashville, Tennessee

BUSY LADY BEEF STEW

2 pounds (1-inch) beef cubes
Flour
Vegetable oil
4 large potatoes, cut into small pieces
1 quart water
16 ounces frozen mixed vegetables
1 large onion, chopped
1 quart canned tomatoes
Salt and pepper to taste
1 envelope beef stew seasoning mix

Coat the beef with flour. Brown in a small amount of oil in a skillet, stirring frequently. Combine the potatoes and water in a 6-quart stockpot. Bring to a boil and cook until tender. Add the mixed vegetables, onion, tomatoes, salt and pepper and mix well. Bring to a boil. Reduce the heat and stir in the beef and seasoning mix. Simmer for 1 hour, stirring occasionally. Ladle into soup bowls. Serves 10.

Rachael Pickett
Cleveland, Tennessee

VEGETABLE BEEF SOUP

1 pound ground beef
1/2 cup (1 stick) margarine
1 quart water
1 quart tomatoes
1 large onion, chopped
2 potatoes, chopped
2 carrots, thinly sliced
1/2 cup corn kernels
1/2 cup sliced okra
1/2 cup shredded cabbage
3 tablespoons chopped green bell pepper
Salt and pepper to taste

Brown the ground beef with the margarine in a large saucepan, stirring until crumbly; drain. Add the water and tomatoes. Cook for 5 to 10 minutes, stirring occasionally. Add the onion, potatoes, carrots, corn, okra, cabbage, bell pepper, salt and pepper and mix well. Bring to a boil. Reduce the heat. Simmer for 45 minutes, stirring occasionally. Ladle into soup bowls. Serves 4 to 6.

Luzenia Queen
Clinton, Tennessee

VEGETABLE BEEF SOUP

$1^1/_2$ pounds ground beef
2 cans condensed cream of celery soup
1 (46-ounce) can vegetable juice cocktail
3 potatoes, peeled and chopped
3 carrots, peeled and chopped
1 can green peas
1 can green beans
1 can lima beans
1 can corn
1 can black-eyed peas
Salt and pepper to taste

Brown the ground beef in a large saucepan, stirring until crumbly; drain. Add the soup, vegetable juice, potatoes, carrots, green peas, green beans, lima beans, corn, black-eyed peas, salt and pepper and mix well. Simmer for 2 to 3 hours or until the potatoes and carrots are tender. Ladle into soup bowls. Serves 8 to 10.

Margie McAlister
Cleveland, Tennessee

BEEF AND CABBAGE SOUP

2 onions, chopped
1 pound ground beef
2 beef bouillon cubes
2 cups water
2 (15-ounce) cans kidney beans, drained
1 can crushed tomatoes
3 cups chopped cabbage

Sauté the onions in a 3-quart saucepan. Add the ground beef and cook until browned and crumbly, stirring constantly; drain. Dissolve the bouillon cubes in the water in a bowl. Stir into the ground beef mixture. Add the kidney beans, tomatoes and cabbage and mix well. Bring to a boil. Reduce the heat and simmer, covered, for 30 to 40 minutes. Ladle into soup bowls. Serves 6 to 8.

Kathleen Price
Rockwood, Tennessee

MEXICAN SOUP

1 pound ground beef
1/2 cup chopped onion
1 can white corn
1 can yellow hominy
1 small can tomato juice
1 can tomatoes with green chiles
1 can ranch-style beans
1 can black beans
1 (16-ounce) jar mild salsa

Brown the ground beef with the onion in a large saucepan, stirring until crumbly; drain. Add the white corn, undrained yellow hominy, tomato juice, undrained tomatoes with green chiles, undrained ranch-style beans, undrained black beans and salsa and mix well. Bring to a boil over medium-low heat. Cook until heated through. Ladle into soup bowls. Serves 12.

John Randolph
Jackson, Tennessee

TACO SOUP

2 pounds ground chuck
1 onion, chopped
Garlic salt to taste
2 small cans tomato sauce
1 large can stewed tomatoes
2 cans white corn, drained
2 cans pinto beans
1 can tomatoes with green chiles
1 envelope ranch salad dressing mix
1 envelope taco seasoning mix
1 tablespoon sugar
1 tablespoon chili powder

Brown the ground beef with the onion in a skillet, stirring until crumbly; drain. Rinse with hot water and drain again. Combine the ground beef mixture, garlic salt, tomato sauce, stewed tomatoes, corn, pinto beans, tomatoes with green chiles, salad dressing mix, taco seasoning mix, sugar and chili powder in a 6-quart saucepan and mix well. Cook until heated through, stirring occasionally. Ladle into soup bowls. Serve with corn bread, tortilla chips and shredded cheese. Serves 8.

Myra Pryor
Troy, Tennessee

WEIGHT WATCHERS TACO SOUP

8 ounces lean ground beef
1 onion, chopped
1 envelope taco seasoning mix
1 envelope ranch salad dressing mix
1 (16-ounce) can dark red kidney beans, drained
1 (15-ounce) can ranch-style beans, drained
1 (11-ounce) can Shoe Peg corn, drained
1 (14-ounce) can tomatoes with green chiles
3 tomato cans water

Brown the ground beef with the onion in a large saucepan, stirring until crumbly; drain. Add the taco seasoning mix and salad dressing mix and mix well. Stir in the kidney beans, ranch-style beans, corn, tomatoes with green chiles and water. Bring to a boil. Reduce the heat and simmer for 5 minutes or until heated through. Ladle into soup bowls. Serve with cornbread, corn chips or shredded Cheddar cheese. Serves 12.

Mackie Jernigan
Memphis, Tennessee

BOHEMIAN CHILI

1 onion, chopped
1 green bell pepper, chopped
3 ribs celery, chopped
2 tablespoons vegetable oil
1 pound ground round
1 can red kidney beans, drained
1 bottle chili sauce
Salt and pepper to taste
1 teaspoon chili powder

Cook the onion, bell pepper and celery in the oil in a large skillet over medium-high heat until tender. Add the ground beef. Cook until the ground beef is browned and crumbly; drain. Add the beans, chili sauce, salt, pepper and chili powder and mix well. Simmer for 45 minutes. Ladle into soup bowls. Serve with crackers. Serves 6.

Ella Mae Hasty
Memphis, Tennessee

CHILI

1 pound ground beef
1 small onion, chopped
1 can kidney beans
1 (15-ounce) can tomato sauce
2 teaspoons chili powder

Brown the ground beef in a skillet, stirring until crumbly; drain. Add the onion and simmer for 5 minutes. Stir in the kidney beans, tomato sauce and chili powder. Cook for 5 minutes. Continue to cook, covered, for 10 to 15 minutes. Ladle into soup bowls. Serves 5.

Juli Simms
Knoxville, Tennessee

CHILI

2 pounds ground beef
1 onion, chopped
1 envelope chili seasoning mix
1 (29-ounce) can pinto beans
1 (29-ounce) can diced tomatoes
2 (15-ounce) cans condensed tomato soup
2 soup cans water
Salt and pepper to taste

Brown the ground beef with the onion in a large saucepan, stirring until crumbly; drain. Add the chili seasoning mix and water using the package directions. Stir in the pinto beans, tomatoes, tomato soup, water, salt and pepper. Simmer for 1 hour. Ladle into soup bowls. Serves 15 to 20.

Helen Wynegar
Powell, Tennessee

WHITE CHILI

2 or 3 chicken breasts, cooked and chopped or shredded
1 (48-ounce) can white beans
1 can tomatoes with green chiles
2 (12-ounce) cans chicken broth
1 small onion, chopped
1 tablespoon cumin (optional)
Shredded Colby Jack cheese

Combine the chicken, white beans, tomatoes, chicken broth, onion and cumin in a saucepan and mix well. Cook over medium-low heat for 30 minutes, stirring occasionally. Ladle into soup bowls and sprinkle with the cheese. Serves 8 to 10.

Kaye Lewis
Joelton, Tennessee

BLACK BEAN SOUP

1 small yellow onion, chopped (about 1/2 cup)
2 garlic cloves, minced
3 tablespoons olive oil
1 teaspoon cumin
1 large rib celery, chopped (about 3/4 cup)
1 large carrot, chopped (about 3/4 cup)
4 cups chicken broth or vegetable broth
3 (15-ounce) cans black beans, rinsed and drained
Juice of 1 lime
1 tablespoon tomato paste
Salt to taste

Cook the onion and garlic in the olive oil in a stockpot until tender, stirring constantly. Stir in the cumin and cook for 1 minute, stirring constantly. Add the celery, carrot, chicken broth and black beans and mix well. Bring to a boil. Reduce the heat to low and simmer, covered, for 15 to 20 minutes. Stir in the lime juice, tomato paste and salt. Ladle into soup bowls and serve with sour cream, salsa and chopped fresh cilantro. You may thicken the soup by puréeing the black beans in a blender or food processor. Serves 8 to 10.

Betty Goan
Morristown, Tennessee

CREAM OF BROCCOLI SOUP

4 teaspoons butter or margarine
3/4 cup chopped onion
2 garlic cloves, minced
1 1/2 pounds broccoli, chopped
2 3/4 cups milk or half-and-half
1 (12-ounce) can evaporated milk
1 teaspoon coriander
3/4 teaspoon salt
White pepper to taste

Melt the butter in a heavy 2-quart saucepan. Cook the onion and garlic in the butter for 3 minutes, stirring constantly. Add the broccoli, milk and evaporated milk. Cook over low heat for 25 minutes, stirring occasionally. Process the soup in batches in a blender until puréed. Return to the saucepan. Stir in the coriander, salt and white pepper. Cook over low heat for 3 minutes, stirring occasionally. Ladle into soup bowls. Serves 4.

Bob Jeffries
Southaven, Mississippi

CHEESE SOUP

3 cups chopped potatoes
1/2 cup chopped celery
1/2 cup chopped carrots
1/4 cup chopped onion
2 tablespoons chopped fresh parsley
2 chicken bouillon cubes
Dash of red pepper
2 tablespoons all-purpose flour
1/2 cup milk
8 ounces Velveeta cheese

Combine the potatoes, celery, carrots, onion, parsley, bouillon cubes, red pepper and just enough water to cover in a saucepan. Simmer for 20 to 30 minutes or until the vegetables are tender. Mix the flour and milk in a bowl and add to the potato mixture. Cook until thickened, stirring occasionally. Add the cheese and stir until melted. Ladle into soup bowls. Serves 6 to 8.

Helen Cole
Knoxville, Tennessee

CHEESY CORN CHOWDER

1 large onion, chopped
2 tablespoons bacon drippings or vegetable oil
1/4 cup all-purpose flour
2 quarts water
6 to 8 potatoes, chopped
1 bay leaf (optional)
1 can condensed cream of chicken or cream of celery soup
1 cup milk
1 1/2 cups (6 ounces) shredded Velveeta cheese
1 1/2 cups (6 ounces) shredded Mexican Velveeta cheese
1 can Mexicorn, drained
Salt and pepper to taste

Sauté the onion in the bacon drippings in a large saucepan until tender. Stir in the flour gradually. Cook for 1 to 2 minutes, stirring constantly. Add the water gradually, stirring constantly. Add the potatoes and bay leaf. Cook until the potatoes are tender. Remove the bay leaf. Add the remaining ingredients and mix well. Cook until the cheeses are melted and the mixture is bubbly, stirring frequently. Serves 10 to 12.

Judy Knowles
Talbott, Tennessee

POTATO SOUP

10 Idaho potatoes, peeled and chopped
2 onions, chopped
2 large carrots, shredded
3 tablespoons dried or chopped fresh parsley
5 cups water
1/2 cup (1 stick) butter
1 (12-ounce) can evaporated milk
1 can condensed cream of chicken soup or cream of celery soup
Salt and pepper to taste

Combine the first 5 ingredients in a saucepan. Cook, covered, over medium heat for 30 minutes or until the potatoes are tender. Add the butter, evaporated milk and soup and mix well. Cook over low heat until heated through. Season with salt and pepper. Serves 12.

Florence Stubblefield
Morristown, Tennessee

IDAHO BAKED POTATO SOUP

2/3 cup butter or margarine
1/2 cup all-purpose flour
7 cups milk
4 large baking potatoes, baked, peeled and chopped (about 4 cups)
4 green onions, sliced
12 slices bacon, crisp-cooked and crumbled
1 1/4 cups (5 ounces) shredded Cheddar cheese
1 cup sour cream
3/4 teaspoon salt
1/2 teaspoon pepper

Melt the butter in a Dutch oven over medium-high heat. Add the flour and stir until smooth. Add the milk gradually, stirring constantly. Cook until thickened, stirring constantly. Add the potatoes and green onions. Bring to a boil, stirring constantly. Reduce the heat and simmer for 10 minutes. Add the bacon, cheese, sour cream, salt and pepper and stir until the cheese is melted. Ladle into soup bowls. You may substitute 1 small onion, chopped, for the green onions. Serves 8 to 10.

Barbara Bearden
Cunningham, Tennessee

CHEESE VEGETABLE SOUP

1 quart water
4 chicken bouillon cubes
1 cup chopped celery
1 cup chopped onion
2 1/2 cups chopped potatoes
1 cup chopped carrots
10 ounces frozen mixed vegetables
2 cans cream of chicken soup
16 ounces Velveeta cheese

Combine the water, bouillon cubes, celery and onion in a saucepan. Simmer, covered, for 20 minutes. Add the potatoes, carrots and mixed vegetables and mix well. Simmer until tender. Add the soup and cheese. Cook until the cheese is melted, stirring constantly. Ladle into soup bowls. Serves 6.

Cathy Funderburk
Knoxville, Tennessee

MAIN DISHES

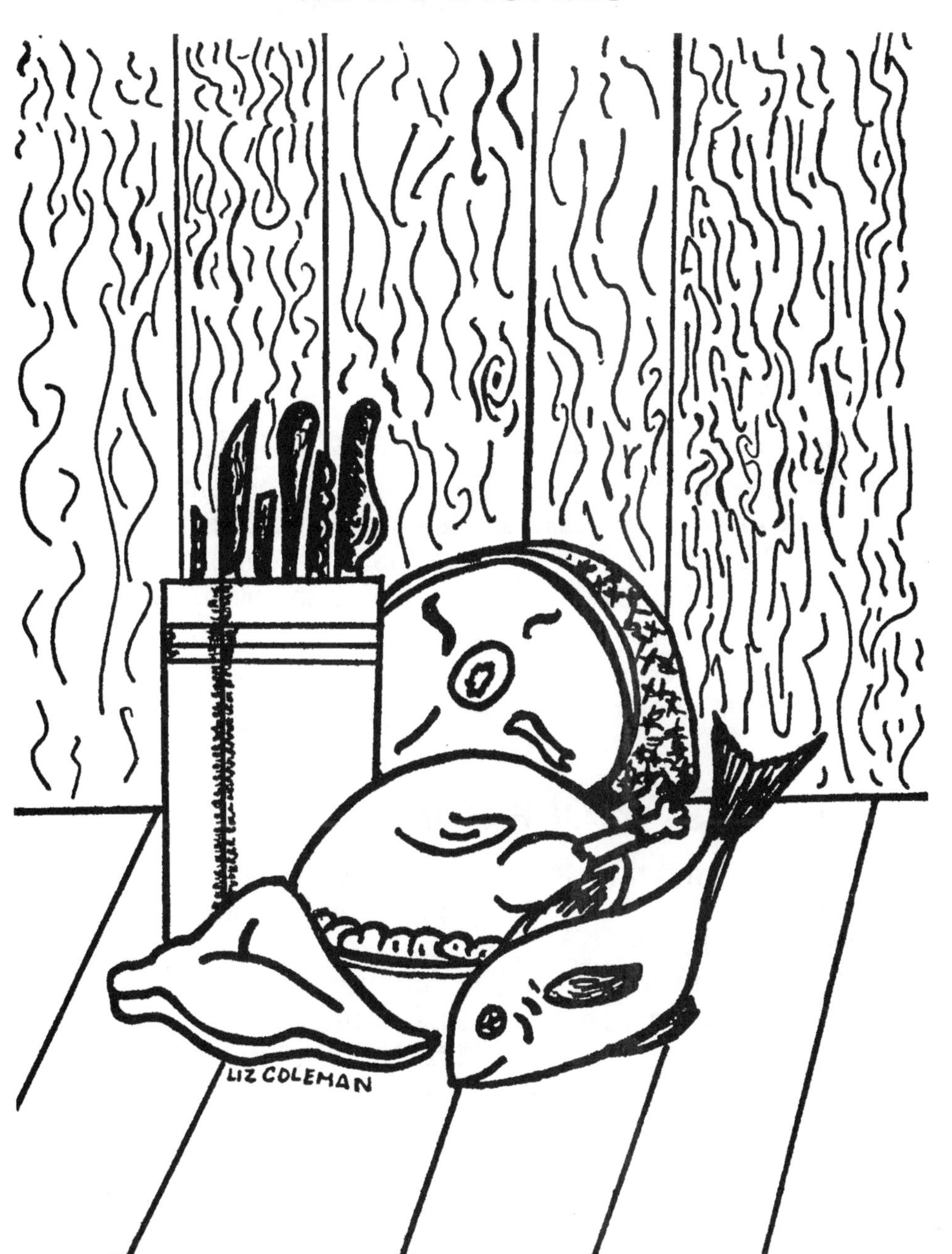

SAFARI ROAST PIG

1 (16-ounce) can whole cranberry sauce
2/3 cup fresh orange juice
1 teaspoon grated orange zest
2 teaspoons balsamic vinegar
1/8 teaspoon salt
1/2 teaspoon pepper
1/4 teaspoon ground allspice
1/8 teaspoon ground cloves
1 1/2 pounds pork tenderloin

Combine the cranberry sauce, orange juice, orange zest, vinegar, salt, pepper, allspice and cloves in a saucepan over medium-high heat. Bring to a boil. Reduce the heat and simmer for 20 minutes.

Cut the pork into slices and arrange in a lightly greased roasting pan or Dutch oven. Pour half the cranberry sauce mixture over the pork. Bake at 425 degrees for 40 minutes or until cooked through, removing the lid during the last 5 minutes of the baking time. Serve with the remaining cranberry sauce mixture. Serves 4 to 6.

Novella Inman Laster
Morristown, Tennessee

PORK ROAST

1 (4- to 5-pound) pork loin roast
1 teaspoon vinegar
1 tablespoon brown sugar
2 teaspoons all-purpose flour
1 teaspoon paprika
1/2 teaspoon salt
1/2 teaspoon pepper
1/4 cup Jack Daniel's whiskey
1/4 cup water
1 bay leaf
2 tablespoons finely chopped fresh parsley

Rub the pork roast with the vinegar. Mix the brown sugar, flour, paprika, salt and pepper in a small bowl. Rub over the entire roast. Place the roast, fat side up, on a rack in a roasting pan. Let stand for 1 hour.

Add the whiskey, water and bay leaf to the bottom of the roasting pan. Sprinkle the parsley over the roast. Place in a 450 degree oven. Reduce the heat to 325 degrees. Roast for 20 to 35 minutes per pound or until a meat thermometer inserted in the thickest part registers 170 degrees. Baste the meat frequently with the pan juices during roasting. Remove the roast to a cutting board and let stand for 15 minutes before carving. Serves 6 to 8.

Glenda Buchanan
College Grove, Tennessee

HERBED PORK MEDALLIONS

2 (3/4 to 1-pound) pork tenderloins
3 tablespoons butter
1 onion, chopped
3 garlic cloves, minced
2 (10-ounce) packages frozen spinach, thawed
1 tablespoon chopped fresh rosemary
2 tablespoons chopped fresh parsley
3/4 cup sour cream
1 egg, beaten
Olive oil
1 envelope béarnaise sauce mix, prepared using the package directions

Butterfly each tenderloin lengthwise on a work surface. Pound to 1/4-inch thickness between sheets of waxed paper.

Melt the butter in a skillet. Add the onion, garlic, spinach, rosemary and parsley and sauté until the liquid evaporates. Remove from the heat and stir in the sour cream and egg. Spread the spinach mixture over the tenderloins. Roll up and secure with kitchen twine. Place in a greased baking dish. Brush with olive oil. Cover with foil.

Bake at 350 degrees for 20 minutes. Remove the foil and bake for 20 minutes longer or until the meat is cooked through. Remove to a cutting board and slice. Spoon the prepared béarnaise sauce over the medallions just before serving. Serves 6 to 8.

Judy Knowles
Talbott, Tennessee

BAKED PORK CHOP CASSEROLE

4 pork chops
Shortening
1/3 cup finely chopped celery
2 tablespoons brown sugar
Juice of 1/2 lemon
1/2 teaspoon salt
1/2 teaspoon dry mustard
1/8 teaspoon pepper
1 (10 3/4-ounce) can condensed tomato soup
2/3 cup water

Brown the pork chops in the shortening in a skillet. Place the chops in a shallow baking dish. Sprinkle with the celery, brown sugar, lemon juice, salt, dry mustard and pepper. Pour a mixture of the soup and water over the chops. Bake, covered, at 350 degrees for 1 1/4 hours or until the meat is cooked though and tender. Serves 4.

Elizabeth Osterholz
Shelbyville, Tennessee

SWEET-AND-SOUR PORK CHOPS

6 (3/4-inch) pork loin chops
1/2 cup pineapple juice
1/2 cup ketchup
1/4 cup water
2 tablespoons white wine vinegar
2 tablespoons honey
1 1/2 teaspoons Dijon mustard
1/4 teaspoon salt
4 teaspoons cornstarch
2 tablespoons water

Arrange the pork chops in a 9x13-inch baking dish. Mix the next 7 ingredients in a bowl. Pour over the chops. Bake, covered, at 350 degrees for 30 minutes. Reduce the heat to 300 degrees. Bake, uncovered, for 30 minutes or until the meat is cooked through and tender. Remove the chops to a serving platter and keep warm. Strain the pan juices into a saucepan. Dissolve the cornstarch in 2 tablespoons water in a small bowl. Add to the pan juices. Cook until thickened and bubbly, stirring constantly. Cook for 2 minutes longer, stirring constantly. Serve immediately over the pork chops. Serves 6.

Lauraette Cheatham
Nashville, Tennessee

PORK CHOP CASSEROLE

1 (10-ounce) can condensed cream of mushroom soup
5 potatoes, peeled, grated
4 pork chops
Salt and pepper to taste

Combine the soup and potatoes in a bowl and mix well. Spoon into a greased baking dish. Season the pork chops with salt and pepper. Arrange on top of the potato mixture. Bake at 375 degrees for 30 minutes. Turn the pork chops and bake for 45 minutes longer or until the meat is cooked through. Serves 4.

Gwen Spalding
Hermitage, Tennessee

UPSIDE-DOWN HAM LOAF

1 tablespoon butter or margarine
1/2 cup packed dark brown sugar
1 (13 1/2-ounce) can crushed pineapple, drained, juice reserved
3 maraschino cherries, quartered
Milk
1 egg
1 cup soft bread crumbs
2 tablespoons mustard
1 teaspoon salt
1/8 teaspoon pepper
1 1/2 pounds ground fully cooked smoked ham
8 ounces ground pork

Melt the butter in a saucepan. Add the brown sugar slowly and cook until smooth, stirring constantly. Pour evenly into the bottom of a loaf pan. Spread the drained pineapple over the brown sugar and dot with the quartered cherries. Add enough milk to the reserved pineapple juice to make 1 cup. Beat the egg in a large bowl. Stir in the milk mixture, bread crumbs, mustard, salt and pepper. Add the ham and pork and mix with hands until well combined. Spoon on top of the pineapple in the loaf pan. Bake at 350 degrees for 1 hour or until the pork is cooked through. Drain off any excess liquid. Invert the loaf onto a serving plate. Serves 8.

Betty Hall
Morristown, Tennessee

STROMBOLI

1/2 cup thinly sliced onion
1/2 cup thinly sliced green bell pepper
1/2 cup chopped mushrooms
1 (10-ounce) can refrigerator pizza dough
1/2 cup shredded mozzarella cheese
1/2 cup shredded Pepper Jack cheese
1/2 cup shredded Monterey Jack cheese
1 cup each thinly sliced beer salami and pepperoni
8 ounces thinly sliced baked ham

Sauté the onion, bell pepper and mushrooms in a nonstick skillet until tender. Stretch or roll the pizza dough into a rectangular shape on a nonstick baking sheet. Layer the cheeses, salami, pepperoni, ham and sautéed vegetables on top of the dough. Roll up starting with the long side, pressing to seal. Cut slits in the top. Bake at 375 degrees until golden brown. Slice and serve. Serves 10.

Carolyn Payne
Jackson, Tennessee

SAUSAGE AND RICE CASSEROLE

1 pound bulk pork sausage
1 onion, chopped
1 bell pepper, chopped
1/2 cup chopped celery
1 cup instant rice
1 (4-ounce) jar chopped pimentos, drained
1 cup shredded sharp Cheddar cheese
1 (10-ounce) can condensed cream of chicken soup
1 (10-ounce) can condensed cream of mushroom soup

Brown the sausage, onion, bell pepper and celery in a skillet, stirring until the sausage is crumbly; drain. Remove from the heat and stir in the remaining ingredients. Spoon into a 2-quart baking dish. Bake at 350 degrees for 35 to 40 minutes, stirring once halfway through baking. Serves 10 to 12.

Rubye Hahn
Bridgeport, Alabama

SAUSAGE AND RICE CASSEROLE

4 1/2 cups water
2 envelopes chicken noodle soup mix with chicken bits
1/2 cup rice
1/4 cup (1/2 stick) butter
3/4 cup chopped onion
1 cup chopped green bell pepper
2 1/2 cups chopped celery
1 pound bulk pork sausage, cooked and drained
1 cup slivered almonds

Bring the water to a boil in a saucepan. Stir in the soup mix, rice and butter. Simmer for 20 minutes; drain. Combine the onion, bell pepper, celery and sausage in a saucepan. Cook until the vegetables are tender. Add the noodles and rice and mix well. Spoon into a greased 9x13-inch baking dish.

Bake at 375 degrees for 20 to 30 minutes. Sprinkle the almonds on top and serve. You can reserve 1 cup chopped celery and sprinkle over the top in place of the almonds, if desired. Serves 6 to 8.

Doris Volz
Memphis, Tennessee

PASTA CASSEROLE

1 pound hot bulk pork sausage
1 pound ground beef
1 (16-ounce) package penne, spiral or macaroni pasta, cooked al dente and drained
1 (26-ounce) jar spaghetti sauce
1 (8-ounce) package each shredded Cheddar cheese and shredded mozzarella cheese

Brown the sausage and ground beef in a skillet, stirring until crumbly; drain. Stir in the pasta and spaghetti sauce. Spoon into a baking dish. Sprinkle with the Cheddar cheese and mozzarella cheese. Bake at 425 degrees until the cheese melts and is golden brown. Serves 8.

Barbara June Borum
Athens, Tennessee

PASTA AND ITALIAN SAUSAGE CASSEROLE

5½ ounces bulk Italian sausage
¼ cup chopped onion
1 garlic clove, minced
¼ cup sliced fresh mushrooms
1 (14-ounce) can whole tomatoes
2 tablespoons chopped green olives
2 tablespoons tomato paste
½ teaspoon sugar
¼ teaspoon basil
1⅓ cups penne pasta, cooked al dente and drained
½ cup shredded mozzarella cheese
1 teaspoon grated Parmesan cheese

Combine the sausage, onion and garlic in a microwave-safe bowl and cover. Microwave on High for 3½ to 6 minutes or until the sausage is cooked through, stirring once during cooking; drain. Stir in the next 6 ingredients and cover. Microwave on High for 2 to 4 minutes. Stir in the pasta. Sprinkle with the mozzarella cheese and Parmesan cheese. Microwave on Medium for 4½ to 7 minutes. Serves 4 to 6.

Peggy McCanless
Nashville, Tennessee

VICKI'S SLOW-COOKER PIZZA

1 (8-ounce) package Kluski noodles
1 (8-ounce) jar pizza sauce
1 (8-ounce) jar spaghetti sauce
8 ounces Italian sausage, casings removed, cooked and drained
8 ounces ground beef, cooked and drained
½ cup chopped onion
½ cup chopped bell pepper
½ cup chopped mushrooms
½ cup chopped black or green olives
8 ounces shredded mozzarella cheese
Sliced pepperoni
Sliced banana or Italian peppers (optional)

Spread the uncooked noodles in the bottom of a slow cooker coated with nonstick cooking spray.

Mix the pizza sauce and spaghetti sauce in a bowl. Pour over the noodles. Top with the next 6 ingredients. Sprinkle with the cheese. Arrange the pepperoni and banana peppers on top of the cheese. Cook on High for 3 hours. Serves 8 to 10.

Vicki Evitts
Nashville, Tennessee

BARBECUED BEEF RIBS

2 pounds beef back ribs, cut into serving pieces
1/2 cup ketchup
2 tablespoons chopped onion
2 garlic cloves, minced
2 tablespoons vinegar
1/2 teaspoon chili powder
1 tablespoon brown sugar
1/2 teaspoon Worcestershire sauce
1/8 teaspoon garlic powder
Dash of hot red pepper sauce

Place the ribs in a large skillet and cover with water. Simmer for 50 to 60 minutes; drain. Arrange the ribs in a greased shallow 2-quart baking dish. Combine the remaining ingredients in a small saucepan and simmer for 10 minutes, stirring occasionally. Pour over the ribs. Bake at 350 degrees for 50 to 60 minutes. Serves 2.

Rosalie Williams
Chattanooga, Tennessee

ROUND STEAK WITH RICH GRAVY

2 1/2 pounds round steak, cut into serving pieces
1 envelope dried onion soup mix
1 (10-ounce) can condensed cream of mushroom soup
1/4 cup water

Arrange the steak in a slow cooker. Sprinkle with the soup mix and spread the soup over the top. Add the water. Cook on Low for 6 to 8 hours. Serves 8.

Betty Ann Webb
Knoxville, Tennessee

CARIBBEAN MEAT LOAF

1 1/2 pounds ground beef
1/2 cup tomato sauce
1 cup bread crumbs
1 egg
2 tablespoons minced onion
2 teaspoons Worcestershire sauce
1/4 teaspoon pepper
Sauce (below)

Combine the ground beef, tomato sauce, bread crumbs, egg, onion, Worcestershire sauce and pepper in a bowl and mix well. Shape into a loaf and place in a 4x8-inch loaf pan sprayed with nonstick cooking spray. Bake at 350 degrees for 65 minutes or until cooked through. Top with the sauce. Bake for 5 minutes longer. Serves 6.

Fruited Sauce

1/2 cup plus 2 tablespoons tomato sauce
1/4 cup drained crushed pineapple
2 tablespoons minced onion
1 1/2 teaspoons brown sugar
1 1/2 teaspoons lime juice
1 teaspoon Worcestershire sauce
1/4 teaspoon ground allspice
1/8 teaspoon salt
1/8 teaspoon ginger
1/8 teaspoon dry mustard

Combine the tomato sauce, pineapple, onion, brown sugar, lime juice, Worcestershire sauce, allspice, salt, ginger and dry mustard in a bowl and mix well.

Bob Jeffries
Southaven, Mississippi

HUNT'S MEAT LOAF

2½ pounds ground beef
1 cup fresh bread crumbs
1 onion, chopped
½ cup chopped celery
½ cup chopped green bell pepper
1¼ teaspoons salt
½ (6-ounce) can Hunt's tomato paste
1 egg, beaten
½ cup milk
Sauce (below)

Combine the ground beef, bread crumbs, onion, celery, bell pepper, salt, tomato paste, egg and milk in a bowl and mix well. Shape into a loaf and place in a baking dish. Pour the sauce over the meat loaf. Bake at 350 degrees for 1¼ hours and 15 minutes, basting occasionally. Serves 6 to 8.

Zesty Sauce

½ (6-ounce) can Hunt's tomato paste
2 tablespoons vinegar
2 tablespoons mustard
2 tablespoons brown sugar
1 cup water

Combine all the ingredients in a saucepan. Heat until bubbly, stirring occasionally.

Betty Holton
Columbia, Tennessee

ENTRÉE MEATBALLS

1 pound ground beef
¾ cup applesauce
1 onion, chopped
1 teaspoon salt
1 teaspoon pepper
1 cup cornflakes, crushed
½ cup ketchup
½ cup water

Mix the ground beef, applesauce, onion, salt, pepper and cornflakes in a bowl until well combined. Shape into 2-inch balls and arrange in a 9x13-inch baking dish. Mix the ketchup and water in a small bowl. Pour over the meatballs. Bake at 375 degrees for 1 hour or until cooked through. Serves 4.

Ethel Ann Burson
Dickson, Tennessee

CRANBERRY MEATBALLS

2 pounds ground beef
1 cup cornflakes
2 tablespoons grated onion
2 tablespoons Worcestershire sauce
1/2 teaspoon garlic powder
1/4 teaspoon pepper
2 eggs
1/2 cup ketchup
1 (12-ounce) can chili sauce
1 (16-ounce) can cranberry sauce
2 tablespoons sugar
2 tablespoons lemon juice

Mix the ground beef, cornflakes, onion, Worcestershire sauce, garlic powder, pepper, eggs and ketchup in a bowl until well combined. Shape gently into balls and arrange in a 9x13-inch baking dish. Mix the chili sauce, cranberry sauce, sugar and lemon juice in a bowl. Pour over the meatballs. Bake at 400 degrees for 35 to 40 minutes or until cooked through.
Serves 8.

Ann Howell Tickle
Morristown, Tennessee

BAKED MEATBALLS

2 pounds lean ground beef
2 eggs or 1/2 cup pasteurized egg substitute
1 tablespoon dried parsley flakes
1 cup bread crumbs
1 cup skim milk
2 teaspoons onion powder
1 teaspoon salt
1/2 teaspoon pepper
1/4 teaspoon nutmeg

Mix the ground beef, eggs, parsley flakes, bread crumbs, milk, onion powder, salt, pepper and nutmeg in a bowl until well combined. Shape into 1 1/2-inch balls and arrange on 2 baking sheets coated with nonstick cooking spray. Bake at 425 degrees for 15 minutes or until cooked through.
Makes 48 meatballs.

Sharon Beason
Spring Hill, Tennessee

HOT TAMALES

2 pounds ground beef
1 (29-ounce) can diced tomatoes, drained
1 (2-ounce) can chili powder
1 envelope chili seasoning mix
2 tablespoons garlic salt
1 (2-pound) package plain cornmeal
4 cups boiling water
1 cup shortening
Tamale papers
Cotton twine, cut into 12-inch lengths

Combine the ground beef, tomatoes, chili powder, seasoning mix and garlic salt in a bowl. Mix with hands until well combined. Shape into balls, using about 2 tablespoons per ball.

Mix the cornmeal, boiling water and shortening gradually together in a bowl to form a ball. Separate the tamale papers and soak in a large pan of water. Add a few drops of vegetable oil to the water, if desired.

Remove a few papers from the water and arrange on a work surface. Place 2 tablespoons of the cornmeal mixture in the center of each paper. Top with a ball of the beef mixture and top with more of the cornmeal. Shape the cornmeal around the beef to form a ball.

Roll up the tamale paper, starting with a corner and tuck as you wrap. Secure the rolls with cotton twine. Repeat with remaining cornmeal, beef and papers. Add the tamales to a large saucepan of boiling water. Boil for 30 to 60 minutes. Makes 36 to 48 tamales.

Helen Wynegar
Powell, Tennessee

AFRICAN CURRY

2 pounds ground beef
4 teaspoons curry powder
2 teaspoons salt
$1\frac{1}{2}$ teaspoons ground cinnamon
$\frac{3}{4}$ teaspoon turmeric
$\frac{1}{2}$ teaspoon nutmeg
1 chicken bouillon cube
1 cup water
Chopped celery
Chopped carrots
Chopped onion
Chopped bell pepper
Pineapple chunks
Chopped watermelon
Chopped cantaloupe
Chopped banana
Chopped apple
Flaked coconut
Peanuts
6 cups hot cooked rice

Brown the ground beef in a skillet, stirring until crumbly; drain. Stir in the curry powder, salt, cinnamon, turmeric and nutmeg. Cook over medium heat, stirring occasionally. Add the bouillon cube and water. Cook until the liquid evaporates, stirring occasionally. Place the celery, carrots, onion, bell pepper, pineapple, watermelon, cantaloupe, banana and apple into separate small bowls. Spoon the rice onto 6 large dinner plates. Top with the meat mixture. Add the vegetables and fruits as desired. Sprinkle with coconut and peanuts. Serves 6.

Kathy Duncan
Memphis, Tennessee

PIZZA CASSEROLE

$1\frac{1}{2}$ pounds ground beef
$\frac{1}{2}$ cup chopped bell pepper
2 ($2\frac{1}{4}$-ounce) cans sliced black olives
$\frac{1}{2}$ cup sliced green olives
$\frac{1}{2}$ onion, chopped
2 (14-ounce) jars pizza sauce
3 ounces sliced pepperoni, cut into quarters
8 to 10 ounces extra-wide noodles, cooked al dente and drained
6 cups (24 ounces) shredded cheese
$\frac{1}{3}$ cup grated Parmesan cheese

Brown the ground beef in a large saucepan, stirring until crumbly; drain. Stir in the bell pepper, black olives, green olives, onion, pizza sauce and pepperoni. Cook until heated through. Spread the noodles in a 9x13-inch baking dish. Sprinkle 1/2 of one package of shredded cheese over the noodles. Add the meat sauce and stir until well mixed. Sprinkle the remaining shredded cheese and Parmesan cheese over the top. Bake at 350 degrees for 30 minutes or until the cheese melts. Serves 12.

Angel Harris
Memphis, Tennessee

BEEF AND BEAN ENCHILADAS

12 ounces lean ground beef
1 cup chopped onion
1 (30-ounce) can refried beans
1/2 teaspoon cumin
1/2 teaspoon chili powder
1 (15-ounce) can enchilada sauce
1/4 teaspoon chopped garlic
1 (15-ounce) can green chile sauce
1/2 teaspoon chopped garlic
12 flour or corn tortillas
1 cup shredded Cheddar cheese

Brown the ground beef in a large saucepan with the onion, stirring until the ground beef is crumbly; drain. Stir in the refried beans, cumin and chili powder. Mix the enchilada sauce and 1/4 teaspoon garlic in a small bowl. Mix the green chile sauce and 1/4 teaspoon garlic in a small bowl. Spread 1/2 the enchilada sauce and 1/2 the green chile sauce in the bottom of a 9x13-inch baking dish coated with nonstick cooking spray. Lay the tortillas on a work surface. Top each with the meat mixture. Roll up and place seam side down in the baking dish. Top with the remaining enchilada sauce and green chile sauce. Bake at 375 degrees for 20 to 25 minutes or until heated through. Sprinkle with the cheese and bake for 5 minutes longer. Serves 12.

Sharon Beason
Spring Hill, Tennessee

TORTILLA SUPREME

1 1/2 pounds ground chuck
1 onion, chopped
1 (16-ounce) can tomatoes
1 (10-ounce) can enchilada sauce
1 (2 1/4-ounce) can sliced black olives
1 teaspoon salt
1/4 teaspoon pepper
1/4 teaspoon garlic powder
1/4 cup vegetable oil
8 corn tortillas
1 cup cottage cheese
1 cup sour cream
8 ounces Monterey Jack cheese, thinly sliced
1/2 cup shredded longhorn cheese

Brown the ground chuck in a large saucepan with the onion, stirring until the beef is crumbly; drain. Stir in the tomatoes, enchilada sauce, olives, salt, pepper and garlic powder. Simmer for 20 minutes. Heat the oil in a skillet. Add the tortillas and cook until softened. Drain on paper towels. Cut each tortilla in half. Beat the cottage cheese and sour cream in a bowl. Spread 1/3 of the meat sauce in the bottom of a shallow baking dish. Top with 1/2 the cottage cheese mixture. Layer with 1/2 the Monterey Jack cheese and arrange 1/2 the tortillas evenly on top. Repeat the layers. Spread the remaining meat sauce on top and sprinkle with the longhorn cheese. Bake at 350 degrees for 45 minutes. Serves 8.

Sadie Tipton
Lafollette, Tennessee

TACO CASSEROLE

2 pounds ground beef
1 envelope taco seasoning mix
1 (8-ounce) can tomato sauce
1 cup (or more) water
1 to 2 cups broken tortilla chips
Shredded cheese

Brown the ground beef in a large skillet, stirring until crumbly; drain. Stir in the seasoning mix, tomato sauce and water. Simmer for 15 to 20 minutes. Remove from the heat and stir in the tortilla chips. Pour into a 9x13-inch baking dish. Top with cheese.

Bake at 350 degrees for 15 minutes or until the cheese melts and the sides are bubbly. Serve with shredded lettuce and diced tomatoes. Serves 6.

Barbara Sneathern
Marion, Arkansas

MEXICAN CASSEROLE

1 pound ground beef
2 tablespoons shortening
1 small onion, chopped
1 (15-ounce) can chili with beans
1 (10-ounce) can condensed tomato soup
1/4 teaspoon salt
1 (10-ounce) package corn chips
1 cup shredded Cheddar cheese
Ketchup

Brown the ground beef in the shortening in a saucepan, stirring until crumbly; drain. Stir in the next 4 ingredients. Simmer, stirring occasionally. Spread 1/2 the corn chips in a large baking dish. Top with the meat mixture. Sprinkle with the cheese. Top with the remaining corn chips and ketchup. Bake at 400 degrees until the cheese melts. Serves 8.

Betty Ann Webb
Knoxville, Tennessee

BEEF TACO BAKE

1 pound ground beef
1 (10 3/4-ounce) can condensed tomato soup
1 cup salsa
1/2 cup milk
6 (6 to 8-inch) flour tortillas, cut into 1-inch pieces
1 cup shredded sharp Cheddar cheese

Brown the ground beef in a large saucepan, stirring until crumbly; drain. Stir in the soup, salsa, milk, tortillas and 1/2 the cheese. Spoon into a 2-quart baking dish. Bake, covered, at 400 degrees for 30 minutes or until hot. Sprinkle with the remaining cheese. Serves 5.

Wanda (Susie) Ladd
Williamsport, Tennessee

7-LAYER CASSEROLE

3 potatoes, peeled and sliced
1 (15-ounce) can whole kernel corn, drained
1 green bell pepper, chopped
1 onion, chopped
1 (15-ounce) can kidney beans, drained
6 ground beef patties
1 (14-ounce) can whole or chopped tomatoes
3 tablespoons beef bouillon

Arrange the potatoes in a 10-inch flat-bottomed baking dish. Layer the corn, bell pepper, onion and kidney beans over the potatoes. Arrange the beef patties on top. Pour a mixture of the tomatoes and bouillon over the beef layer. Bake at 350 degrees for 30 minutes or until the potatoes are tender and the meat is cooked through. Serves 8.

Carolyn Payne
Jackson, Tennessee

MANICOTTI

2 (9-ounce) packages frozen creamed spinach
15 ounces ricotta cheese
8 ounces shredded mozzarella cheese
1 teaspoon salt
1/4 teaspoon pepper
1 (12-ounce) package jumbo macaroni shells, cooked al dente, drained
1 1/2 pounds ground beef
1 (32-ounce) jar spaghetti sauce
1 (8-ounce) can herb-seasoned tomato sauce

Cook the creamed spinach according to the package directions. Pour into a bowl and let cool slightly. Stir in the ricotta cheese, mozzarella cheese, salt and pepper. Stuff the shells with the spinach mixture. Arrange the stuffed shells in a 9x13-inch baking dish. Brown the ground beef in a 10-inch skillet, stirring until crumbly; drain. Stir in the sauces. Cook until hot, stirring occasionally. Pour over the stuffed shells. Bake at 350 degrees for 30 minutes. Serves 12.

Allison Turner
Memphis, Tennessee

SPAGHETTI SAUCE

2 pounds ground chuck
4 (15-ounce) cans tomato sauce
1 (12-ounce) can tomato paste
2 tablespoons olive oil
1 large onion, chopped
1 cup dried parsley flakes
2 teaspoons crushed garlic
1/2 teaspoon oregano
Salt and pepper to taste
Hot cooked spaghetti

Brown the ground chuck in a large saucepan, stirring until crumbly; drain. Stir in the tomato sauce, tomato paste, olive oil, onion, parsley flakes, garlic and oregano. Season with salt and pepper. Bring to a boil and reduce the heat. Simmer for 1 1/2 hours, stirring frequently. Serve over hot spaghetti and add a salad and garlic bread for a complete meal. Serves 6.

Jane Burchfield
Knoxville, Tennessee

BEEF AND MACARONI CASSEROLE

1 pound ground beef
Canola oil
1 onion, chopped
1 cup macaroni, cooked al dente and drained
1 (14 1/2-ounce) can tomatoes
1 (8-ounce) can tomato sauce
1 (8-ounce) can whole kernel corn
1 1/2 cups shredded Cheddar cheese
Salt and pepper to taste
1/2 cup shredded Cheddar cheese

Brown the ground beef in a small amount of oil in a skillet, stirring until crumbly, drain. Sauté the onion in a small amount of oil in a skillet until tender. Combine the beef, onion, macaroni, tomatoes, tomato sauce, corn and 1 1/2 cups cheese in a large bowl. Season with salt and pepper. Stir to mix well. Spoon into a 9x13-inch baking dish. Bake at 400 degrees for 30 minutes. Sprinkle with 1/2 cup cheese and bake until the cheese melts. Serves 6 to 8.

Judy Barton
Clarksville, Tennessee

HAMBURGER ITALIANO

1/4 cup (1/2 stick) margarine
1/2 cup chopped onion
1/2 cup chopped green bell pepper
1 1/2 pounds ground chuck
1 1/2 teaspoons salt
1/4 teaspoon pepper
1/2 teaspoon oregano
2 tablespoons Worcestershire sauce
1 (8-ounce) package macaroni, cooked al dente and drained
1 (3-ounce) can button mushrooms, drained
1 (10-ounce) can condensed tomato soup
1 tomato, chopped
1/2 cup grated Parmesan cheese

Melt the margarine in a large skillet over medium heat. Add the onion and bell pepper and sauté until tender. Add the ground chuck and cook, stirring until crumbly; drain. Stir in the salt, pepper, oregano and Worcestershire sauce. Place the macaroni in a 2 1/2-quart baking dish. Add the meat mixture, mushrooms, soup and chopped tomato and stir to mix well. Bake, covered, at 375 degrees for 40 minutes. Sprinkle with the cheese and bake until the cheese melts. Serves 6 to 8.

Betty Hall
Morristown, Tennessee

GROUND BEEF IN SOUR CREAM

2 tablespoons vegetable oil
1 cup chopped onion
1 pound ground beef
3 cups medium noodles
3 cups tomato juice
2 teaspoons Worcestershire sauce
1 teaspoon salt
1 1/2 teaspoons celery salt
1/4 to 1/2 cup chopped green bell pepper
1 cup sour cream
1 (3-ounce) can broiled, sliced mushrooms, drained
Pepper to taste

Heat the oil in a skillet. Add the onion and sauté until tender but not browned. Add the ground beef and cook, stirring until crumbly; drain. Spread the noodles over the ground beef mixture.

Mix the tomato juice, Worcestershire sauce, salt and celery salt in a bowl. Pour over the noodles. Bring to a boil and reduce the heat. Simmer, covered, over low heat for 20 minutes. Add the bell pepper.

Simmer, covered, for 10 minutes or until the noodles are tender. Stir in the sour cream and mushrooms. Cook just until heated through. Season with pepper and top with bell pepper rings. Serves 6.

Bernice Curtis
Knoxville, Tennessee

SKILLET SUPPER

1 pound ground beef
1 large onion, chopped
1 (10-ounce) can condensed tomato soup
1 (10-ounce) can condensed chili beef soup or 1 (15-ounce) can chili with beans
1 1/4 cups water
1 (7-ounce) package macaroni, cooked al dente and drained
1 cup shredded Cheddar cheese

Brown the ground beef in a large skillet with the onion, stirring until the ground beef is crumbly; drain. Stir in the tomato soup, chili beef soup, water and macaroni. Pour into a baking dish. Top with the cheese. Bake at 350 degrees for 20 to 30 minutes or until bubbly. Serves 6.

Janis and Pam Barker
Chattanooga, Tennessee

TAKE-ALONG

1 pound ground beef
1 onion, chopped
1/4 cup chopped green bell pepper
1 (4-ounce) can chopped green olives, drained
1 tablespoon vinegar
1 (8-ounce) can tomato sauce
1 teaspoon garlic salt
8 ounces shredded Cheddar cheese
4 sourdough French rolls, split

Brown the ground beef in a skillet, stirring until crumbly; drain. Stir in the onion, bell pepper, olives, vinegar, tomato sauce and garlic salt. Simmer for 30 minutes.

Remove from the heat and stir in the cheese. Spoon equal amounts into the rolls and wrap in foil. Bake at 400 degrees for 30 minutes. Serves 4.

Lou Hames
Shelbyville, Tennessee

BARBECUE SAUCE

1/2 cup (1 stick) butter
1 1/2 cups ketchup
3/4 cup cold water
1/2 cup white vinegar
1 large onion, finely chopped
1 1/2 tablespoons Worcestershire sauce
1 1/2 tablespoons sugar
1 1/2 teaspoons pepper
1 1/4 teaspoons paprika
3/4 teaspoon garlic salt

Mix the butter, ketchup, water, vinegar, onion, Worcestershire sauce, sugar, pepper, paprika and garlic salt in a saucepan. Cook over medium heat for 15 to 25 minutes or until the onion is tender, stirring occasionally. Use on beef, pork or chicken. Makes about 3 1/2 cups.

Nancy Bassett
Nashville, Tennessee

CHICKEN AND STEAK MARINADE

2 cups soy sauce
2 cups pineapple juice
1 cup vegetable oil
1/2 cup packed brown sugar
8 teaspoons ginger
4 teaspoons garlic powder
4 teaspoons dry mustard
2 teaspoons pepper

Mix the soy sauce, pineapple juice, oil, brown sugar, ginger, garlic powder, dry mustard and pepper in a saucepan. Bring to a boil. Reduce the heat and cover. Simmer for 5 minutes.

Remove from the heat and let cool. Use as an overnight marinade for steak or chicken. Makes about 3 1/2 cups.

Bonnie Chadwell
Nashville, Tennessee

TEXAS TWO-STEP CHICKEN PICANTE

1 1/2 cups picante sauce
3 tablespoons brown sugar
1 tablespoon Dijon mustard
4 boneless skinless chicken breasts
3 cups hot cooked rice

Mix the picante sauce, brown sugar and mustard in a bowl. Arrange the chicken in a shallow 2-quart baking dish. Pour the sauce over the chicken.

Bake at 400 degrees for 20 minutes or until the chicken is cooked through. Serve with the rice. Serves 4.

Martha Hammonds
Nashville, Tennessee

PATTI'S CHICKEN ROLL-UPS

2 (8-count) cans refrigerator crescent rolls
4 boneless skinless chicken breasts, cooked
1 cup milk
2 (10-ounce) cans condensed cream of chicken soup
4 ounces shredded Colby cheese

Separate the crescent rolls into 8 pieces on a work surface. Press the seam between rolls to seal. Cut the chicken breasts in half lengthwise. Place 1 chicken piece on each dough rectangle. Roll up and arrange in a 9x12-inch baking dish. Pour a mixture of the milk, soup and cheese over the chicken rolls. Bake at 350 degrees for 45 minutes. Serves 8.

Bobbie Latta
Columbia, Tennessee

CHICKEN CONTINENTAL

1 onion, chopped
4 ribs celery, chopped
1 (7-ounce) can water chestnuts, drained and chopped
1 (7-ounce) can mushrooms, drained and chopped
4 chicken breasts, cooked, deboned and chopped
1/2 cup mayonnaise
1 (10-ounce) can condensed cream of mushroom soup
Salt and pepper to taste
1 cup crushed potato chips
1 cup (4 ounces) shredded Cheddar cheese
1 (2-ounce) package sliced almonds

Combine the onion, celery, water chestnuts and mushrooms in a saucepan. Cook over medium heat for 15 minutes or until tender, stirring frequently. Combine the chicken, mayonnaise and soup in a bowl and mix well. Add the onion mixture and mix well. Season with salt and pepper. Spoon into a 3-quart baking dish. Sprinkle with the potato chips, cheese and almonds. Bake at 350 degrees for 30 minutes. Serves 15 to 20.

Helen Wynegar
Powell, Tennessee

SAVORY CHICKEN PASTA DINNER

1 cup all-purpose flour
1 teaspoon salt
1/2 teaspoon pepper
1 1/4 pounds boneless skinless chicken breasts, cut into short strips
3 tablespoons olive oil or canola oil
1 to 2 ounces thinly sliced ham
8 ounces sliced fresh mushrooms
1 (14-ounce) can diced tomatoes
1 teaspoon thyme
Salt and pepper to taste
12 ounces linguine, cooked al dente and drained

Mix the flour, salt and pepper in a shallow dish. Dredge the chicken in the flour mixture. Heat the olive oil in a 12-inch skillet over high heat for 1 minute. Add the chicken and sauté for 3 minutes or until golden brown and cooked through. Remove the chicken with a slotted spoon to a plate and set aside. Add the ham and mushrooms to the skillet. Sauté over high heat until the mushrooms begin to brown. Stir in the tomatoes and thyme and sauté for 1 to 2 minutes. Stir in the chicken, salt and pepper. Serve over the hot linguine. Serves 4.

Martha Hammonds
Nashville, Tennessee

CHICKEN FRICASSEE

1 cup condensed cream of chicken soup
1 cup milk
8 ounces Velveeta cheese, cubed
2 cups egg noodles, cooked al dente and drained
1 (15-ounce) can green peas, drained
2 cups cooked chicken

Combine the soup, milk and cheese in a large saucepan. Cook over low heat until the cheese melts, stirring often. Add the noodles and toss to mix. Stir in the peas and chicken. Serves 4.

Cathy Funderbunk
Knoxville, Tennessee

SLOW-COOKER CHICKEN AND DRESSING

2 1/2 cups torn corn bread
1 cup torn white bread or biscuits
2 eggs
1 onion, chopped
3/4 cup chopped celery
1 tablespoon sage
Salt and pepper to taste
2 (10-ounce) cans condensed cream of chicken soup
Chicken broth
1 (3- to 4-pound) chicken, cooked, boned and cut into cubes

Mix the first 8 ingredients in a large bowl. Stir in 1 can soup and enough chicken broth to moisten. Spread 1/2 can soup in the bottom of a slow cooker. Top with a 1/3 of the chicken and 1/2 the dressing. Repeat the layers and top with the remaining chicken. Spread the remaining soup over the top. Cook on Low for 3 hours. Serves 4.

Ruby Rigsby
Soddy-Daisy, Tennessee

CHICKEN AND DUMPLINGS

1 (3- to 4-pound) chicken
3 cups self-rising flour
Dash of salt
1/4 cup shortening
1/2 cup ice water
Salt and pepper to taste

Boil the chicken with water to cover in a large saucepan until cooked through. Remove the chicken and let cool. Reserve the broth. Bone the chicken. Cover and chill. Mix the flour and dash of salt in a bowl. Cut in the shortening with a pastry blender or fork until crumbly. Stir in the water to form a dough. Roll out the dough between floured sheets of waxed paper. Let stand for 30 minutes. Heat the reserved chicken broth to boiling. Add water, margarine or chicken bouillon if needed. Cut the dough into short pieces and drop in the boiling broth 1 at a time. Cook for 15 minutes. Add the cooked chicken and season with salt and pepper. Cook until the chicken is heated through, stirring occasionally. Serves 4 to 6.

Nancy Bassett
Nashville, Tennessee

EASY CHICKEN POTPIE

1 (2-crust) pie pastry
1 (2 1/2-pound) chicken, cooked, boned and chopped
1 (10-ounce) can condensed cream of mushroom soup
1 (10-ounce) can condensed cream of celery soup
1 onion, chopped
1 (10-ounce) package frozen mixed vegetables, thawed
Salt and pepper to taste
1 cup all-purpose flour
1 cup milk
1/2 cup (1 stick) butter, melted

Fit the pie dough in the bottom of a 9x13-inch baking pan, pressing the seams to seal. Combine the chicken, mushroom soup, celery soup, onion and vegetables in a bowl. Season with salt and pepper and mix well. Pour over the dough. Mix the flour, milk and melted butter in a bowl until smooth. Pour over the filling. Bake at 350 degrees for 1 hour or until the top is golden brown. Serves 10 to 12.

Mildred Hensley
Lake City, Tennessee

CHICKEN POTPIE

1/2 cup (1 stick) margarine
1 (10-ounce) can condensed cream of celery soup
1 (10-ounce) can condensed chicken broth
1 pound boneless chicken breasts, cooked and cut into bite-size pieces
Salt and pepper to taste
1 cup baking mix
1 cup milk

Combine the margarine, soup and broth in a small saucepan. Cook until heated through, stirring often. Spread the chicken in a 9x13-inch baking dish. Season with salt and pepper. Pour the soup mixture over the chicken. Stir the baking mix and milk in a small bowl until well mixed. Pour evenly over the soup mixture. Bake at 350 degrees for 35 minutes. Serves 8.

Juli Simms
Knoxville, Tennessee

ARTICHOKE CHICKEN CASSEROLE

2 (14-ounce) cans artichoke hearts, drained and quartered
$2^1/_2$ cups chopped cooked chicken breasts
1 (14-ounce) can condensed cream of chicken soup
1 tablespoon lemon juice
1 cup mayonnaise
$1^1/_2$ teaspoons curry powder
$1^1/_2$ cups shredded Cheddar cheese
$1^1/_2$ cups bread crumbs
$^1/_4$ cup ($^1/_2$ stick) margarine, melted
Hot cooked rice

Spread the artichoke hearts in a greased 9x13-inch baking dish. Top with the chicken. Mix the next 4 ingredients in a bowl. Pour over the chicken. Sprinkle with the cheese. Toss the bread crumbs and melted margarine in a bowl. Sprinkle over the cheese. Bake at 350 degrees for 25 minutes. Serve over cooked white rice. Serves 6.

Addie Downs
Antioch, Tennessee

JEAN'S 1-2-3 CHICKEN DISH

1 (10-ounce) can condensed cream of chicken soup
4 boneless skinless chicken breasts
1 (10-ounce) can condensed cream of celery soup
2 tablespoons sherry
2 cups shredded sharp Cheddar cheese
1 (16-ounce) package herb-seasoned stuffing
$^1/_2$ cup (1 stick) butter, melted

Spread the chicken soup in the bottom of a 9x13-inch baking dish. Arrange the chicken on top. Mix the celery soup and sherry in a small bowl. Spread over the chicken. Top with the cheese. Sprinkle the stuffing over the cheese. Pour the melted butter over the stuffing. Cover with foil. Bake at 350 degrees for 1 hour or until the chicken is cooked through. Serves 4.

Jean Mayo
Ashland City, Tennessee

CHICKEN CASSEROLE

1 pound boneless skinless chicken breasts, cooked and cut into cubes
2 (10½-ounce) cans condensed cream of chicken soup
1 cup sour cream
1 sleeve (about 36) butter crackers
½ cup (1 stick) butter or margarine, melted

Spread the chicken in a baking dish. Mix the chicken soup and sour cream in a small bowl. Pour over the chicken. Crumble the crackers over the soup mixture. Pour the melted butter evenly over the crackers. Bake at 350 degrees until bubbly and beginning to brown. Serves 4.

Peggy Burr
Nashville, Tennessee

WHITE CHICKEN CASSEROLE

4 chicken breasts (or other chicken parts)
1 (10-ounce) can condensed cream of chicken soup
1 (10-ounce) can condensed cream of mushroom soup
1 (10-ounce) can condensed cream of onion soup
1 cup sour cream
½ (6-ounce) package stuffing mix
Several pats of margarine

Boil the chicken with water to cover in a saucepan until cooked through. Remove the chicken and reserve the broth. Cut the chicken into bite-size pieces and spread in a 9x11-inch baking dish. Mix the chicken soup, mushroom soup, onion soup and sour cream in a bowl. Pour over the chicken. Top with the stuffing mix. Sprinkle with some of the reserved chicken broth. Arrange the margarine on top. Cover with foil. Bake at 350 degrees for 30 minutes. Remove the foil and bake for 10 minutes longer. Serves 8 to 10.

Rachael Pickett
Cleveland, Tennessee

HOT CHICKEN SALAD

3 boneless chicken breasts, cooked, cut into bite size pieces
4 hard-cooked eggs, diced
1 1/2 cups mayonnaise
1 cup diced celery
1/2 cup slivered almonds
2 (4-ounce) jars chopped pimentos, drained
2 tablespoons lemon juice
1 tablespoon finely chopped onion
1 teaspoon salt
1/2 teaspoon MSG
1 1/2 cups crushed potato chips
1 cup shredded sharp Cheddar cheese

Combine the first 10 ingredients in a large bowl. Stir to mix well. Cover and chill overnight. Add the potato chips and cheese and stir to mix well. Spoon into a 9x13-inch baking dish. Bake at 400 degrees for 25 minutes. Serves 12.

Ann Wooten
Cordova, Tennessee

HOT CHICKEN SALAD CASSEROLE

4 cups diced cooked chicken
3/4 cup chicken broth or milk
1 (10-ounce) can condensed cream of chicken soup
1 (10-ounce) can condensed cream of mushroom soup
1 onion, chopped
1 cup diced celery
2 cups slivered almonds
1 cup mayonnaise
1 cup shredded cheese
4 teaspoons lemon juice
1/2 teaspoon pepper
1 sleeve (about 30) saltine crackers, crushed
1/4 cup (1/2 stick) margarine, melted

Combine the first 11 ingredients in a large bowl. Stir to mix well. Spoon into a 9x13-inch baking dish. Mix the cracker crumbs and margarine in a bowl. Sprinkle over the chicken mixture. Bake at 350 degrees for 30 minutes. Serves 12.

Ruby Rigsby
Soddy-Daisy, Tennessee

EASY CHICKEN CASSEROLE

1 pound boneless skinless chicken breasts, cooked and cubed
8 ounces egg noodles, cooked al dente in chicken broth and drained
1 envelope chicken noodle soup mix
1/2 cup wild rice, cooked
6 ounces frozen corn
1 (8-ounce) can water chestnuts, drained
1 (10-ounce) can condensed cream of chicken soup
1 (10-ounce) can condensed cream of mushroom soup
1/2 cup sour cream
1/2 to 3/4 teaspoon seasoned salt
1 teaspoon Worcestershire sauce
1 teaspoon pepper

Combine all the ingredients in a large bowl. Stir to mix well. Spoon into a greased 2-quart baking dish. Bake at 350 degrees for 45 minutes. Serves 6 to 8.

Wendy O'Neal
Maryville, Tennessee

CHICKEN CASSEROLE

4 to 6 chicken breasts
1 (10-ounce) can each condensed cream of chicken soup and cream of celery soup
1 cup sour cream
1 (16-ounce) package herb-seasoned stuffing
1/2 cup (1 stick) butter, melted

Simmer the chicken in water in a saucepan for 2 hours. Remove the chicken and reserve 1 cup of the broth. Remove the meat from the bones and arrange in a greased baking dish. Mix the soups and sour cream in a bowl. Pour over the chicken. Sprinkle the stuffing over the soup mixture and pour the butter evenly over the stuffing. Pour the reserved broth evenly over the top. Bake at 350 degrees for 1 hour. Serves 8 to 10.

Gwen Spalding
Hermitage, Tennessee

CHICKEN AND RICE CASSEROLE

- $2^1/_2$ pounds cooked chicken, cut into bite-size pieces
- 2 (10-ounce) cans condensed cream of chicken soup
- 1 ($14^1/_2$-ounce) can low-sodium chicken broth
- 1 small onion, minced
- $^1/_2$ cup mayonnaise
- 1 (8-ounce) can sliced water chestnuts, drained and chopped
- 1 ($6^1/_3$-ounce) package instant rice, cooked using the package directions
- 2 cups broccoli florets, cooked

Mix all the ingredients in a large bowl. Spread evenly into 2 lightly greased 8x8-inch baking dishes. Freeze 1 casserole wrapped in heavy-duty foil for later use. Bake the remaining casserole at 350 degrees for 55 minutes or until thoroughly heated. Thaw the other casserole overnight in the refrigerator before baking. Serves 4 per casserole.

Billie Carson
Lafollette, Tennessee

CHICKEN BROCCOLI CASSEROLE

- 1 cup mayonnaise
- 1 ($10^3/_4$-ounce) can condensed cream of mushroom soup
- 1 (8-ounce) can sliced water chestnuts, drained
- 1 cup cubed Velveeta cheese
- 3 cups cubed cooked chicken
- 1 (16-ounce) bag frozen chopped broccoli, cooked using the package directions
- $^1/_2$ cup cubed Velveeta cheese
- 1 sleeve (about 36) butter crackers, crushed
- 3 tablespoons margarine, melted

Mix the first 5 ingredients in a large bowl. Spread in the bottom of a large baking dish. Top with the broccoli and $^1/_2$ cup cheese. Cover with the cracker crumbs and drizzle with the margarine. Bake at 350 degrees for 30 minutes. Serves 8 to 10.

Barbara Bearden
Cunningham, Tennessee

CLUB CHICKEN CASSEROLE

1/4 cup (1/2 stick) butter
1/4 cup all-purpose flour
1 cup chicken broth
1 (12-ounce) can evaporated milk
1/2 cup water
1 1/2 teaspoons salt
2 1/2 cups diced cooked chicken
3 cups cooked white rice
1 (3-ounce) can sliced mushrooms, drained
1/3 cup chopped green bell pepper
1/4 cup chopped pimento
1/2 cup slivered almonds, toasted

Melt the butter in a large skillet. Stir in the flour. Stir in the broth, evaporated milk and water. Cook over low heat until thick, stirring constantly. Stir in the salt, chicken, rice, mushrooms, bell pepper and pimento. Pour into a greased 8x11-inch baking dish. Bake at 350 degrees for 30 minutes. Sprinkle with the almonds. Serves 10.

Martha Williams
Hollow Rock, Tennessee

CHICKEN AND WILD RICE CASSEROLE

3 cups cooked chicken
1 small package long grain and wild rice, prepared using the package directions
1 cup mayonnaise
1 onion, chopped
1 (10-ounce) can condensed cream of celery soup
1 (8-ounce) can sliced water chestnuts, drained
2 cups green beans

Combine the chicken, rice, mayonnaise, onion, soup, water chestnuts and beans in a large bowl. Stir to mix well. Spoon into one 9x13-inch baking dish or two 8x8-inch baking dishes. Bake at 350 degrees for 25 to 30 minutes or until heated through. Serves 12.

Allison Turner
Memphis, Tennessee

CHEESY CHICKEN SPAGHETTI

1 (3- to 4-pound) chicken
1 (16-ounce) package spaghetti
1/2 cup (1 stick) butter
1 onion, chopped
1 small bell pepper, chopped
1 cup chopped celery
1 (10-ounce) can condensed cream of chicken soup
16 ounces Velveeta cheese, cubed
1 (10-ounce) can tomatoes with green chiles

Boil the chicken in water to cover in a large saucepan until cooked through. Remove the chicken and let cool. Reserve the broth. Bone the chicken and place in a large baking dish. Cook the spaghetti in the reserved broth according to the package directions; drain. Add to the chicken. Melt the butter in a skillet. Add the onion, bell pepper and celery and sauté until the vegetables are tender. Add to the chicken mixture. Combine the soup and cheese in a saucepan. Cook until the cheese melts, stirring often. Add to the chicken mixture. Add the tomatoes with green chiles and stir to mix well. Bake at 350 degrees until bubbly. Serves 6 to 10.

Joyce Neely
Jackson, Tennessee

OVEN-FRIED CHICKEN LEGS

1/4 cup all-purpose flour
1/2 teaspoon salt
1/8 teaspoon pepper
2 pounds chicken legs
5 1/3 tablespoons butter or margarine, melted

Combine the flour, salt and pepper in a large sealable plastic bag. Seal the bag and shake to mix. Add the chicken, 2 legs at a time, and seal the bag. Shake until well coated. Arrange the chicken in a single layer in a large baking dish. Drizzle the melted butter over the chicken. Bake at 425 degrees for 45 minutes or until the chicken is cooked through and tender. Serves 4.

Trilby Williams
Morristown, Tennessee

POPPY SEED CHICKEN

4 boneless chicken breasts, cooked and shredded
1 teaspoon poppy seeds
2 cups sour cream
1 (10-ounce) can condensed cream of celery soup
1 (10-ounce) can condensed cream of mushroom soup
40 butter crackers, crushed
1/2 cup (1 stick) butter, cut into small pieces

Mix the chicken, poppy seeds, sour cream, celery soup and mushroom soup in a large bowl. Spoon into a 7x11-inch or 8x8-inch baking dish. Top with the crushed crackers and dot with the butter.

Bake at 350 degrees for 30 to 45 minutes or until bubbly. Serves 6 to 8.

Emily Taylor
Jackson, Tennessee

FRIED CHICKEN LIVERS

1 pound chicken livers, drained
1 cup buttermilk
1 cup self-rising flour
Vegetable oil for deep-frying

Combine the chicken livers and buttermilk in a bowl. Let stand for 10 minutes. Drain in a colander.

Dredge the chicken livers in the flour. Heat oil in a heavy saucepan or deep-fryer to 350 degrees. Add the chicken livers. Fry for 3 to 4 minutes or until golden brown. Remove to paper towels to drain. Serves 4.

Marie Guy
Clinton, Tennessee

STUFFED CORNISH GAME HENS

2 Cornish game hens
Salt and pepper to taste
6 tablespoons unsalted butter
1 rib celery with leaves, coarsely chopped
1 onion, chopped
6 to 10 mushrooms, sliced
1 garlic clove, minced
1/4 cup dry white wine
3 cups dried bread cubes
1 teaspoon sage
1 1/2 teaspoons thyme
2 tablespoons chopped fresh parsley
Melted butter for basting

Rub the outside of the game hens with salt and pepper. Melt 6 tablespoons butter in a skillet. Add the celery, onion, mushrooms, garlic and wine and sauté just until the vegetables are tender. Remove to a bowl. Add the bread cubes, sage, thyme and parsley. Season with salt and pepper. Toss to mix. Taste and add more seasonings, if desired. Stuff the game hens with the bread mixture. Spoon any leftover stuffing into a covered baking dish. Tuck the wings under the game hens and tie the legs together with kitchen twine. Place the game hens, breast side up, in a shallow roasting pan. Place in a 450 degree oven. Reduce the heat to 350 degrees. Roast for about 1 hour or until tender and cooked through, basting occasionally with melted butter. Remove the twine and serve. Leftover stuffing can be baked during the last 30 minutes of roasting or chilled and used at another time. Serves 2.

Patricia Ray
Shelbyville, Tennessee

MARINATED FRIED TURKEY

1 (2-ounce) bottle onion juice
1 (2-ounce) bottle garlic juice
1 (10-ounce) bottle Worcestershire sauce
1 (2-ounce) bottle Tabasco sauce
1 (8-ounce) bottle lemon juice
1/2 cup plus 1 tablespoon salt
Water
1 (12-pound) turkey
Tony's Cajun Seasoning Mix
Peanut oil for deep-frying

Combine the onion juice, garlic juice, Worcestershire sauce, Tabasco sauce, lemon juice and salt with enough water to make 2 quarts in a large bowl or pitcher. Stir until the salt dissolves.

Inject at least 1 cup of marinade into the turkey. Sprinkle the outside of the turkey with Cajun seasoning.

Heat oil to 400 degrees in turkey-fryer according to manufacturer's directions. Add the turkey carefully and maintain the oil at 375 degrees. Cook for 50 minutes or until cooked through. Serves 12.

Joanne Taylor
Jackson, Tennessee

LOBSTER ALFREDO PRIMAVERA

1 tablespoon olive oil
1 cup diced zucchini
1 cup sliced fresh mushrooms
1/2 cup diced red bell pepper
1 tablespoon chopped garlic
1/2 cup dry white wine
1 (16-ounce) jar Alfredo sauce
1 (6- to 8-ounce) package imitation lobster meat
1 teaspoon basil
1 teaspoon lemon juice
3 cups penne, cooked al dente and drained

Heat the olive oil in a large saucepan over medium heat. Add the zucchini, mushrooms and bell pepper and sauté for 1 to 2 minutes. Add the garlic and sauté for a few seconds. Stir in the wine.

Stir in the Alfredo sauce, lobster, basil and lemon juice. Cook until heated through. Serve over the hot pasta. Serves 4.

Glenda Buchanan
College Grove, Tennessee

MANDARIN SHRIMP STIR-FRY

2 cups chopped eggplant
1/4 cup vegetable oil
2 garlic cloves, crushed
2 cups chopped zucchini
2 cups chopped broccoli
1 cup julienned carrots
1 cup fresh pea pods or thawed frozen pea pods
1 (8-ounce) can sliced water chestnuts, drained
1 tablespoon ginger
1 1/2 pounds shrimp, peeled and deveined
Sauce (below)
Hot cooked rice or pasta

Combine the eggplant and enough salted water to cover in a bowl. Let stand for 20 minutes; drain. Heat half the oil in a wok or large skillet over medium-high heat. Stir-fry the eggplant, garlic, zucchini, broccoli, carrots, pea pods, water chestnuts and ginger in the hot oil until the vegetables are tender. Remove to a bowl. Add the remaining oil to the wok. Stir-fry the shrimp in the oil for 4 to 5 minutes or until pink. Return the vegetables to the wok. Add the sauce. Cook until the sauce is thickened and bubbly, stirring constantly. Serve over rice. Serves 6 to 8.

Sauce

2 tablespoons cornstarch
1 1/4 cups water
1/3 cup soy sauce
3 cups dark corn syrup
2 tablespoons sherry or white wine
2 teaspoons crushed red pepper flakes

Dissolve the cornstarch in the water in a bowl. Add the soy sauce, corn syrup, sherry and red pepper flakes and mix well.

Bob Jeffries
Southaven, Mississippi

SHRIMP/OYSTER SAUCE

1 (12-ounce) bottle chili sauce
1 (12-ounce) bottle ketchup
2 tablespoons grated onion
2 tablespoons Worcestershire sauce
1 tablespoon horseradish
1 tablespoon lemon juice
1 tablespoon mustard
Salt and pepper to taste
2 tablespoons cognac or bourbon

Combine the chili sauce, ketchup, onion, Worcestershire sauce, horseradish, lemon juice and mustard in a bowl. Season with salt and pepper. Stir to mix well. Stir in the cognac just before serving. Makes about 3³/4 cups.

Barbara Johnson
Collierville, Tennessee

SALMON PATTIES

2 eggs, beaten
1/4 cup milk
1 (16-ounce) can pink salmon, drained and flaked
1/3 cup finely crushed crackers
1/2 teaspoon pepper
3 tablespoons vegetable oil

Mix the eggs and milk in a bowl. Stir in the salmon. Add the crushed crackers and pepper. Stir to mix well.

Shape into 6 patties. Heat the oil in a cast-iron skillet. Add the patties and brown on both sides. Serves 6.

Nancy Bassett
Nashville, Tennessee

SALMON LOAF

- 1 (1 1/4-ounce) package white sauce mix, prepared using the package directions
- 1 (16-ounce) can salmon, drained and flaked
- 1/2 cup mayonnaise-style salad dressing
- 1 egg, beaten
- 1 cup bread crumbs
- 1/2 cup chopped celery
- 1/2 cup chopped onion
- 1/4 cup chopped green bell pepper
- 1 tablespoon lemon juice
- 1 teaspoon salt
- Cucumber Sauce (below)

Combine the white sauce, salmon, salad dressing, egg, bread crumbs, celery, onion, bell pepper, lemon juice and salt in a large bowl. Stir to mix well. Shape into a loaf and place in a shallow baking dish. Bake at 350 degrees for 1 hour. Serve the salmon loaf with the Cucumber Sauce. Serves 6.

Cucumber Sauce

- 1 (1 1/4-ounce) package sour cream sauce mix, prepared using the package directions
- 1/4 cup mayonnaise-style salad dressing
- 1/4 cup chopped cucumber

Combine the sour cream sauce, salad dressing and cucumber in a bowl. Stir to mix well.

Patricia Ray
Shelbyville, Tennessee

PARMESAN TILAPIA

- 1/2 cup grated Parmesan cheese
- 1/4 cup (1/2 stick) butter, softened
- 3 tablespoons mayonnaise
- 2 tablespoons lemon juice
- 1/4 teaspoon basil
- 1/4 teaspoon pepper
- 1/8 teaspoon onion powder
- 2 pounds fresh tilapia fillets

Combine the cheese, butter, mayonnaise, lemon juice, basil, pepper and onion powder in a small bowl and mix well.

Arrange the fillets on a broiler pan coated with nonstick cooking spray. Broil a few inches from the heat source for 2 to 3 minutes. Turn the fillets and broil for 2 to 3 minutes on the other side.

Spread the cheese mixture over the fish. Broil for 2 minutes or until the topping is golden brown. Do not overcook the fish. Serves 5.

Lee and Toni Trice
Henderson, Tennessee

SCOTCH EGGS

1 egg
1 pound bulk pork sausage, cooked and drained
8 hard-cooked eggs, peeled
All-purpose flour
2 cups bread crumbs
4 cups vegetable oil

Mix the egg and sausage in a bowl. Divide into 8 equal portions. Roll the hard-cooked eggs in flour to coat.

Wrap 1 portion of sausage around each hard-cooked egg to form a thin coating. Roll each coated egg in bread crumbs to coat.

Heat the oil in a deep saucepan over medium heat to 375 degrees. Fry the eggs, 4 at a time, for 5 to 6 minutes or until golden brown, turning often to brown all sides. Drain on paper towels. Serves 8.

Bill and Audrey Hembree
Clinton, Tennessee

SAUSAGE AND EGG CASSEROLE

1 pound mild bulk pork sausage, cooked and drained
1 cup shredded sharp cheese
1/4 cup (1/2 stick) margarine, melted
6 eggs, beaten
1/2 teaspoon salt
1/4 teaspoon pepper
1/2 teaspoon dry mustard (optional)
1 cup shredded sharp cheese

Spread the sausage in a 9x13-inch baking dish. Sprinkle with 1 cup cheese. Mix the margarine, eggs, milk, salt, pepper and dry mustard in a bowl. Pour over the sausage mixture. Sprinkle 1 cup cheese over the top. Bake at 325 degrees for 35 minutes. You may also use hot sausage or a combination of hot and mild sausage. Serves 8 to 10.

Kathy Duncan
Memphis, Tennessee

VERA'S SAUSAGE HASH BROWN CASSEROLE

1/2 cup (1 stick) margarine
1 (2-pound) bag frozen shredded hash brown potatoes
1 pound hot or mild bulk pork sausage, cooked and drained
10 eggs
1 cup milk
Salt and pepper to taste
2 cups shredded Cheddar cheese

Melt the margarine in a skillet. Add the potatoes and fry until golden brown. Spread the potatoes in a 9x13-inch baking dish. Crumble the sausage over the potatoes. Beat the eggs and milk in a bowl. Season with salt and pepper. Pour over the potato mixture. Sprinkle the cheese over the top. Cover and chill overnight. Bake, uncovered, at 350 degrees for 1 hour. Cover with foil and bake 20 minutes longer. Serves 12.

Vera Raines
Lake City, Tennessee

SALES MEETING BREAKFAST CASSEROLE

1 pound bulk pork sausage, cooked and drained
1 1/2 bunches green onions, chopped
4 ounces fresh mushrooms, sliced
2 tomatoes, diced
2 cups shredded mozzarella cheese
12 eggs, well beaten
1 1/4 cups baking mix
1 cup milk
1 teaspoon oregano
Salt and pepper to taste

Spread the sausage in a 9x13-inch baking dish. Layer the green onions, mushrooms and tomatoes on top of the sausage. Sprinkle the cheese over the tomatoes. Combine the eggs, baking mix, milk and oregano in a large bowl. Season with salt and pepper and mix well. Pour over the cheese. Bake at 350 degrees for 30 to 35 minutes or until firm and the edges are golden brown. Serves 8.

Sonya Van Cleave
Memphis, Tennessee

BREAKFAST CASSEROLE

1 (8-count) can refrigerator crescent rolls
1 pound bulk pork sausage, cooked and drained
1 cup shredded cheese
4 eggs
3/4 cup milk
1/4 teaspoon salt
1/8 teaspoon pepper

Unroll the crescent dough and fit in the bottom of a buttered 9x13-inch baking pan. Press the seams together to seal. Spread the sausage over the dough and sprinkle the cheese over the sausage. Beat the eggs, milk, salt and pepper in a bowl. Pour over the cheese. Bake at 425 degrees for 15 minutes. Serves 6 to 8.

Arizona Powell
Lafollette, Tennessee

BREAKFAST CASSEROLE

1 (8-count) can refrigerator crescent rolls
1 pound bulk pork sausage, cooked and drained
4 eggs
$^2/_3$ cup milk
$1^1/_2$ cups shredded Monterey Jack cheese
$1^1/_2$ cups shredded Cheddar cheese

Unroll the crescent dough and fit in the bottom of a greased 9x13-inch baking pan. Press the seams together to seal. Spread the sausage over the dough. Beat the eggs and milk in a bowl. Pour over the sausage. Sprinkle the Monterey Jack cheese and Cheddar cheese on top. Bake at 350 degrees for 20 to 30 minutes or until set and lightly browned. Serve hot.
Serves 8.

Nancy Bassett
Nashville, Tennessee

BREAKFAST CASSEROLE

1 (8-count) can refrigerator crescent rolls
1 pound bulk pork sausage, cooked and drained
$1^1/_2$ to 2 cups shredded Cheddar cheese
5 eggs, well beaten
$^3/_4$ cup milk
Salt and pepper to taste

Unroll the crescent dough and fit in the bottom of a 9x13-inch baking dish. Press the seams together to seal. Spread the sausage over the dough and sprinkle the cheese over the sausage. Mix the eggs and milk in a bowl. Season with salt and pepper. Pour evenly over the cheese. Bake at 350 degrees for 25 to 30 minutes or until set. Remove to a wire rack and let stand for 10 minutes before serving.
Serves 8 to 10.

Kaye Lewis
Joelton, Tennessee

MUSHROOM BREAKFAST CASSEROLE

2 1/4 cups seasoned croutons
1 1/2 pounds bulk pork sausage, cooked and drained
4 eggs, beaten
2 1/4 cups milk
1 (4-ounce) can sliced mushrooms, drained
1 (10-ounce) can condensed cream of mushroom soup
3/4 teaspoon dry mustard
2 cups shredded Cheddar cheese
Cherry tomatoes and parsley for garnish

Spread the croutons in a lightly greased 9x13-inch baking dish. Sprinkle the sausage over the croutons. Combine the eggs, milk, mushrooms, soup and dry mustard in a bowl and mix well. Pour over the sausage. Cover and chill for at least 2 hours or overnight. Let stand at room temperature for 30 minutes before baking. Bake, uncovered, at 325 degrees for 45 minutes. Sprinkle the cheese on top and bake for 5 to 10 minutes longer. Garnish with cherry tomatoes and parsley. Serves 10.

Addie Downs
Antioch, Tennessee

SAUSAGE PIE

1 pound hot bulk pork sausage, cooked and drained
1 pound sharp Cheddar cheese, shredded
4 eggs, beaten
1/2 cup milk
Salt and pepper to taste
1 unbaked (9-inch) pie shell

Combine the sausage, cheese, eggs and milk in a bowl. Season with salt and pepper and mix well. Pour into the pie shell. Bake at 350 degrees for 30 minutes. Serve with a salad or fresh fruit and sauce. Serves 6 to 8.

Peggy Burr
Nashville, Tennessee

BREAKFAST QUICHE

2 patties hot bulk pork sausage, cooked, drained and crumbled
4 slices bacon, crisp-cooked and chopped
1/2 cup chopped ham
1/4 cup chopped green onions
1/4 cup sliced black olives
1/4 cup heavy cream
1 cup (4 ounces) shredded Cheddar cheese
Salt and pepper to taste
4 eggs, well beaten
1 unbaked pie shell

Combine the sausage, bacon, ham, green onions, black olives, cream, cheese, salt and pepper in a bowl and mix well. Stir in the eggs. Pour into the pie shell. Bake at 350 degrees for 1 hour or until golden brown. Serve with sour cream. Serves 6 to 8.

Jean Perryman
Clinton, Tennessee

BROCCOLI QUICHE

1 (10-ounce) can condensed cream of mushroom soup
1 cup mayonnaise
1 small onion, finely chopped, or 2 green onions, finely chopped
1 cup shredded mild Cheddar cheese
2 eggs, beaten
2 (10-ounce) packages frozen chopped broccoli, cooked using the package directions
1 sleeve (about 36) butter crackers, crushed

Mix the soup, mayonnaise, onion and cheese in a large bowl. Stir in the eggs. Fold in the broccoli and pour into a buttered quiche dish. Sprinkle the crushed crackers on top. Bake at 350 degrees for 1 hour. Serves 8.

Ina Burkhalter
Springfield, Tennessee

ZUCCHINI FRITTATA

1 teaspoon vegetable oil
1/2 onion, chopped
1 heaping cup grated zucchini
3 eggs, beaten
1/4 teaspoon salt
1 cup shredded Cheddar cheese

Heat the oil in an 8-inch ovenproof skillet over medium heat. Add the onion and zucchini and sauté for 2 to 3 minutes. Pour the eggs over the vegetables and sprinkle with the salt. Cook, covered, for 6 to 7 minutes or until almost set. Remove from the heat and sprinkle with the cheese. Bake at 325 degrees until the cheese melts. Serves 2.

Willie White
Germantown, Tennessee

ALFREDO PASTA SUPREME

2 tablespoons margarine
1 cup chopped onion
1 bell pepper, chopped
1 (8-ounce) can mushrooms, drained
1 cup sliced black olives
1 cup sliced green salad olives
3 cups fresh deveined peeled shrimp
3 cups chopped ham
1 (16-ounce) jar Alfredo sauce
1 cup water
2 cups (8 ounces) shredded cheese
12 to 16 ounces thin spaghetti, cooked al dente and drained

Melt the margarine in an electric skillet. Add the next 7 ingredients. Sauté for 5 minutes or until the shrimp turn pink. Stir in the Alfredo sauce. Pour the water into the empty sauce jar. Replace the lid and shake to mix. Add to the skillet. Bring to a boil, stirring occasionally. Sprinkle the cheese over the top and cook until the cheese melts. Serve over the hot pasta. Serves 6 to 8.

Angel Harris
Memphis, Tennessee

ONION-SMOTHERED PASTA

3 cups pasta
2 tablespoons olive oil
4 onions, cut into 1/4-inch slices
1/4 cup dry red wine or beef broth
1/2 cup beef broth
1 teaspoon basil
1/2 teaspoon oregano
1 (8-ounce) can tomato paste

Cook the pasta using the package directions; drain. Heat the olive oil in a 3-quart saucepan over medium heat. Cook the onions in the hot oil for 8 to 10 minutes or until tender, stirring constantly. Stir in the wine, broth, basil, oregano and tomato paste. Cook until heated through. Spoon over the pasta in a serving dish. Serve immediately. Serves 4 to 6.

Bob Jeffries
Southaven, Mississippi

PESTO

4 garlic cloves
1 cup fresh basil, stems removed
1/4 cup fresh parsley, stems removed
1/8 teaspoon salt
3/4 cup extra-virgin olive oil
1/2 cup grated Parmesan cheese
1/4 cup pine nuts or pecans

Combine the garlic, basil, parsley and salt in a food processor and process for 20 to 30 seconds or until finely chopped. Add the olive oil slowly with the machine running to make a smooth paste. Add the cheese slowly with the machine running to make the consistency of thick tomato sauce. Add more olive oil if the mixture seems too thick. Add more cheese or basil if the mixture seems too thin. Add the pine nuts and pulse 2 to 3 times or for a few seconds. Spoon over your favorite hot cooked pasta or fish or freeze in ice cube trays for quick meals. You may add 1 tomato and use 1/2 the basil and 1/2 the olive oil or add 1/2 cup cooked chicken to the original recipe and process. Serves 4.

George DeBaby
Maryville, Tennessee

ENCHILADAS VERDE

1 pound tomatillos, husks and stems removed
2 garlic cloves
1 or 2 serrano chiles
1/4 white onion, coarsely chopped
1 cup fresh cilantro leaves
1/4 cup unsalted chicken broth
2 teaspoons fresh lime juice
1/2 teaspoon salt
Vegetable oil for frying
12 (6-inch) corn tortillas
12 ounces shredded Monterey Jack cheese
6 ounces shredded Colby cheese or Cheddar cheese
1/2 cup crème fraîche or sour cream

Bring a large saucepan of water to a boil. Add the tomatillos, garlic and chiles. Boil for 7 minutes. Remove 1/2 cup of the cooking liquid and reserve. Drain the remaining liquid.

Combine the tomatillo mixture and reserved liquid in a food processor or blender. Add the onion, cilantro, broth, lime juice and salt. Process until slightly chunky. Add more salt, if desired. Remove to a shallow bowl.

Heat 1/4- to 1/2-inch oil in a large saucepan over medium heat until hot but not smoking. Heat 1 tortilla in the oil for 10 seconds or until limp but not browned. Remove the tortilla with tongs and dip in the tomatillo sauce to coat both sides. Place on a platter and spoon 1/4 cup Monterey Jack cheese down the center of the tortilla. Roll up and place seam side down in a baking dish large enough to hold the enchiladas in a single layer. Repeat with the remaining tortillas, tomatillo sauce and Monterey Jack cheese.

Pour the remaining tomatillo sauce over the enchiladas and sprinkle with the Colby cheese. Cover with foil. Bake at 375 degrees for 20 minutes. Remove the foil and bake for 5 minutes longer. Drizzle with the crème fraîche and serve. Serves 4.

Olivia Murley
Jackson, Tennessee

FRIED GREEN TOMATO SANDWICH

1/2 cup cornmeal
2 tablespoons grated Parmesan cheese
1/2 teaspoon salt
Dash of cayenne pepper
2 eggs
2 large green tomatoes, thinly sliced
1/4 cup (1/2 stick) butter
Lettuce
Cooked bacon slices
Sandwich bread
Ranch salad dressing

Mix the cornmeal, cheese, salt and cayenne pepper in a shallow dish. Beat the eggs in a shallow dish. Dip the tomato slices in the egg and then dredge in the cornmeal mixture to coat.

Melt the butter in a skillet over medium heat. Add the tomatoes in batches and fry for 2 minutes per side or until golden brown. Drain on paper towels.

Layer the lettuce, bacon, and fried tomatoes on bread. Drizzle with salad dressing and top with bread. Serve immediately. Serves 4.

Alene White
Nashville, Tennessee

SIDE DISHES

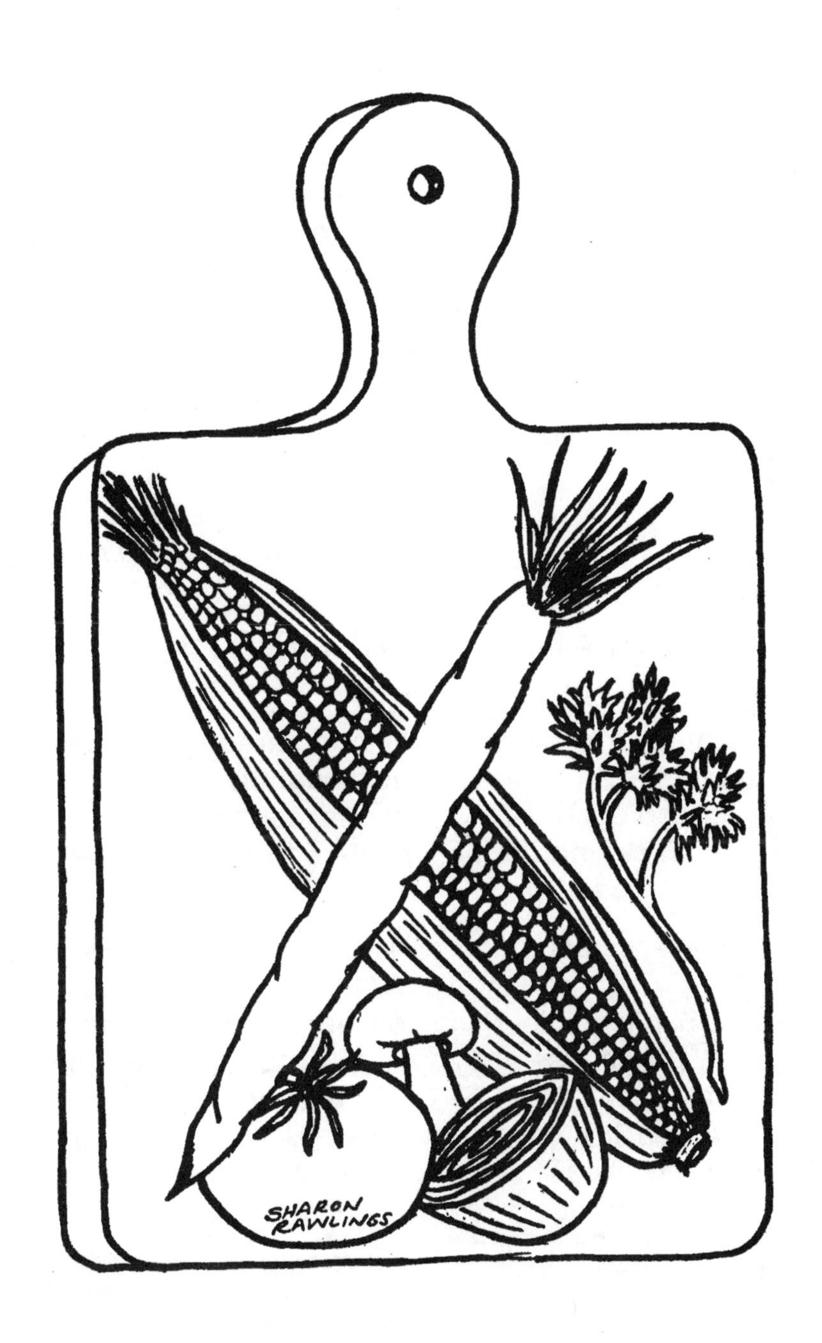

ASPARAGUS CASSEROLE

1 (14 1/2-ounce) can cut asparagus
1 (17-ounce) can small green peas
1 (2-ounce) jar diced pimento
1 cup (4 ounces) shredded cheese
3 hard-cooked eggs, chopped
Salt and pepper to taste
1 (10 1/2-ounce) can condensed cream of mushroom soup
Butter cracker crumbs
1/4 cup (1/2 stick) margarine

Layer the asparagus, peas, pimento, 3/4 cup of the cheese, eggs, salt and pepper in a greased 1 3/4-quart baking dish. Pour the soup over the layers. Sprinkle with the cracker crumbs. Dot with the margarine and sprinkle with the remaining 1/4 cup cheese. Bake at 350 degrees for 30 minutes. Serves 8 to 10.

Margaret Bivens
Memphis, Tennessee

ASPARAGUS AU GRATIN

1 (15-ounce) can asparagus tips, heated, drained and liquid reserved
3 hard-cooked eggs, sliced
1/4 cup (1/2 stick) margarine
1/4 cup all-purpose flour
Milk
1/4 cup shredded cheese
1/2 teaspoon salt
Pepper to taste
Buttered bread crumbs

Arrange the asparagus and eggs in alternating layers in a buttered 8x8-inch baking dish. Melt the margarine in a saucepan. Stir in the flour and cook for several minutes. Add enough milk to the reserved asparagus liquid to make 2 cups. Stir into the flour mixture. Cook until thickened, stirring constantly. Add the cheese and salt. Season with pepper. Cook until the cheese melts, stirring constantly. Pour over the asparagus mixture. Top with bread crumbs. Bake at 400 degrees for 15 minutes. Serves 8.

Betty Gainous
Tullahoma, Tennessee

BAKED ASPARAGUS

1 tablespoon vegetable oil
1 (10-ounce) package frozen asparagus spears, partially thawed
1 teaspoon salt
2 tablespoons water
Pimento slices for garnish

Spread the oil in a 9x13-inch baking dish. Add the asparagus and roll to coat in the oil. Sprinkle with the salt and water. Cover dish with foil. Bake at 375 degrees for 35 minutes. Garnish with sliced pimentos. Serves 4.

Catherine Grice
Nashville, Tennessee

VEGETABLE CASSEROLE DELIGHT

2 (14 1/2-ounce) cans asparagus spear cuts, drained
10 ounces extra sharp Cheddar cheese, shredded or thinly sliced
1 (17-ounce) can green peas, drained
1 (4-ounce) jar pimentos, drained and finely chopped
Salt and pepper to taste
1 (10-ounce) can condensed cream of celery soup
1/2 cup milk
1 cup sour cream
8 ounces sliced Swiss cheese
4 hard-cooked eggs, finely chopped
5 tablespoons butter, melted
1 cup seasoned croutons, finely crushed

Spread the asparagus evenly in a buttered shallow 3-quart baking dish. Sprinkle with the Cheddar cheese. Top with the peas and pimentos. Season with salt and pepper. Mix the soup, milk and sour cream in a bowl. Pour over the vegetables. Top with the Swiss cheese. Sprinkle with the eggs. Mix the butter and crouton crumbs in a bowl. Sprinkle over the egg layer. Bake at 350 degrees for 25 minutes or until bubbly and lightly browned. Serves 8.

Louise Stuart
White Bluff, Tennessee

TEX-MEX BEANS

2 slices bacon, chopped
1 onion, chopped
2 tomatoes, chopped
2 jalapeño chiles, seeded and chopped
3 (16-ounce) cans beans
3/4 cup beer
1/2 cup water
1/2 cup fresh cilantro leaves

Fry the bacon in a saucepan until almost cooked though. Add the onion and sauté until tender.

Stir in the tomatoes and jalapeños and cook for 5 minutes. Stir in the beans, beer, water and cilantro. Bring to a boil and reduce the heat. Simmer for 30 minutes. Serves 6.

Olivia Murley
Jackson, Tennessee

BAKED BEANS

1 1/2 pounds ground beef
1 onion, chopped
2 (14-ounce) cans pork and beans
1/2 cup molasses
1 cup ketchup
1 cup barbecue sauce
4 heaping teaspoons brown sugar
Dash of cola
1 slice bacon (optional)

Brown the ground beef in a saucepan, stirring until crumbly; drain. Stir in the onion, pork and beans, molasses, ketchup, barbecue sauce, brown sugar and cola. Pour into a 9x13-inch baking dish and place the bacon on top.

Bake, covered, at 325 degrees for 1 hour and 15 minutes. Uncover and bake for 15 minutes longer. You can cook the ground beef in Dale's Steak Sauce, if desired. Serves 6 to 8.

Kathy Duncan
Memphis, Tennessee

GREEN BEAN CASSEROLE

2 (14-ounce) cans French-style green beans, drained
1 (14-ounce) can Shoe Peg corn, drained
1 (10-ounce) can condensed cream of celery soup
1/2 cup sour cream
1/4 cup chopped onion
1/2 cup (2 ounces) shredded Cheddar cheese
Pinch of salt
1/2 cup (1 stick) margarine, melted
1 cup crushed butter crackers
1/2 cup sliced almonds

Mix the beans, corn, soup, sour cream, onion, cheese and salt in a large bowl. Pour into a 1 1/2 or 2-quart baking dish. Mix the margarine, crushed crackers and almonds in a bowl. Sprinkle on top of the bean mixture. Bake at 350 degrees for 30 minutes. Serves 6 to 8.

Mildred and Henry Hensley
Lake City, Tennessee

SWEET-AND-SOUR BEANS

2 tablespoons butter or margarine
2 tablespoons all-purpose flour
2 tablespoons sugar
2 tablespoons vinegar
1 (16-ounce) can French-style or regular-cut green beans, drained and liquid reserved

Melt the butter in a saucepan. Stir in the flour and cook for several minutes. Stir in the sugar and vinegar. Stir in enough of the reserved bean liquid to make a sauce. Cook until thickened, stirring constantly. Stir in the beans. Cook until heated through. To increase the recipe, add 1 tablespoon each of butter, flour, sugar and vinegar for each can of beans. Serves 2.

Elizabeth Osterholz
Shelbyville, Tennessee

JOE'S GREEN BEAN CASSEROLE

2 (14-ounce) cans French-style green beans, drained
1 (10-ounce) can condensed cream of mushroom soup
1 (8-ounce) can sliced water chestnuts, drained
1/2 cup (1 stick) butter, softened
3/4 cup (3 ounces) shredded mild Cheddar cheese
2/3 cup slivered almonds
17 butter crackers, crushed
3 butter crackers, crushed
1/4 cup shredded mild Cheddar cheese

Mix the beans, soup, water chestnuts, butter, 3/4 cup cheese and almonds in a baking dish. Sprinkle with 17 crushed crackers. Bake, covered, at 350 degrees for 30 minutes, stirrring once or twice. Sprinkle 3 crushed crackers and 1/4 cup cheese over the top. Bake, uncovered, for 5 minutes longer or until the cheese melts. Serves 8.

Joe Huffman
Nashville, Tennessee

GREEN BEANS

8 slices bacon
5 (14-ounce) cans French-style green beans, drained
1/2 onion, sliced
1 cup sugar
1 cup vinegar

Cook the bacon in a large skillet until crisp. Remove to paper towels to drain; crumble. Remove the bacon drippings to a bowl. Spread the beans in a baking dish. Sprinkle the bacon and onion over the beans. Add the sugar and vinegar to the bacon drippings and mix well. Pour over the bean mixture. Bake, covered, at 500 degrees for 1 hour. Serves 8.

Paula Hartley
Franklin, Tennessee

PINEAPPLE BEETS

2 tablespoons brown sugar
1 tablespoon cornstarch
1/4 teaspoon salt
1 (8-ounce) can pineapple tidbits
1 (16-ounce) can sliced beets, drained
1 tablespoon margarine
1 tablespoon lemon juice

Combine the sugar, cornstarch and salt in a saucepan. Stir in the pineapple. Bring to a boil, stirring constantly. Cook for 2 minutes or until thickened, stirring constantly.

Stir in the beets, margarine and lemon juice. Cook over medium heat for 5 minutes, stirring occasionally. Serves 8.

Ruby Rigsby
Soddy-Daisy, Tennessee

BROCCOLI, CHEESE AND RICE CASSEROLE

2 (10-ounce) packages frozen chopped broccoli, partially thawed
1 1/2 cups instant rice
1/2 cup chopped onion
1/2 cup chopped celery
1 (10-ounce) can condensed cream of mushroom soup
1 (15-ounce) jar Cheez Whiz
1/2 cup (1 stick) margarine

Break apart the broccoli and place in a large bowl. Stir in the rice, onion, celery and soup.

Combine the Cheez Whiz and margarine in a small saucepan. Cook until melted, stirring occasionally. Stir into the broccoli mixture. Spoon into a baking dish. Bake at 350 degrees for 30 minutes. Serves 10.

Edna Lindsey
Maryville, Tennessee

RICE BROCCOLI CASSEROLE

4 cups cooked rice
1 (10-ounce) package frozen chopped broccoli, cooked using the package directions
1 (8-ounce) jar Cheez Whiz
1 (10-ounce) can condensed cream of mushroom soup
1 (10-ounce) can condensed cream of chicken soup

Spread the rice in a baking dish and top with the broccoli. Mix the Cheez Whiz, mushroom soup and chicken soup in a bowl. Pour over the broccoli. Bake at 350 degrees for 20 minutes. Serves 6 to 8.

Ina Burkhalter
Nashville, Tennessee

BROCCOLI CASSEROLE

1 (10-ounce) package frozen chopped broccoli, cooked using the package directions
1/2 cup (2 ounces) shredded sharp Cheddar cheese
1/2 cup mayonnaise
1 tablespoon grated onion
1 (10-ounce) can condensed cream of chicken soup
1 egg, beaten
Salt and pepper to taste
1 (12-ounce) package cheese crackers, crushed

Combine the broccoli, cheese, mayonnaise, onion, soup and egg in a large bowl. Season with salt and pepper and mix well.

Spoon into a buttered 9x13-inch baking dish. Sprinkle the crushed crackers over the top. Bake at 400 degrees for 20 minutes. Serves 10.

Billie Moore
Knoxville, Tennessee

BAKED CABBAGE

1 large head cabbage, cut into 8 wedges
1/4 cup (1/2 stick) butter
1/2 cup finely chopped green bell pepper
1/2 cup finely chopped green onions
1/2 cup all-purpose flour
1/2 teaspoon salt
1/2 teaspoon pepper
3/4 to 1 cup milk
1/2 cup mayonnaise
3/4 cup (3 ounces) shredded Cheddar cheese
3 tablespoons chili sauce

Cook the cabbage in a saucepan of boiling water for 10 minutes; drain. Arrange the cabbage in 9x13-inch baking dish. Melt the butter in a saucepan. Add the bell pepper and green onions and sauté until the vegetables are tender. Stir in the flour, salt and pepper. Cook for several minutes, stirring constantly. Add the milk. Cook until thickened and bubbly, stirring constantly. Pour over the cabbage. Bake at 375 degrees for 20 minutes. Mix the mayonnaise, cheese and chili sauce in a small bowl. Spoon over the cabbage. Bake for 5 minutes longer.
Serves 8.

Janice Cude
Franklin, Tennessee

CARROTS ELEGANTE

1 pound carrots, thinly sliced
1/4 cup golden raisins
1/4 cup butter-flavored vegetable oil spread
3 tablespoons honey
1 tablespoon lemon juice
1/4 teaspoon ginger
1/4 cup sliced almonds

Cook the carrots covered with 1/2 inch of boiling water in a saucepan for 8 minutes; drain. Place the carrots in a 1-quart baking dish. Stir in the raisins, vegetable oil spread, honey, lemon juice and ginger. Bake at 375 degrees for 35 minutes, stirring once or twice. Sprinkle with the almonds and serve.
Serves 4.

Madeline McCamy
Cleveland, Tennessee

PARTY CARROTS

2 pounds carrots, sliced
2 cups chicken broth
8 ounces Velveeta cheese, cubed
2 tablespoons butter
1 cup sour cream
1 small bunch green onions, chopped
Salt and pepper to taste

Cook the carrots in the broth in a saucepan until tender; drain. Cook the cheese and butter in a saucepan over low heat until melted, stirring occasionally. Stir in the sour cream and green onions. Season with salt and pepper. Stir in the carrots.

Spoon into an 8x8-inch baking dish. Bake at 350 degrees until heated through. Serves 9.

Addie Downs
Antioch, Tennessee

CAULIFLOWER CASSEROLE

2 cups cauliflower florets or 1 (10-ounce) package frozen cauliflower florets
2 tablespoons butter
4 ounces Velveeta cheese, cubed
2 tablespoons butter, melted
12 butter crackers, crumbled

Cook the cauliflower in a saucepan of boiling water until tender; drain well. Place in a bowl.

Cook 2 tablespoons butter and the cheese in a saucepan over low heat until melted, stirring occasionally. Pour over the cauliflower and stir to mix. Pour into a greased baking dish.

Mix 2 tablespoons melted butter and the crumbled crackers in a bowl. Sprinkle over the cauliflower. Bake at 350 degrees for 20 minutes. Serves 3 to 4.

Ann Harville
Talbott, Tennessee

CORN PUDDING SQUARES

2 (15 1/4-ounce) cans whole kernel corn
2 (14 3/4-ounce) cans cream-style corn
2 cups sour cream
1 cup (2 sticks) butter or margarine, melted
2 (8 1/2-ounce) packages corn bread mix
3 eggs

Combine the whole kernel corn, cream-style corn, sour cream, melted butter, corn bread mix and eggs in a large bowl and stir just until mixed.

Pour into 2 greased 9x13-inch baking dishes. Bake at 350 degrees for 40 to 45 minutes or until a wooden pick inserted in the center comes out clean. Remove to a wire rack and let cool for 15 minutes before cutting. Serve warm.
Serves 20 to 24.

Ruby Rigsby
Soddy-Daisy, Tennessee

CORN PUDDING

1/4 cup sugar
3 tablespoons all-purpose flour
2 teaspoons baking powder
2 teaspoons salt
6 eggs
2 cups heavy cream
1/2 cup (1 stick) butter or margarine, melted
6 cups fresh corn kernels

Mix the sugar, flour, baking powder and salt together. Beat the eggs in a large bowl. Stir in the cream and melted butter. Mix in the dry ingredients gradually, stirring constantly until smooth. Stir in the corn.

Pour into a lightly greased 9x13-inch baking dish. Bake at 350 degrees for 45 minutes or until set and a deep golden brown. Remove to a wire rack and let stand for 5 minutes before serving. Serves 8.

Deborah Thurman
Nashville, Tennessee

CORN PUDDING

1 cup self-rising cornmeal
1 (14-ounce) can cream-style corn
1 cup sour cream
1/2 cup vegetable oil
2 eggs, beaten

Combine the cornmeal, corn, sour cream, oil and eggs in a bowl and stir just until mixed.

Pour into a 9x13-inch baking dish. Bake at 375 degrees for 40 to 50 minutes. Serves 10 to 12.

Mildred and Henry Hensley
Lake City, Tennessee

THE BEST CORN CASSEROLE

16 ounces cream cheese, softened
1/2 cup (1 stick) margarine, melted
1 (16-ounce) bag frozen baby white corn
2 (10-ounce) cans tomatoes with green chiles, drained

Stir the cream cheese and melted margarine together in a large bowl until smooth. Add the corn and tomatoes with green chiles and stir to mix well.

Pour into a buttered 2-quart baking dish. Bake at 350 degrees for 30 minutes. Serves 8.

Wanda (Susie) Ladd
Williamsport, Tennessee

CORN CASSEROLE

1/2 cup (1 stick) margarine
1 onion, finely chopped
1 or 2 jalapeño chiles, seeded and finely chopped
2 (14-ounce) cans cream-style corn
2 eggs, beaten
1 cup corn bread stuffing mix
1/2 cup water
1/4 cup sugar
Salt and pepper to taste
Shredded Cheddar cheese

Melt the margarine in a skillet. Add the onion and jalapeños and sauté until the vegetables are tender. Remove to a large bowl. Add the corn, eggs, stuffing mix, water and sugar. Season with salt and pepper and mix well. Pour into a baking dish. Bake at 325 degrees for 50 minutes. Top with cheese and bake for 10 minutes longer. Serves 10.

Sonya Van Cleave
Memphis, Tennessee

CORN CASSEROLE

9 ears corn
4 or 5 slices bacon
2 cups chopped onions
2 cups shredded Cheddar cheese
1 cup half-and-half
1 (4-ounce) jar chopped pimentos, drained
3/4 teaspoon ginger
Salt and pepper to taste

Cut the kernels from the corn, cutting only halfway through the kernels. Remove to a bowl. Scrape the remaining corn from the cobs into the bowl. Cook the bacon in a large saucepan until crisp. Remove to paper towels to drain; crumble. Add the onions to the bacon drippings. Sauté until tender but not browned. Add the corn kernels, corn scrapings and cheese. Cook for 10 minutes, stirring constantly. Stir in the half-and-half, pimentos and ginger. Season with salt and pepper. Pour into a 2-quart baking dish. Bake at 350 degrees until bubbly. This casserole freezes well. Serves 6 to 8.

Peggy Burr
Nashville, Tennessee

CORN CASSEROLE

1 (8-ounce) package corn bread mix
1 cup sour cream
1 (15-ounce) can whole kernel corn, drained
1 (14-ounce) can cream-style corn
1/2 cup (1 stick) butter, melted

Combine the corn bread mix, sour cream, whole kernel corn, cream-style corn and melted butter in a large bowl and mix well. Pour into a baking dish. Bake at 350 degrees for 1 hour. Serves 10.

Billie Moore
Knoxville, Tennessee

HOMINY CASSEROLE

1 (30-ounce) can hominy, rinsed and drained
2 tablespoons chopped onion
1 (10-ounce) can condensed cream of celery soup
Shredded cheese

Combine the hominy, onion and soup in a bowl and mix well. Pour into a 2-quart baking dish. Top with cheese. Bake at 350 degrees for 35 minutes or until bubbly. Serves 6 to 8.

Madeline McCamy
Cleveland, Tennessee

FRIED OKRA

3 pounds okra
1 1/2 cups plain or self-rising cornmeal
1 1/2 teaspoons salt
Canola oil for frying

Cut the okra crosswise into 1/2-inch slices. Mix the cornmeal and salt in a shallow dish. Coat the okra slices in the cornmeal mixture. Heat 1/4 inch oil in a large skillet over high heat until hot. Add the okra and cook until golden brown and crisp, turning occasionally. Remove to paper towels to drain and serve immediately. If using self-rising cornmeal, reduce the amount of salt. Yellow squash or peeled eggplant can be used instead of okra. Cut into 1/4-inch slices. Serves 8.

Martha Hammonds
Nashville, Tennessee

OKRA SIDE DISH

1 tablespoon olive oil
1 small onion, chopped
2 cups sliced okra
1/4 cup Italian-style seasoned bread crumbs
1 cup chopped tomato

Heat the olive oil in a skillet. Add the onion and sauté for 3 to 4 minutes. Add the okra and sauté for 5 to 10 minutes. Add the bread crumbs and sauté for 5 minutes. Stir in the tomato and simmer to blend flavors. Serves 4.

Zoerita Proctor
McEwen, Tennessee

VIDALIA ONION SOUFFLÉ

2 tablespoons butter
4 cups finely chopped Vidalia onions
10 slices white bread, toasted and cubed
1 (12-ounce) can evaporated milk
3 eggs, well beaten
1 cup (4 ounces) grated Parmesan cheese
Salt to taste
1/4 cup (1 ounce) grated Parmesan cheese

Melt the butter in a skillet over medium heat. Add the onions and sauté for 10 to 15 minutes or until tender. Remove to a large bowl. Add the bread cubes and toss gently to mix. Add the evaporated milk, eggs and 1 cup cheese. Season with salt. Stir gently to mix. Pour into a greased 2-quart baking dish. Sprinkle with 1/4 cup cheese. Bake at 350 degrees for 30 minutes or until the edges are golden brown. Serves 8.

Sonya Van Cleave
Memphis, Tennessee

TWICE-BAKED POTATOES

7 large baking potatoes
1/2 cup (1 stick) butter or margarine, softened
2 cups (8 ounces) shredded Cheddar cheese
2 cups sour cream
2 ounces bacon bits
10 green onions, chopped
Salt and pepper to taste
Paprika

Wrap the potatoes in foil. Bake at 375 degrees for 2 hours or until soft. Remove to a wire rack and let cool. Slice off the top 1/4 of the potatoes lengthwise. Scoop out the potato pulp into a bowl, keeping the shells intact. Mash the potatoes. Add the next 5 ingredients. Season with salt and pepper. Mix until no lumps remain. Fill 6 of the potato shells with the potato mixture and discard the remaining shell. Sprinkle with paprika and place on a baking sheet. Bake at 350 degrees until heated through. Serves 6.

Glenda Buchanan
College Grove, Tennessee

RED CHEESE POTATOES

1/2 cup (1 stick) butter, melted
15 red-skinned potatoes, cooked
Velveeta cheese slices
10 slices bacon, crisp-cooked and crumbled
2 tablespoons chopped onion

Spread 1/2 of the butter in a 9x13-inch baking dish. Arrange 1/2 of the potatoes on the butter. Cover with cheese and sprinkle with 1/2 the bacon. Sprinkle 1/2 the onion over the bacon. Repeat the layers to use the remaining butter, potatoes, cheese, bacon and onion. Bake at 350 degrees for 30 minutes. Serves 8.

Cathy Funderburk
Knoxville, Tennessee

SCALLOPED POTATOES

3 tablespoons butter or margarine
2 tablespoons all-purpose flour
1 1/2 teaspoons salt
1/8 teaspoon pepper
3 cups milk
1 1/2 cups shredded American cheese
6 potatoes, peeled and thinly sliced
2 tablespoons chopped onion

Melt the butter in a saucepan. Stir in the flour, salt and pepper. Cook for a few minutes stirring constantly. Stir in the milk. Cook until it begins to thicken, stirring constantly. Stir in the cheese. Cook until the cheese melts, stirring frequently. Arrange 1/2 of the potatoes in a greased 2-quart baking dish. Sprinkle with 1/2 of the onion. Cover with 1/2 of the cheese sauce. Repeat the layers to use the remaining potatoes, onion and cheese sauce. Bake, covered, at 350 degrees for 1 hour. Uncover and bake for 30 minutes longer. Serves 6 to 8.

Martha Hammonds
Nashville, Tennessee

SCALLOPED POTATOES

2 tablespoons butter
3 tablespoons all-purpose flour
1 1/2 teaspoons salt
2 cups milk
2 tablespoons chopped fresh parsley
2 tablespoons chopped pimento
3 cups diced cooked potatoes
1/2 cup (2 ounces) shredded cheese
1/2 cup buttered bread crumbs
1/4 teaspoon paprika

Melt the butter in a saucepan. Stir in the flour and salt. Cook for a few minutes, stirring constantly. Add the milk gradually, stirring constantly. Cook over low heat until thickened, stirring constantly. Stir in the parsley, pimento and potatoes. Pour into a 2-quart baking dish. Sprinkle with the cheese, bread crumbs and paprika. Bake at 400 degrees for 20 minutes. Serves 4.

Catherine Grice
Nashville, Tennessee

SCALLOPED POTATOES AND VEGETABLES

1 (10-ounce) can condensed cream of onion soup
1 cup milk
1 (16-ounce) bag frozen mixed vegetables
26 ounces frozen shredded hash brown potatoes, or 32 ounces frozen diced potatoes
2 cups (8 ounces) shredded Cheddar cheese

Mix the soup and milk in a large bowl. Stir in the mixed vegetables, potatoes and 1/2 of the cheese. Spoon into a 9x13-inch baking dish. Bake, covered, at 350 degrees for 45 minutes. Uncover and bake for 30 minutes longer or until the potatoes are tender. Sprinkle with the remaining cheese and let stand for 5 minutes before serving. Serves 12.

Martha Hammonds
Nashville, Tennessee

HOT POTATO SALAD

6 slices bacon, cut into 2-inch pieces
1 small onion, chopped
6 to 8 unpeeled small potatoes, cooked and cubed
Mayonnaise
2 teaspoons celery salt
1 teaspoon Worcestershire sauce
Dash of sugar
Salt and pepper to taste
1/2 cup (2 ounces) cubed Cheddar cheese

Sauté the bacon and onion in a skillet until the onions are tender and the bacon is beginning to brown. Remove to a bowl. Add the potatoes. Toss with enough mayonnaise to moisten the mixture. Add the celery salt, Worcestershire sauce and sugar. Season with salt and pepper. Toss gently to mix. Spoon into an ungreased 4-quart baking dish. Add the cheese and stir to mix. Bake at 350 degrees for 40 minutes. Serves 8 to 10.

Sonya Van Cleave
Memphis, Tennessee

CHEESE POTATOES

1 (5 1/2-ounce) package potatoes au gratin, prepared using the package directions
1 (15-ounce) can whole kernel corn, drained
1 green bell pepper, chopped
1/4 cup mayonnaise
1/4 cup bread crumbs
1 tablespoon butter, melted

Place the uncooked prepared potatoes in a 2-quart baking dish. Stir in the corn, bell pepper and mayonnaise. Bake at 400 degrees for 25 minutes. Mix the bread crumbs and melted butter in a small bowl. Sprinkle over the potatoes. Bake for 10 to 15 minutes longer or until the potatoes are tender. Serves 6.

Charlotte James
Beech Bluff, Tennessee

POTATO CASSEROLE

6 to 8 large potatoes
1 (6-ounce) jar mayonnaise
Velveeta cheese slices
Bacon bits

Peel the potatoes and cut into chunks. Cook in a saucepan of boiling water until tender; drain. Combine the potatoes and mayonnaise in a large bowl and stir until well mixed.

Spoon into a large baking dish. Arrange cheese slices on top and sprinkle with bacon bits. Bake at 350 degrees for 40 minutes. Serves 10 to 12.

Charlotte James
Beech Bluff, Tennessee

HASH BROWN CASSEROLE

1 (2-pound) bag frozen hash brown potatoes
1/2 cup chopped onion
5 1/3 tablespoons margarine, melted
2 1/2 cups (10 ounces) shredded Cheddar cheese
1 (10-ounce) can condensed cream of chicken soup
1 cup sour cream
Salt and pepper to taste

Combine the potatoes, onion, melted margarine, cheese, soup and sour cream in a large bowl. Season with salt and pepper and mix well.

Spoon into a large baking dish. Bake at 350 degrees for 1 hour. Serves 10 to 12.

Charlotte James
Beech Bluff, Tennessee

POTATO CASSEROLE

1 (2-pound) bag frozen country-style hash brown potatoes
1/2 cup (1 stick) margarine, melted
2 1/2 cups (10 ounces) shredded Cheddar cheese
1/2 cup chopped onion
1 (10-ounce) can condensed cream of chicken soup
2 cups sour cream
1/4 teaspoon salt

Combine the potatoes, melted margarine, cheese, onion, soup, sour cream and salt in a large bowl and mix well. Spoon into a 9x13-inch baking dish. Bake at 350 degrees for 1 hour or until golden brown and the potatoes are tender. Serves 10.

Mackie Jernigan
Memphis, Tennessee

CREAMY POTATO CASSEROLE

1 (30-ounce) bag frozen shredded hash brown potatoes, thawed
2 cups sour cream
2 cups (8 ounces) shredded sharp Cheddar cheese
1 (10-ounce) can condensed cream of chicken soup
1/2 cup chopped onion
1/4 cup (1/2 stick) butter, melted
2 tablespoons chopped fresh parsley
1/2 teaspoon pepper
1/4 teaspoon salt

Combine the potatoes, sour cream, cheese, soup, onion, melted butter, parsley, pepper and salt in a large bowl and mix well. Spoon into an ungreased 2-quart baking dish. Bake at 350 degrees for 1 hour or until heated through. Serves 8 to 10.

Rubye Hahn
Bridgeport, Alabama

BAKED HASH BROWN POTATOES

1 (2-pound) bag frozen hash brown potatoes, partially thawed
1/2 cup chopped onion
1/2 cup (1 stick) butter or margarine, melted
1 (10-ounce) can condensed cream of celery, cream of mushroom or cream of chicken soup
1 cup sour cream
1 cup (4 ounces) shredded Cheddar cheese
1/2 teaspoon salt
1/2 teaspoon pepper
1/4 cup milk (optional)
1 cup cornflake crumbs or bread crumbs
1/2 cup (1 stick) margarine, melted

Combine the potatoes, onion, 1/2 cup melted butter, soup, sour cream, cheese, salt and pepper in a large bowl and mix well. Stir in the milk if the mixture seems too thick. Spoon into a 9x13-inch baking dish. Sprinkle with the cornflake crumbs and drizzle 1/2 cup melted margarine over the top. Bake at 350 degrees for 1 hour. Serves 12.

Louise Stuart
White Bluff, Tennessee

POTATO CASSEROLE

1 (2-pound) bag frozen shredded hash brown potatoes, thawed
1/2 cup chopped onion
1 (10-ounce) can condensed cream of chicken soup
2 cups sour cream
10 ounces shredded American cheese
1 teaspoon salt
1/2 teaspoon pepper
2 cups cornflakes, crushed
1/2 cup (1 stick) margarine, melted

Mix the first 7 ingredients in a large bowl. Spoon into a greased 9x13-inch baking dish. Mix the cornflakes and melted margarine in a bowl. Sprinkle over the potato mixture. Bake at 350 degrees for 45 minutes. Serves 12.

Louise Spahr
Knoxville, Tennessee

FANCY MASHED POTATOES

5 large potatoes, peeled and diced
1/4 cup milk
1/2 teaspoon seasoned salt
2 tablespoons margarine
1 cup sour cream
3 ounces cream cheese, softened
1 teaspoon dried chives
1 tablespoon margarine, melted
1/2 cup crushed butter crackers
1/4 cup (1 ounce) shredded Cheddar cheese

Cook the potatoes in a saucepan of boiling water until tender; drain. Remove to a bowl. Beat the potatoes, milk, seasoned salt and 2 tablespoons margarine until fluffy. Add the sour cream, cream cheese and chives and mix well. Pour into a buttered baking dish. Mix 1 tablespoon melted margarine and the crushed crackers in a small bowl. Sprinkle over the potato mixture. Bake at 350 degrees for 20 minutes. Sprinkle with the Cheddar cheese and bake for 10 minutes longer. Serves 6.

Ann Montgomery
Sevierville, Tennessee

OLD-FASHIONED POTATO PANCAKES

3 cups mashed cooked potatoes
1 small onion, chopped
2 eggs, lightly beaten
1/8 teaspoon nutmeg
1/4 cup all-purpose flour
3 tablespoons vegetable oil
Chopped fresh parsley

Mix the potatoes, onion, eggs and nutmeg in a bowl. Shape into 10 patties. Coat the patties in the flour. Heat the oil in a large skillet over medium-high heat until hot. Fry the patties a few at a time for 3 minutes per side or until golden brown, turning once. Remove to paper towels to drain. Sprinkle with chopped parsley and serve immediately. Serves 5.

Martha Hammonds
Nashville, Tennessee

EASY SPINACH SOUFFLÉ

6 eggs
2 cups cottage cheese
2 tablespoons butter, melted
8 ounces Cheddar cheese, shredded
6 tablespoons all-purpose flour
1 (10-ounce) package frozen chopped spinach, thawed and drained
1/8 teaspoon salt

Beat the eggs in a large bowl. Add the cottage cheese and stir to mix well. Add the melted butter and Cheddar cheese and stir to mix well. Add the flour, spinach and salt and stir to mix well.

Spoon into an ungreased 9x13-inch baking dish. Bake at 350 degrees for 1 hour. Serves 6.

Barbara Duncan
Memphis, Tennessee

SPINACH MARIA

1 tablespoon butter or margarine
1 onion, finely chopped
8 ounces cream cheese, softened
1 cup (4 ounces) grated Parmesan cheese
2 (10-ounce) packages frozen chopped spinach, cooked and well drained
1/2 teaspoon cayenne pepper

Melt the butter in a saucepan. Add the onion and sauté until tender. Stir in the cream cheese and Parmesan cheese. Stir in the spinach and cayenne pepper.

Pour into a greased 9x13-inch baking dish. Bake at 350 degrees for 30 minutes. Serves 10 to 12.

Allison Turner
Memphis, Tennessee

ITALIAN SPINACH

2 (10-ounce) packages frozen chopped spinach, thawed and drained
2 tablespoons canola oil
2 eggs, beaten
1 tablespoon garlic powder
3/4 cup (3 ounces) grated Parmesan cheese

Combine the spinach, oil, eggs, garlic powder and cheese in a bowl and mix well. Pour into a skillet and cook until the eggs are set and cooked through. Serves 8.

Ella Mae Hasty
Memphis, Tennessee

BUTTERNUT SQUASH

2 cup mashed cooked butternut squash
3 eggs
3/4 cup sugar
1 teaspoon ginger
5 1/3 tablespoons butter, softened
1/2 teaspoon coconut extract
Topping (below)

Combine the squash, eggs, sugar, ginger, butter and coconut extract in a bowl and mix well. Pour into a lightly greased 8x8-inch baking dish. Bake at 350 degrees for 35 minutes. Sprinkle the Topping over the baked squash. Bake at 350 degrees for 10 minutes. Serves 4 to 6.

Topping

1 1/2 cups cornflake crumbs
3/4 cup packed brown sugar
1/2 cup chopped pecans
1/4 cup (1/2 stick) butter, melted

Combine the cornflake crumbs, brown sugar, pecans and melted butter in a bowl and mix well.

Peggy Burr
Nashville, Tennessee

MEXICAN SQUASH

6 to 8 yellow squash, sliced
1/4 cup chopped onion
1/2 cup (2 ounces) shredded cheese
1 (10-ounce) can tomatoes with green chiles
1/4 cup (1/2 stick) margarine, softened
Salt and pepper to taste
3/4 cup finely crushed crackers
2 tablespoons margarine

Cook the squash and onion in a saucepan of boiling water until tender; drain. Remove to a bowl. Add the cheese, tomatoes with green chiles and 1/4 cup margarine. Season with salt and pepper and mix gently.

Spoon into a buttered 2-quart baking dish. Sprinkle with the crushed crackers and dot with 2 tablespoons margarine. Bake at 350 degrees for 30 minutes. Serves 6 to 8.

Willie White
Germantown, Tennessee

SQUASH DRESSING

1/2 cup (1 stick) butter
1 onion, chopped
2 cups cooked squash
1 (10-ounce) can condensed cream of chicken soup
2 cups crumbled corn bread
2 eggs, well beaten
1/2 teaspoon sage
Salt and pepper to taste

Melt the butter in a skillet. Add the onion and sauté until tender. Remove to a bowl. Add the squash, soup, corn bread, eggs and sage. Season with salt and pepper and mix well.

Spoon into a baking dish. Bake at 350 degrees for 30 minutes or until golden brown and bubbly. Serves 6.

Jimmie Ruth Humberd
Cleveland, Tennessee

SQUASH CASSEROLE

2 pounds yellow squash, sliced
1 large yellow onion, chopped
1 (4-ounce) jar sliced pimentos, drained
4 cups (16 ounces) shredded Cheddar cheese
2 (10-ounce) cans condensed cream of chicken soup
1 (8-ounce) package herb-seasoned stuffing
Garlic salt to taste
Salt and pepper to taste
1/2 cup (1 stick) butter

Cook the squash and onion in a saucepan of boiling water until tender; drain. Remove to a bowl. Add the pimentos, cheese, soup and 3/4 of the stuffing. Season with garlic salt, salt and pepper and mix well. Spoon into a large baking dish. Sprinkle with the remaining stuffing and dot with the butter. Bake at 400 degrees for 20 to 25 minutes or until browned. Serves 12.

Kaye Lewis
Joelton, Tennessee

SQUASH CASSEROLE

1 1/2 pounds yellow squash, sliced
1 onion, sliced
1/4 cup (1/2 stick) margarine
1 (10-ounce) can condensed cream of chicken soup
1 egg, beaten
2 cups (8 ounces) shredded Cheddar cheese
Salt and pepper to taste
1 (2-ounce) can French-fried onions (optional)

Cook the squash and onion in a saucepan of boiling water over medium heat until tender; drain well. Remove to a bowl. Add the margarine and let melt. Stir in the soup, egg and 1 cup of the cheese. Season with salt and pepper. Spoon into a baking dish. Bake at 350 degrees for 30 minutes. Sprinkle with the remaining cheese and the French-fried onions and bake for 5 minutes longer. Serves 8 to 10.

Deborah Horton
Nashville, Tennessee

YELLOW SQUASH CASSEROLE

1 teaspoon margarine
1/2 cup finely chopped onion
3 cups cooked chopped yellow squash
1 (10-ounce) can condensed low-fat cream of mushroom soup
1 tablespoon beef bouillon granules
1 teaspoon pepper
1 teaspoon Tabasco sauce
1/2 teaspoon salt
1 cup plus 2 tablespoons bread crumbs
3 3/4 ounces 1/3-reduced fat Cheddar cheese, shredded

Melt the margarine in a small skillet. Add the onion and sauté until tender. Remove to a bowl. Add the next 6 ingredients and mix well. Spread 1/3 of the bread crumbs in a baking dish coated with nonstick cooking spray. Top with 1/2 the squash mixture. Sprinkle with 1/2 the cheese. Repeat the layers and top with the remaining bread crumbs. Bake at 350 degrees for 20 minutes. Serves 6.

Betty Shields
Morristown, Tennessee

BUTTERSCOTCH SWEET POTATOES

2 cups sugar
1 cup (2 sticks) butter
1/2 cup light cream
1 teaspoon vanilla extract
1 cup toasted pecans
3 cups hot mashed cooked sweet potatoes
Brown sugar to taste
2 cups heavy cream

Combine the sugar and butter in a cast-iron skillet. Cook until the mixture turns a deep tan color, stirring constantly. Stir in the light cream slowly and cook for 2 minutes, stirring often. Stir in the vanilla and pecans. Keep warm. Place the hot potatoes in a 2-quart baking dish. Stir in brown sugar to taste. Stir in the heavy cream. Make a well in the center of the potatoes. Pour the butterscotch sauce into the well. Serves 6 to 8.

Addie Downs
Antioch, Tennessee

SWEET POTATO CASSEROLE

3 cups mashed cooked sweet potatoes
1/3 cup milk
1/2 cup (1 stick) butter, softened
1 cup sugar
1 egg, lightly beaten
1 teaspoon vanilla extract
1 cup packed brown sugar
1/2 cup all-purpose flour
5 1/3 tablespoons butter, softened
1 cup nuts, chopped

Combine the potatoes, milk, 1/2 cup butter, sugar, egg and vanilla in a large bowl and mix well. Pour into a buttered 9x13-inch baking dish. Combine the brown sugar, flour, 5 1/3 tablespoons butter and nuts in a bowl and mix well. Sprinkle over the potato mixture. Bake at 350 degrees for 30 to 40 minutes. Serves 6.

Zoerita Proctor
McEwen, Tennessee

SWEET POTATO CASSEROLE

6 large sweet potatoes
6 tablespoons margarine
3/4 cup sugar
1/4 cup orange juice
1 teaspoon vanilla extract
1/2 cup honey
1 1/2 cups miniature marshmallows

Cook the potatoes in a 2-quart saucepan of boiling water for 30 minutes or until tender. Drain and let cool. Peel the potatoes and place in a large bowl. Mash the potatoes with a large spoon. Stir in the margarine, sugar, orange juice and vanilla.

Spoon into an 8x11-inch baking dish. Bake at 300 degrees for 30 to 35 minutes. Drizzle the honey over the potato mixture and bake for 10 minutes longer. Sprinkle the marshmallows over the top and bake for 5 minutes longer or until the marshmallows are lightly browned. Serves 6 to 8.

Rebecca Cook
Mt. Pleasant, Tennessee

SWEET POTATO CASSEROLE

3 cups grated fresh sweet potatoes
$1^1/_2$ cups sugar
1 tablespoon all-purpose flour
6 tablespoons margarine, melted
3 eggs, well beaten
1 (8-ounce) can crushed pineapple
1 cup flaked coconut
1 teaspoon vanilla extract

Combine the potatoes, sugar, flour, margarine, eggs, pineapple, coconut and vanilla in a large bowl and mix well. Pour into a 2-quart baking dish. Bake at 325 degrees for 45 minutes. Serves 6 to 8.

Liz Moore
Cedar Hill, Tennessee

BAKED TOMATOES

6 tomatoes, peeled and cut into $^1/_4$-inch slices
1 cup bread crumbs
$^1/_3$ cup grated Parmesan cheese
1 teaspoon sugar
$^1/_2$ teaspoon oregano
$^1/_4$ teaspoon pepper
Pinch of dry mustard
$^1/_4$ cup ($^1/_2$ stick) butter, melted

Arrange half the tomatoes in a single layer in a shallow baking dish. Mix the bread crumbs, cheese, sugar, oregano, pepper and dry mustard in a bowl. Add the butter and stir to mix well. Sprinkle half the bread crumb mixture over the tomatoes in the baking dish. Arrange the remaining tomatoes in a single layer on top of the bread crumb mixture. Sprinkle with the remaining bread crumb mixture. Bake at 350 degrees for 20 minutes. Serves 4.

Martha Hammonds
Nashville, Tennessee

TOMATO PIE

2 cups baking mix
2/3 cup milk
1/2 teaspoon basil
1/2 teaspoon oregano
1/2 teaspoon garlic powder
1/2 teaspoon parsley flakes
1/2 teaspoon salt
1/2 teaspoon pepper
3 to 4 tomatoes, sliced
1 cup mayonnaise
2 cups (8 ounces) favorite shredded cheese

Stir the baking mix and milk in a bowl to form a dough. Roll out on a floured work surface. Fit into a pie plate and crimp the edges. Mix the basil, oregano, garlic powder, parsley flakes, salt and pepper in a small bowl. Alternate layers of tomatoes and the seasoning mixture in the pastry shell. Spread the mayonnaise over the top and sprinkle with the cheese. Bake at 350 degrees for 30 minutes or until the crust is golden brown. You may use an unbaked pie shell instead of the baking mix and milk. Bake at 400 degrees. Serves 6 to 8.

Marie Guy
Clinton, Tennessee

FRIED GREEN TOMATOES

1/2 cup cornmeal
1/2 teaspoon salt
1/4 teaspoon sugar
1/8 teaspoon pepper
6 green tomatoes, cut into 1/4-inch slices
1/2 cup (about) canola oil

Mix the cornmeal, salt, sugar and pepper in a shallow dish. Coat the tomato slices in the cornmeal mixture. Heat the oil in a large skillet to 375 degrees. Add the tomatoes and fry until golden brown on each side. Remove to paper towels to drain. You may also use firm ripe tomatoes. Serves 6.

Martha Hammonds
Nashville, Tennessee

FRIED GREEN TOMATOES AND OKRA

2 tablespoons (or more) olive oil
1 large sweet onion, chopped
1 tablespoon garlic salt
1 teaspoon pepper
2 green tomatoes, diced
1 pound okra, diced
Cornmeal

Heat the olive oil in a skillet. Add the onion, garlic salt and pepper and sauté until the onion is golden brown. Toss the tomatoes and okra with enough cornmeal in a bowl to coat. Add to the skillet. Sauté until golden brown and tender, adding more oil, if needed. Remove to paper towels to drain. Serves 4.

Marie Guy
Clinton, Tennessee

GREEN TOMATO CASSEROLE

3 large green tomatoes, thinly sliced
1 large sweet onion, thinly sliced
Salt and pepper to taste
Bread crumbs
Olive oil

Arrange alternating layers of tomatoes and onion in a greased 2-quart baking dish, seasoning each layer with salt and pepper. Cover the top with a light layer of bread crumbs. Drizzle olive oil over the bread crumbs. Bake at 350 degrees for 40 to 45 minutes. Serves 6.

Sonya Van Cleave
Memphis, Tennessee

GREEN TOMATO CASSEROLE

$1^1/_2$ teaspoons salt
$^1/_2$ teaspoon pepper
3 tablespoons chopped chives or onion
1 cup bread crumbs, toasted
8 green tomatoes, sliced
Lemon juice
Butter
$^1/_3$ cup grated Parmesan cheese

Mix the salt, pepper, chives and bread crumbs in a small bowl. Arrange layers of tomatoes in a 9x13-inch baking dish, sprinkling each layer with the bread crumb mixture and lemon juice. Dot the top with butter and sprinkle with the cheese. Bake at 350 degrees for 45 minutes. Serves 12.

Rosalie Williams
Chattanooga, Tennessee

JAMAICAN YAMS

1 (23-ounce) can yams
1 banana, cut into thick slices
$^1/_4$ cup orange juice
$^1/_2$ teaspoon salt
$^1/_8$ teaspoon pepper
2 tablespoons flaked coconut, toasted if preferred
Crushed pecans (optional)

Arrange the yams and bananas in an oiled 1-quart baking dish. Drizzle with the orange juice and sprinkle with the salt and pepper. Top with the coconut and pecans. Bake, covered, at 350 degrees for 30 minutes. Serves 2.

Bob Jeffries
Southaven, Mississippi

ZUCCHINI BAKE

2 to 3 onions, sliced and separated into rings
2 cups (8 ounces) each shredded Cheddar and mozzarella cheese
4 zucchini, sliced
1 (15 1/2-ounce) jar mushroom spaghetti sauce

Layer the onions, 1/2 of the Cheddar cheese, 1/2 of the mozzarella cheese, the zucchini and spaghetti sauce in a 9x13-inch baking pan coated with nonstick cooking spray. Top with the remaining cheeses. Bake, covered, at 350 degrees for 45 minutes or until the zucchini is tender. Cool on a wire rack for 5 to 10 minutes before cutting. Serves 12.

Betty Shields
Morristown, Tennessee

VISA VEGGIES

1 bunch broccoli, cut into bite-size pieces
2 tablespoons butter
8 ounces fresh mushrooms, sliced
1/2 cup mayonnaise
1/2 cup sour cream
1/2 cup grated Parmesan cheese
1 (14-ounce) can artichoke hearts, drained and cut into bite-size pieces
1/2 cup chopped Roma tomatoes
Salt and pepper to taste
1/2 cup bread crumbs
1/4 cup (1/2 stick) butter, melted

Boil or steam the broccoli in a saucepan of water until tender-crisp; drain. Melt 2 tablespoons butter in a skillet. Add the mushrooms and sauté until tender. Mix the mayonnaise, sour cream and cheese in a large bowl. Stir in the broccoli, mushrooms and artichoke hearts. Spoon into a greased 9x13-inch baking dish. Sprinkle the tomatoes on top. Season with salt and pepper. Toss the bread crumbs with 1/4 cup melted butter in a small bowl. Sprinkle over the tomatoes. Bake at 325 degrees for 20 minutes. Serves 10 to 12.

Barbara Duncan
Memphis, Tennessee

PINEAPPLE CASSEROLE

2 (20-ounce) cans pineapple chunks, drained, juice reserved
1 cup sugar
6 tablespoons all-purpose flour
10 ounces sharp Cheddar cheese, shredded
1 sleeve (about 36) butter crackers, crushed
1/2 cup (1 stick) margarine, melted

Place the pineapple and 1/2 cup reserved juice in a 9x13-inch baking dish.

Mix the sugar and flour in a small bowl. Add to the pineapple and stir to mix.

Combine the cheese and crushed crackers in a bowl and stir to mix. Sprinkle over the pineapple mixture. Drizzle the melted margarine over the top. Bake at 350 degrees for 30 minutes. Serves 12.

Betty Ann Webb
Knoxville, Tennessee

SCALLOPED PINEAPPLE

2 cups sugar
1 cup (2 sticks) butter, softened
3 eggs, beaten
1 (20-ounce) can crushed pineapple
4 cups bread cubes

Mix the sugar, butter and eggs in a large bowl until well blended. Stir in the pineapple and bread cubes. Pour into a baking dish. Bake at 350 degrees for 1 hour. Serves 8.

Ella Mae Hasty
Memphis, Tennessee

PINEAPPLE NOODLE PUDDING

1/2 cup apple juice
2 eggs, beaten
1/2 cup crushed pineapple in juice
2 tablespoons sugar
1/4 cup raisins
2 teaspoons vegetable oil
1/2 teaspoon vanilla extract
Pinch of ground cinnamon
Pinch of nutmeg
6 ounces egg noodles, cooked
2 teaspoons reduced-calorie soft margarine

Combine the apple juice, eggs, pineapple, sugar, raisins, oil, vanilla, cinnamon, nutmeg and noodles in a bowl and mix well. Spoon into an 8x8-inch baking pan sprayed with nonstick cooking spray. Dot with the margarine. Bake at 350 degrees for 35 to 40 minutes or until set and light brown. Serves 4.

Betty Shields
Morristown, Tennessee

FAYE'S MAC AND CHEESE

1 (16-ounce) package macaroni
16 ounces Velveeta cheese, sliced
1/4 cup (1/2 stick) butter, cut into 6 slices
1 1/2 cups (6 ounces) shredded mild Cheddar cheese
1 egg
1 1/2 cups milk
1/4 teaspoon salt

Cook the macaroni in a saucepan of boiling water until al dente; drain. Spread half the hot macaroni in a 9x13-inch baking dish coated with nonstick cooking spray. Top with half the Velveeta cheese and put 3 slices of butter down the center. Sprinkle with half the Cheddar cheese. Repeat the layers to use the remaining macaroni, Velveeta cheese, butter and Cheddar cheese. Beat the egg, milk and salt in a bowl. Pour over the top. Bake at 450 degrees for 15 to 20 minutes or until bubbly in the center. Serves 12.

Linda (Faye) Perkins
Nashville, Tennessee

DELUXE MAC AND CHEESE CASSEROLE

1 (8-ounce) package macaroni, cooked al dente and drained
1/4 cup chopped onion
1/4 cup chopped green bell pepper
1/4 cup chopped pimento
1 small can mushrooms, drained and chopped
2 (10-ounce) cans condensed cream of mushroom soup
1 cup mayonnaise
3 to 4 cups (12 to 16 ounces) shredded cheese
Salt and pepper to taste
Buttered bread crumbs

Combine the first 7 ingredients and most of the cheese in a large bowl. Season with salt and pepper. Spoon into a 9x13-inch baking dish or 2 smaller baking dishes. Sprinkle with bread crumbs and top with the remaining cheese. Bake at 375 degrees for 45 minutes. Serves 12.

C. Jane Burchfield
Knoxville, Tennessee

CORN BREAD DRESSING

2 cups chopped onions
2 cups chopped celery
8 cups crumbled corn bread
8 cups crumbled toasted bread
1 (14-ounce) can (or more) chicken broth
1 (10-ounce) can condensed cream of chicken soup
2 eggs, beaten
2 tablespoons rubbed fresh sage
1 teaspoon pepper
1 teaspoon salt

Sauté the onions and celery in a nonstick skillet until tender. Remove to a large bowl. Add the next 8 ingredients and mix well, adding additional broth if needed to make of a consistency that can be dropped from a spoon. Spoon onto a baking sheet coated with nonstick cooking spray. Bake at 350 degrees for 30 minutes or until golden brown. Store in an airtight container in the refrigerator. Warm before serving. Serves 12.

George Price
Athens, Tennessee

BREAD DRESSING

1 pound ground beef
1 pound ground pork or bulk pork sausage
1 large onion, chopped
1 large bell pepper, chopped
3 ribs celery, chopped
1 (10-ounce) can condensed cream of mushroom soup
1 (10-ounce) can condensed cream of chicken soup
1 1/3 cups water
1/2 cup chopped fresh parsley
1 teaspoon salt
1/2 teaspoon cayenne pepper
1/2 teaspoon black pepper
1/2 teaspoon garlic powder
2 (7-ounce) boxes seasoned croutons

Brown the ground beef and pork in a skillet, stirring until crumbly; drain. Remove to a large bowl. Sauté the onion, bell pepper and celery in a skillet until tender. Add to the meat mixture. Add the next 8 ingredients and mix well. Add the croutons and mix well. Spoon into a 9x13-inch baking dish. Bake at 350 degrees for 35 minutes. Serves 12.

Lewis Miller
Memphis, Tennessee

COUSCOUS WITH LEMON

1 1/3 cups water
8 ounces couscous
1/2 teaspoon salt
2 tablespoons (or more) minced fresh flat-leaf parsley
2 tablespoons finely chopped fresh mint leaves
2 tablespoons lemon juice
Pepper to taste

Bring the water to a boil in a saucepan. Stir in the couscous and salt and remove from the heat. Let stand for 5 minutes or until the liquid is absorbed. Add the parsley, mint and lemon juice. Season with pepper. Mix gently with a fork. Serves 4.

Betty Shields
Morristown, Tennessee

MEXICAN RICE

2 tablespoons vegetable oil
1 cup rice
1/4 cup chopped onion
3 cups water
1 tablespoon Knorr Caldo de Tomate (tomato bouillon)

Heat the oil in a medium saucepan. Add the rice and cook for 5 minutes or until light brown, stirring constantly.

Add the onion and sauté for 1 minute. Stir in the water and bouillon. Bring to a boil, reduce the heat and cover. Simmer for 25 minutes. Serves 8.

Olivia Murley
Jackson, Tennessee

CHEESE GRITS

6 cups water
1 1/2 cups quick-cooking grits
1 tablespoon seasoned salt
3/4 cup (1 1/2 sticks) butter
1 pound sharp cheese, shredded
3 eggs, beaten
Tabasco sauce to taste
Paprika

Bring the water to a boil in a saucepan. Stir in the grits and seasoned salt. Reduce the heat and cover. Simmer until thickened.

Remove from the heat. Add the butter and cheese and stir until melted. Let cool slightly and stir in the eggs gradually. Season with Tabasco sauce.

Pour into a greased baking dish. Sprinkle with paprika. Bake at 350 degrees for 30 to 40 minutes or until set. Serves 12.

Peggy McCanless
Nashville, Tennessee

GRITS CASSEROLE

6 cups water
$1^1/_2$ cups grits
2 teaspoons salt
1 pound Cheddar cheese, chopped
3 eggs, beaten
2 tablespoons margarine
1 pound bulk pork sausage, cooked and drained
1 teaspoon paprika

Bring the water to a boil in a saucepan. Stir in the grits and salt. Reduce the heat and cover. Simmer until thick. Remove from the heat and stir in the cheese. Add the eggs gradually, stirring constantly. Add the margarine and sausage and mix well. Pour into a 3-quart baking dish. Sprinkle with the paprika. Bake at 350 degrees for 1 hour. Serves 12.

Bill and Audrey Hembree
Clinton, Tennessee

GARLIC GRITS

4 cups water
1 cup quick-cooking grits
1 teaspoon salt
6 tablespoons margarine
1 (6-ounce) tube garlic cheese
Milk
2 eggs, beaten
Cornflake crumbs or plain or Italian-style seasoned bread crumbs
Melted margarine

Bring the water to a boil in a saucepan. Stir in the grits and salt. Reduce the heat and cover. Simmer for 20 to 25 minutes or until thick. Remove from the heat and add the margarine and cheese and stir until melted. Add enough milk to the eggs to make 1 cup. Stir into the grits. Pour into a greased 9x13-inch baking dish. Mix the crumbs with enough melted margarine to moisten in a bowl. Sprinkle over the grits. Bake at 350 degrees for 1 hour. Serves 10 to 12.

Louise Spahr
Knoxville, Tennessee

BREADS

NO-KNEADING DINNER ROLLS

1 cake yeast
1/4 cup lukewarm water
1 cup boiling water
1 egg
2 tablespoons sugar
1/4 cup shortening
1 1/4 teaspoons salt
3 1/2 cups all-purpose flour

Dissolve the yeast in the lukewarm water in a large bowl. Add the boiling water and egg and mix well. Combine the sugar, shortening, salt and flour in a bowl and mix well. Add to the yeast mixture and mix well. Fill greased muffin cups 3/4 full. Bake at 425 degrees for 20 minutes. Makes 1 dozen rolls.

Rosalie Williams
Chattanooga, Tennessee

ELECTRIC MIXER ROLLS

3 envelopes dry yeast
1 cup lukewarm water
1 cup shortening
3/4 cup sugar
1 teaspoon salt
1 cup boiling water
2 eggs
5 cups all-purpose flour

Dissolve the yeast in the lukewarm water in a small bowl. Combine the shortening, sugar and salt in a large bowl. Beat with an electric mixer until light and fluffy. Beat in the boiling water. Beat in the eggs and dissolved yeast. Beat in the flour, 1/2 cup at a time.

Shape the dough into a ball and place in a greased bowl. Cover and chill for at least 6 hours or up to 5 days. Shape the dough into small balls and arrange on a nonstick baking sheet. Bake at 375 degrees for 10 to 15 minutes.
Makes 2 to 3 dozen rolls.

Nancy Bassett
Nashville, Tennessee

SPOON ROLLS

1 envelope dry yeast
2 cups warm water
3/4 cup (1 1/2 sticks) margarine, melted
1/4 cup sugar
1 egg, beaten
4 cups self-rising flour

Dissolve the yeast in the warm water in a large bowl. Mix the margarine and sugar in a small bowl. Stir into the yeast mixture. Stir in the egg. Stir in the flour. Remove the dough to an airtight container and chill until cold. Spoon the dough into greased muffin cups, filling 1/2 full. Bake at 350 degrees for 25 minutes or until golden brown. Makes 2 dozen rolls.

Jan Moore
Jackson, Tennessee

DOZEN MAYO ROLLS

2 cups self-rising flour
1/4 cup sugar
1/4 cup mayonnaise
1 cup milk

Combine the flour, sugar, mayonnaise and milk in a bowl and mix well. Pour into 12 nonstick muffin cups. Bake at 400 degrees for 15 minutes. Makes 1 dozen rolls.

Betty Reddick
Knoxville, Tennessee

MAYONNAISE ROLLS

1 cup self-rising flour
1/2 cup milk
1 tablespoon mayonnaise

Combine the flour, milk and mayonnaise in a bowl and mix well with a fork. Pour into 6 nonstick muffin cups. Bake at 450 degrees until light golden brown. Makes 6 rolls.

Juli Simms
Knoxville, Tennessee

BROCCOLI CORN BREAD

3/4 cup (1 1/2 sticks) butter or margarine
2 packages corn muffin mix
1 (10-ounce) package frozen chopped broccoli, thawed
1 onion, chopped
10 ounces cottage cheese
4 eggs
1/2 cup (2 ounces) shredded Cheddar cheese

Melt the butter in a 9x13-inch baking pan in a 375-degree oven. Maintain the oven temperature. Combine the corn muffin mix, undrained broccoli, onion, cottage cheese and eggs in a bowl and mix well. Pour into the prepared baking pan. Sprinkle with the Cheddar cheese. Bake for 30 minutes or until brown. Serves 10 to 12.

Emily Taylor
Jackson, Tennessee

CORN LIGHT BREAD

1 1/2 cups cornmeal
1/2 cup all-purpose flour
1/2 cup sugar
1/2 teaspoon baking soda
1/2 teaspoon salt
1 1/2 cups buttermilk
1/2 cup (1 stick) butter, melted

Combine the cornmeal, flour, sugar, baking soda, salt, buttermilk and butter in a large bowl and mix well. Let stand for 20 minutes, or 30 minutes for a finer textured bread. Pour into a greased loaf pan.

Bake at 350 degrees for 1 hour or until a wooden pick inserted in the center comes out clean. Remove to a wire rack and cool in the pan. Serves 8 to 10.

Nancy Bassett
Nashville, Tennessee

TENNESSEE CORN BREAD

2 cups self-rising cornmeal
1/3 cup boiling water
1 egg
1/4 cup vegetable oil
1 teaspoon sugar
1 1/4 cups milk

Place 12 greased muffin cups in a 450-degree oven. Place the cornmeal in a bowl. Remove 2 tablespoons of the cornmeal to a small bowl and stir in the boiling water.

Add the egg, oil, sugar and milk to the dry cornmeal and mix well. Add the hot cornmeal mixture and mix well. Pour into the very hot muffin cups.

Bake at 450 degrees for 15 minutes or until golden brown. Remove to a wire rack to cool. Serves 12.

Martha Williams
Hollow Rock, Tennessee

MEXICAN CORN BREAD

3 eggs
2 cups self-rising cornmeal
1/4 cup sugar
1/2 teaspoon baking soda
2/3 cup vegetable oil
1 cup buttermilk
1 small onion, chopped
1 small bell pepper, chopped
3 or 4 jalapeño chiles, chopped
1 cup whole kernel corn
1 cup (4 ounces) shredded cheese

Place a greased 9x12-inch baking pan in a 400-degree oven. Combine all the ingredients in a bowl and mix well. Pour into the hot baking pan.

Bake at 400 degrees for 40 minutes or until a wooden pick inserted in the center comes out clean. Remove to a wire rack to cool. Serves 8.

Olivia Murley
Jackson, Tennessee

MEXICAN CORN BREAD

1 cup yellow self-rising cornmeal
1/2 cup chopped green chiles
2 eggs, well beaten
1 cup milk
1 (14-ounce) can cream-style corn
2 teaspoons sugar
3 or 4 slices bacon, crisp-cooked and crumbled or 2 tablespoons bacon bits
1/2 cup bacon drippings or vegetable oil
8 ounces ground chuck
1 onion, chopped
1 cup (4 ounces) shredded Cheddar cheese

Mix the first 8 ingredients in a large bowl. Brown the ground chuck in a large skillet with the onion, stirring until the beef is crumbly; drain. Pour half the cornmeal mixture into a warm well-greased cast-iron skillet. Top with the meat mixture and sprinkle with the cheese. Top with the remaining cornmeal mixture. Bake at 350 degrees for 55 minutes. You may use one 4-ounce can chopped green chiles plus 2 tablespoons chopped jalapeño chiles instead of green chiles. Serves 8.

Faye Richardson
Memphis, Tennessee

JALAPEÑO CORN BREAD

2 (8 1/2-ounce) packages corn bread mix
2 eggs, lightly beaten
2/3 cup low-fat milk
2 (7-ounce) cans whole kernel corn, drained
2 cups (8 ounces) shredded sharp Cheddar cheese
2 jalapeño chiles, seeded and finely chopped

Stir the corn bread mix, eggs, milk, corn, cheese and jalapeño chiles in a large bowl just until moistened. Pour into a 9x13-inch baking pan coated lightly with nonstick cooking spray. Bake at 400 degrees for 12 to 15 minutes or until golden brown and the center springs back when lightly touched. Remove to a wire rack and let cool in the pan. Serves 12.

Betty Goan
Morristown, Tennessee

ANGEL CORN MUFFINS

1 cup self-rising cornmeal
1 cup self-rising flour
1 envelope dry yeast
1 tablespoon sugar
1/2 teaspoon baking soda
2 eggs, beaten
1/2 cup corn oil
1 1/2 cups buttermilk

Mix the cornmeal, flour, yeast, sugar and baking soda in a bowl. Add the eggs, oil and buttermilk and stir to mix well.

Fill greased muffin cups. Bake at 450 degrees for 15 to 20 minutes. Remove to a wire rack to cool. Makes 12 to 15 muffins.

Florence Stubblefield
Morristown, Tennessee

ANGEL CORN MUFFINS

1 cup self-rising cornmeal
1 cup self-rising flour
2 tablespoons sugar
1/2 teaspoon baking soda
1 envelope dry yeast
1/2 cup vegetable oil
2 eggs, beaten
1 1/2 cups buttermilk

Combine the cornmeal, flour, sugar, baking soda, yeast, oil, eggs and buttermilk in a bowl and mix well.

Fill greased muffin cups. Bake at 400 degrees for 10 minutes. Remove to a wire rack to cool. Makes 12 to 15 muffins.

Ruby Rigsby
Soddy-Daisy, Tennessee

GENERAL BUSINESS HUSH PUPPIES

1 cup all-purpose flour
1/2 cup cornmeal
2 tablespoons baking powder
Dash of sugar
Salt to taste
1 onion, chopped, or to taste
1 bell pepper, chopped, or to taste
1 egg, well beaten
Hot water
Cayenne pepper to taste
Thyme to taste
Finely chopped jalapeño chiles to taste
Vegetable oil for frying

Mix the flour, cornmeal, baking powder and sugar in a bowl. Season with salt. Stir in the onion and bell pepper. Stir in the egg and enough hot water to make a soft dough. Season with cayenne, thyme and jalapeños and shape into balls. Heat oil in a heavy saucepan or deep-fryer to 350 degrees. Fry the dough balls until golden brown on all sides. Remove to paper towels to drain. Serves 4.

Sonya Van Cleave
Memphis, Tennessee

ONE-PAN BANANA BREAD

3 very brown ripe bananas
1 1/2 cups sugar
2 eggs
1/2 cup vegetable oil
1 1/2 cups all-purpose flour
1/4 cup buttermilk
1 teaspoon baking soda
1 teaspoon vanilla extract
1 cup chopped pecans

Mash the bananas in a bowl. Add the sugar, eggs, oil, flour, buttermilk, baking soda, vanilla and pecans, mixing well after each addition. Pour into a greased and floured loaf dish. Bake at 325 degrees for 1 hour or until a wooden pick inserted in the center comes out clean. Remove to a wire rack to cool. Serves 12.

Peggy McCanless
Nashville, Tennessee

BLACKBERRY PECAN MUFFINS

1/4 cup (1/2 stick) margarine, softened
3/4 cup sucralose
1 teaspoon sugar
1 egg
1/2 cup sour cream
Juice of 1 small orange
1/2 cup self-rising flour
1/2 cup self-rising cornmeal
Dash each of baking soda, cinnamon, allspice and nutmeg
1/2 cup pecans, chopped
1 cup blackberries

Beat the margarine, sucralose and sugar in a bowl until light and fluffy. Stir in the egg, sour cream and orange juice. Mix the next 6 ingredients in a bowl. Stir in the pecans and blackberries. Add to the sour cream mixture and stir lightly with a fork. Fill nonstick muffin cups 3/4 full. Bake at 425 degrees for 20 minutes or until the muffins test done. Cool on a wire rack. Makes 9 muffins.

Teresa Flach and James Parrish
Nashville, Tennessee

BRAN MUFFINS

1 cup All-Bran cereal
1 cup boiling water
1/4 cup vegetable or olive oil
2 1/2 cups self-rising flour
2 1/2 teaspoons baking soda
1 teaspoon salt
2 eggs
1 1/2 cups sugar
2 cups buttermilk
2 cups All-Bran cereal
Raisins or sweetened dried cranberries (optional)

Combine 1 cup cereal and the water in a bowl. Stir until the cereal dissolves and add the oil. Sift the flour, baking soda and salt together. Beat the eggs in a large bowl. Beat in the sugar. Stir in the flour mixture. Stir in the buttermilk and 2 cups cereal. Add the dissolved cereal mixture and raisins and stir to mix well. Cover and chill for at least 24 hours or up to 7 weeks. Fill greased muffin cups. Bake at 400 degrees for 15 to 20 minutes. Cool on a wire rack. Makes 3 dozen muffins.

Janice Cude
Franklin, Tennessee

BREAKFAST MUFFINS

2 cups all-purpose flour
$1^1/_4$ cups sugar
2 teaspoons baking soda
2 teaspoons cinnamon
$^1/_2$ teaspoon salt
3 eggs, beaten
1 cup vegetable oil
2 teaspoons vanilla extract
2 cups grated carrots
$^1/_2$ cup raisins
$^1/_2$ cup pecans
$^1/_2$ cup flaked coconut
1 apple, peeled, cored and grated

Mix the flour, sugar, baking soda, cinnamon and salt together. Mix the eggs, oil and vanilla in a large bowl. Stir in the carrots, raisins, pecans, coconut and apple. Add the dry ingredients and stir just until mixed. Fill well greased muffin cups full. Bake at 350 degrees for 20 to 25 minutes. Remove to a wire rack to cool. Makes 16 large muffins.

Jean Mayo
Ashland City, Tennessee

ORANGE BREAD

2 (11-ounce) cans refrigerator biscuits
3 ounces cream cheese, cut into 20 cubes
$^3/_4$ cup sugar
$^1/_2$ cup chopped pecans
1 tablespoons grated orange zest
$^1/_2$ cup (1 stick) margarine, melted
1 cup confectioners' sugar
2 tablespoons orange juice

Separate the biscuits and gently separate each biscuit in half. Place 1 cube of cream cheese between 2 halves and pinch the edges to seal. Mix the sugar, pecans and orange zest in a shallow dish. Dip the biscuits in the margarine and coat in the sugar mixture. Stand the biscuits on end in a lightly greased 12-cup bundt pan. Drizzle the remaining margarine over the biscuits and sprinkle the remaining sugar mixture over the top. Bake at 350 degrees for 45 minutes or until golden brown. Invert immediately onto a serving plate. Drizzle a mixture of the confectioners' sugar and orange juice over the warm bread. Serve immediately. Serves 10 to 12.

Wanda (Susie) Ladd
Williamsport, Tennessee

EASY LEMON POPPY SEED BREAD

2 packages lemon poppy seed muffin mix
2 eggs, beaten
2/3 cup milk
1/4 cup vegetable oil

Combine the muffin mix, eggs, milk and oil in a bowl and mix well. Pour into an oiled loaf pan.

Bake at 350 degrees for 45 to 50 minutes or until a wooden pick inserted in the center comes out clean. Remove to a wire rack to cool. Serves 8 to 10.

Bobbie Latta
Columbia, Tennessee

PUMPKIN NUT BREAD

2 cups all-purpose flour
2 teaspoons baking powder
1/2 teaspoon baking soda
1 teaspoon salt
1 teaspoon nutmeg
1/2 teaspoon cinnamon
2 eggs
1 cup sugar
1 cup canned or mashed cooked pumpkin
1/2 cup milk
1/4 cup (1/2 stick) butter, softened
1 cup chopped walnuts or pecans

Mix the flour, baking powder, baking soda, salt, nutmeg and cinnamon together. Beat the eggs, sugar, pumpkin and milk in a large bowl. Beat in the butter. Beat in the dry ingredients. Stir in the walnuts. Pour into 2 greased 5x9-inch loaf pans.

Bake at 350 degrees for 45 to 55 minutes or until a wooden pick inserted in the center comes out clean. Cool in the pans for 5 minutes. Remove to a wire rack to cool. Serve warm, cold or toasted and spread with cream cheese. Serves 12.

Billie Carson
Lafollette, Tennessee

PUMPKIN BREAD

1 3/4 cups all-purpose flour
3/4 teaspoon salt
1 teaspoon baking soda
1/4 teaspoon baking powder
1/2 teaspoon ground cinnamon
1/2 teaspoon nutmeg
1/2 teaspoon cloves
1/4 teaspoon mace
2 eggs
1 1/2 cups sugar
1/2 cup vegetable oil
1 cup canned or mashed cooked pumpkin
1/3 cup water
1/2 teaspoon vanilla extract

Sift the flour, salt, baking soda, baking powder, cinnamon, nutmeg, cloves and mace together. Beat the eggs and sugar in a large bowl. Stir in the oil and pumpkin. Stir in the dry ingredients alternately with the water. Stir in the vanilla. Pour into 2 greased 1-pound coffee cans. Bake at 350 degrees for 1 hour or until a wooden pick inserted in the center comes out clean. Remove to a wire rack to cool. Serves 24.

Paula Hartley
Franklin, Tennessee

PUMPKIN BREAD

2 cups sugar
3/4 cup vegetable oil
4 eggs, beaten
1 (15-ounce) can pumpkin
3 1/2 cups sifted all-purpose flour
1/2 teaspoon baking powder
2 teaspoons baking soda
1 teaspoon salt
2 teaspoons pumpkin pie spice
1 teaspoon cinnamon
1 teaspoon nutmeg
2/3 cup water
2 teaspoons vanilla extract

Mix all the ingredients in a large bowl. Pour into 2 nonstick 5x9-inch loaf pans. Bake at 350 degrees for 1 hour or until a wooden pick inserted in the center comes out clean. Remove to a wire rack to cool. Serves 24.

Carolyn Carter
Antioch, Tennessee

PUMPKIN BREAD

3 1/3 cups all-purpose flour
2 teaspoons baking soda
1 1/2 teaspoons salt
1 teaspoon cinnamon
1 teaspoon nutmeg
4 eggs, well beaten
3 cups sugar
1 cup vegetable oil
2 cups canned or mashed cooked pumpkin
2/3 cup water
1 cup chopped nuts

Mix the first 5 ingredients together. Beat the eggs and sugar in a large bowl. Beat in the oil and pumpkin. Beat in the dry ingredients alternately with the water. Stir in the nuts. Pour into two 5x9-inch loaf pans coated with nonstick cooking spray. Bake at 350 degrees for 60 to 70 minutes or until a wooden pick inserted in the center comes out clean. Remove to a wire rack and cool in the pans. Serves 24.

Rubye Morrison
Shelbyville, Tennessee

PUMPKIN MUFFINS

1 (15-ounce) can solid-pack pumpkin
4 eggs
1 1/2 cups vegetable oil
2 cups sugar
3 cups all-purpose flour
2 teaspoons baking powder
2 teaspoons baking soda
2 teaspoons ground cinnamon
Dash of salt
1 1/2 cups black walnuts
2 to 3 cups raisins

Mix the pumpkin, eggs, oil and sugar in a large bowl. Combine the flour, baking powder, baking soda, cinnamon and salt in a bowl and mix well. Combine the walnuts and raisins in a bowl. Add a small amount of the flour mixture and toss to coat. Add the flour mixture and walnut mixture to the pumpkin mixture and stir just until moistened. Fill muffin cups sprayed with nonstick cooking spray 3/4 full with the batter. Bake at 350 degrees for 20 minutes. Makes 36 muffins.

Ann Harville
Talbott, Tennessee

CHOCOLATE ZUCCHINI BREAD

2 1/2 cups all-purpose flour
1/2 cup baking cocoa
1 teaspoon salt
1 teaspoon baking soda
1/4 teaspoon baking powder
1 teaspoon ground cinnamon
3 eggs
1 cup vegetable oil
2 cups sugar
1 tablespoon vanilla extract
2 cups shredded zucchini

Mix the flour, baking cocoa, salt, baking soda, baking powder and cinnamon together. Beat the eggs, oil, sugar and vanilla in a large bowl. Stir in the zucchini. Add the dry ingredients and stir to mix well. Pour into 2 greased 4x8-inch loaf pans. Bake at 350 degrees for 45 minutes or until a wooden pick inserted in the center comes out clean. Remove to a wire rack to cool. Serves 24.

Amy Bible
Knoxville, Tennessee

ZUCCHINI BREAD

3 cups all-purpose flour
1 teaspoon baking soda
1/4 teaspoon baking powder
1 teaspoon salt
4 teaspoons ground cinnamon
3 eggs
2 1/4 cups sugar
1 cup vegetable oil
1 tablespoon vanilla extract
2 cups grated zucchini
1 1/2 cups pecans

Sift the flour, baking soda, baking powder, salt and cinnamon together. Beat the eggs in a large bowl. Beat in the sugar, oil and vanilla. Stir in the zucchini. Add the dry ingredients and stir to mix well. Stir in the pecans. Pour into 2 greased and floured loaf pans. Bake at 325 degrees for 1 hour and 10 minutes or until a wooden pick inserted in the center comes out clean. Remove to a wire rack to cool. Serves 20.

Betty Shields
Morristown, Tennessee

CHEESE GARLIC BISCUITS

2 cups baking mix
2/3 cup milk
1/2 cup (2 ounces) shredded Cheddar cheese
1/2 cup (1 stick) margarine, melted
1/4 teaspoon garlic powder

Combine the baking mix, milk and cheese in a bowl. Stir until a soft dough forms. Beat for 30 seconds. Drop by spoonfuls onto an ungreased baking sheet. Mix the melted margarine and garlic powder in a small bowl. Brush on the biscuits. Bake at 450 degrees for 8 to 10 minutes or until golden brown. Makes 2 dozen biscuits.

Lewis Miller
Memphis, Tennessee

ANGEL BISCUITS

1 envelope dry yeast
2 tablespoons lukewarm water
5 cups self-rising flour
1/4 cup sugar
1 cup shortening
2 cups buttermilk
6 tablespoons butter, melted

Dissolve the yeast in the lukewarm water in a small bowl. Let stand for 5 minutes or until bubbly. Mix the flour and sugar in a large bowl. Cut in the shortening with a pastry blender until crumbly. Add the yeast mixture and buttermilk and stir just until moistened. Cover and chill for 8 to 10 hours. Knead the dough on a floured work surface 10 to 12 times. Roll the dough 1/2 inch thick. Cut with a biscuit cutter. Dip the biscuits in the melted butter and fold in half. Place on a greased baking sheet. Let rise for 2 hours. Bake at 400 degrees for 12 to 15 minutes or until golden brown.
Makes 2 1/2 dozen biscuits.

Ann Howell Tickle
Morristown, Tennessee

SALES MEETING FRENCH TOAST

1 loaf French bread, cut into 1-inch slices
8 eggs, beaten
2 cups half-and-half
1 cup milk
2 tablespoons sugar
1 teaspoon vanilla extract
1/4 teaspoon ground cinnamon
1/4 teaspoon nutmeg
Dash of salt
Maple syrup (optional)

Arrange the bread slices in a slightly overlapping layer in a buttered 9x13-inch baking dish. Stir the next 8 ingredients in a bowl just until blended. Pour evenly over the bread. Cover and chill overnight. Bake, uncovered, at 350 degrees for 40 minutes or until puffed and golden brown. Serve with maple syrup. Serves 8.

Sonya Van Cleave
Memphis, Tennessee

CREAM CHEESE DANISH

2 (8-ounce) cans refrigerator crescent rolls
16 ounces cream cheese, softened
3/4 cup sugar
1 egg yolk
1 tablespoon vanilla extract
1 tablespoon lemon juice
1 egg white, lightly beaten
1 tablespoon butter, softened
1 cup confectioners' sugar
Water or lemon juice

Unroll 1 can of crescent roll dough and fit in the bottom of a 9x13-inch baking pan. Press the seams to seal. Combine the next 5 ingredients in a bowl. Beat until smooth. Spread over the dough in the baking dish. Unroll the remaining can of crescent dough and press the seams to seal. Place on top of the cream cheese layer. Brush with the egg white. Bake at 350 degrees for 25 minutes or until golden brown. Remove to a wire rack. Cream the butter and confectioners' sugar in a small bowl. Beat in enough water to make a glaze. Drizzle the glaze over the hot pastry. Serves 10.

Kathy Duncan
Memphis, Tennessee

BAKED BLUEBERRY PECAN FRENCH TOAST

1 (24-inch) baguette, cut into 20 (1-inch) slices
6 eggs
3 cups milk
3/4 cup packed brown sugar
1/2 teaspoon grated fresh nutmeg
1 teaspoon vanilla extract
1 cup (about 3 ounce) pecans
1 teaspoon unsalted butter
1/4 teaspoon salt
2 cups blueberries
1/4 cup (1/2 stick) unsalted butter, cut into pieces
1/4 cup packed brown sugar
1 cup blueberries
1/2 cup maple syrup
1 tablespoon fresh lemon juice

Arrange the bread slices in a single layer in a buttered 9x13-inch baking dish. Whisk the eggs, milk, 3/4 cup brown sugar, nutmeg and vanilla in a bowl. Pour evenly over the bread. Cover and chill for at least 8 hours or until the liquid has been absorbed. Spread the pecans in a shallow baking pan. Bake at 350 degrees for 8 minutes or until toasted and fragrant. Add 1 teaspoon butter and the salt and toss to coat.

Sprinkle the pecans and 2 cups blueberries over the bread mixture. Combine 1/4 cup butter and 1/4 cup brown sugar in a small saucepan. Cook until the butter melts, stirring constantly. Drizzle over the bread mixture. Bake at 400 degrees for 20 minutes or until any blueberry juice is bubbly. Combine 1 cup blueberries and the maple syrup in a small saucepan. Cook over medium heat for 3 minutes or until the berries burst, stirring often. Pour through a sieve over a bowl, pressing to remove all liquid. Discard the solids. Stir the lemon juice into the syrup and pour into a small heatproof pitcher. Serve with the hot French toast.

The blueberry syrup can be made 1 day ahead. Cover and chill. Reheat before serving. Serves 6 to 8.

Linda Giles
Knoxville, Tennessee

SOUR CREAM COFFEE CAKE

1 (18-ounce) package butter-flavor cake mix
1/4 cup sugar
3/4 cup vegetable oil
4 eggs
1 cup sour cream
1 cup chopped pecans
1/4 cup packed brown sugar
1/4 teaspoon cinnamon

Mix the first 5 ingredients in a bowl. Combine the pecans, brown sugar and cinnamon in a bowl and mix well. Sprinkle 1/3 of the pecan mixture over the bottom of a greased tube pan or bundt pan. Spoon 1/2 of the batter over the pecan mixture. Sprinkle with 1/2 of the remaining pecan mixture. Add the remaining batter. Sprinkle with the remaining pecan mixture. Bake at 325 degrees for 55 minutes. Invert onto a serving plate. Serves 8 to 12.

Kathy Duncan
Memphis, Tennessee

BLUEBERRY "EVERYTHING" SAUCE

1 pint fresh blueberries
1 cup sugar
Dash of water

Bring the blueberries, sugar and water to a boil in a saucepan and cook for 2 to 3 minutes, stirring occasionally. Serve on pancakes, waffles, biscuits and toast. Makes about 2 cups.

Faye Richardson
Memphis, Tennessee

HONEY BUTTER

1/2 cup (1 stick) unsalted butter, softened
1/4 cup honey
Pinch of ground cinnamon

Beat the butter in a bowl with a wooden spoon or with an electric mixer in a mixing bowl until creamy. Beat the honey and cinnamon in a bowl. Add to the butter and mix well. Chill, tightly covered, until serving time. Makes 3/4 cup.

Barbara Johnson
Collierville, Tennessee

DESSERTS

POL'S APPLE CAKE

3 eggs
$1^1/_4$ cups vegetable oil
2 cups sugar
$2^1/_2$ cups self-rising flour
2 apples, peeled, cored and chopped
1 cup chopped walnuts or pecans
1 cup flaked coconut
Topping (below)

Beat the eggs, oil and sugar in a mixing bowl until creamy. Add the flour gradually, stirring constantly; the batter will be stiff. Fold in the apples, walnuts and coconut. Pour into a greased and floured tube pan. Bake at 350 degrees for 1 hour or until a wooden pick inserted in the center comes out clean. Cool in the pan for 30 minutes. Invert onto a serving plate. Pour the topping evenly over the cake. Serves 16.

Brown Sugar Topping

$^1/_4$ cup ($^1/_2$ stick) butter
$^1/_3$ cup milk
$^1/_2$ cup packed brown sugar

Combine the butter, milk and brown sugar in a saucepan. Bring to a boil. Cook for 3 minutes, stirring frequently.

Myrtle Curtis
Lenoir City, Tennessee

FRESH APPLE CAKE

$2^1/_2$ cups all-purpose flour
2 teaspoons baking powder
1 teaspoon baking soda
1 teaspoon salt
1 cup vegetable oil
2 cups sugar
3 eggs
1 teaspoon vanilla extract
3 cups chopped peeled apples
1 cup chopped pecans
Frosting (page 189)

Sift the flour, baking powder, baking soda and salt together. Beat the oil and sugar in a mixing bowl. Beat in the eggs 1 at a time. Stir in the dry ingredients and vanilla.

Fold in the apples and pecans. Pour into a nonstick 9x13-inch cake pan. Bake at 325 degrees for 25 to 40 minutes or until a wooden pick inserted in the center comes out clean. Cool in the pan on a wire rack. Spread the frosting over the cake. Serves 12.

Vanilla Frosting

6 tablespoons butter, softened
2 cups confectioners' sugar
1 teaspoon vanilla extract
Milk

Beat the butter, confectioners' sugar and vanilla in a mixing bowl until well blended. Add a small amount of milk if needed to reach the desired consistency.

Bob and Barbara Burton
Clinton, Tennessee

AMAZING APPLE RAISIN CAKE

3 cups sifted all-purpose flour
2 cups sugar
2 teaspoons ground cinnamon
1/2 teaspoon nutmeg
1/2 teaspoon salt
1/4 teaspoon ground cloves
1 cup mayonnaise
1/3 cup milk
2 eggs
3 cups chopped peeled apples
1 cup raisins
1/2 cup coarsely chopped walnuts

Combine the flour, sugar, cinnamon, nutmeg, salt, cloves, mayonnaise, milk, eggs, apples, raisins and walnuts in a bowl and mix well. Pour into a nonstick 9x13-inch cake pan. Bake at 350 degrees for 25 to 35 minutes or until a wooden pick inserted in the center comes out clean. Cool in the pan on a wire rack. Serve with whipped topping. Serves 12.

Ina Burkhalter
Springfield, Tennessee

CARROT CAKE

2 1/4 cups all-purpose flour
2 teaspoons baking soda
1 teaspoon salt
2 teaspoons ground cinnamon
1/4 teaspoon nutmeg
1/4 teaspoon ground allspice
3 eggs
2 cups sugar
1 1/2 cups vegetable oil
2 teaspoons vanilla extract
2 cups shredded carrots
2 cups flaked coconut
1 (8-ounce) can crushed pineapple
1 1/2 cups chopped pecans
1 cup raisins
Icing (below)

Sift the flour, baking soda, salt, cinnamon, nutmeg and allspice together. Beat the eggs, sugar, oil and vanilla in a mixing bowl. Add the dry ingredients and mix well. Stir in the carrots, coconut, pineapple, pecans and raisins. Pour into 3 greased and floured 9-inch cake pans. Bake at 350 degrees for 50 minutes or until a wooden pick inserted in the center comes out clean. Cool in the pans for 10 minutes. Remove to a wire rack to cool completely. Spread the icing between the layers and over the top and side of the cake. Serves 12.

Cream Cheese Icing

12 ounces cream cheese, softened
1/4 cup (1/2 stick) butter, softened
1 teaspoon vanilla extract
1 (16-ounce) package confectioners' sugar

Beat the cream cheese, butter and vanilla in a mixing bowl until smooth. Beat in the confectioners' sugar.

Joanne Taylor
Jackson, Tennessee

CHOCOLATE CAKE

1/2 cup (1 stick) butter, softened
1 cup granulated sugar
1 cup packed brown sugar
2 eggs, well beaten
1/4 teaspoon salt
2 ounces chocolate
1/2 cup boiling water
2 cups sifted all-purpose flour
1 teaspoon baking soda
1 cup buttermilk
1 teaspoon vanilla extract
Frosting (below)

Beat the butter, granulated sugar and brown sugar in a mixing bowl until light and fluffy. Beat in the eggs and salt. Melt the chocolate in the boiling water in a small bowl. Stir into the butter mixture. Mix the flour and baking soda together. Add the dry ingredients alternately with the buttermilk to the chocolate mixture, mixing well after each addition. Stir in the vanilla. Pour into 2 greased and floured cake pans. Bake at 350 degrees for 40 minutes or until a wooden pick inserted in the center comes out clean. Cool in the pans for 10 minutes. Remove to a wire rack to cool partially. Spread the frosting between the layers and over the top and side of the warm cake. Note: This may be baked in a 9x13-inch baking pan. Serves 12.

Cocoa Brown Sugar Frosting

1/4 cup (1/2 stick) butter
1 cup packed brown sugar
3 tablespoons baking cocoa
1/4 cup cream
1 teaspoon vanilla extract

Melt the butter in a saucepan. Stir in the brown sugar, baking cocoa and cream. Cook over low heat until the sugar is dissolved. Bring to a boil and boil for 1 minute. Remove from the heat and stir in the vanilla. Beat until the mixture begins to lose its gloss.

Luzenia Queen
Clinton, Tennessee

CHOCOLATE FANTASY CAKE

2 1/2 cups all-purpose flour
3 cups sugar
1 cup plus 2 tablespoons baking cocoa
2 1/4 teaspoons baking soda
2 1/4 teaspoons baking powder
1 1/2 teaspoons salt
3 eggs
1 1/2 cups milk
3/4 cup vegetable oil
1 tablespoon vanilla extract
1 1/2 cups boiling water
Frosting (below)

Combine the flour, sugar, baking cocoa, baking soda, baking powder and salt in a mixing bowl and beat at low speed until well mixed. Beat in the eggs 1 at a time. Add the milk, oil and vanilla gradually, beating constantly. Beat at medium speed for a few minutes. Add the boiling water in a slow stream, beating constantly at low speed. Beat until well mixed; the batter will be very thin. Pour into 3 greased 9-inch cake pans. Bake at 350 degrees for 20 to 30 minutes or until a wooden pick inserted in the center comes out clean. Cool in the pans on a wire rack. Remove from the pans and wrap in plastic wrap. Freeze until firm. Spread the frosting between the layers and over the top and side of the frozen cake. Serves 16.

Chocolate Cream Cheese Frosting

16 ounces cream cheese, softened
1 cup (2 sticks) unsalted butter, softened
2 teaspoons vanilla extract
1 cup baking cocoa
8 cups confectioners' sugar

Beat the cream cheese and butter in a bowl until light and fluffy. Beat in the vanilla. Beat in the baking cocoa and confectioners' sugar and beat until smooth.

Donna Burns
Dickson, Tennessee

CHOCOLATE PUDDING CAKE

1 (2-layer) package butter-recipe cake mix
1 (6-ounce) package chocolate instant pudding mix
4 eggs
1 cup vegetable oil
1 tablespoon vanilla extract
1/4 cup water
1 cup sour cream
1 cup (6 ounces) chocolate chips
Confectioners' sugar

Combine the cake mix, pudding mix, eggs, oil, vanilla, water, sour cream and chocolate chips in a mixing bowl and mix well. Pour into a well-greased bundt pan. Bake at 325 degrees for 1 hour or until a wooden pick inserted in the center comes out clean. Cool in the pan for 10 to 15 minutes. Invert onto a serving plate and dust with confectioners' sugar.
Serves 10 to 12.

Sarah F. Parker
Germantown, Tennessee

CHOCOLATE CHIP KAHLÚA CAKE

1 (2-layer) package devil's food cake mix
1 (6-ounce) package instant chocolate pudding mix
4 eggs
3/4 cup vegetable oil
2 cups sour cream
1/3 to 1/2 cup Kahlúa
1 cup chocolate chips

Combine the cake mix, pudding mix, eggs, oil, sour cream and Kahlúa in a mixing bowl and beat until well blended and thick. Stir in the chocolate chips. Pour into a nonstick bundt pan. Bake at 350 degrees for 20 to 30 minutes or until a wooden pick inserted in the center comes out clean. Cool in the pan for 10 to 15 minutes. Remove to a wire rack and let stand until completely cool. Serves 10 to 12.

Nina Morris and Lisa Overstreet
Carthage, Tennessee

TOFFEE-TOPPED RICH CHOCOLATE CAKE

1 (2-layer) package German chocolate cake mix
1 1/3 cups water
1/2 cup vegetable oil
3 eggs
1 (14-ounce) can sweetened condensed milk
1 (16- to 17-ounce) jar caramel, butterscotch or fudge ice cream topping
1 (8-ounce) container frozen whipped topping, thawed
1 (8-ounce) package toffee chips or bits

Combine the cake mix, water, oil and eggs in a mixing bowl and beat for 2 minutes. Grease the bottom of a 9x13-inch cake pan. Pour the batter into the prepared pan. Bake at 350 degrees for 33 to 38 minutes or until a wooden pick inserted in the center comes out clean. Remove to a wire rack and let stand to cool for 15 minutes.

Poke holes every 1/2 inch in the warm cake with the handle of a wooden spoon. Drizzle the sweetened condensed milk evenly over the cake. Let stand until absorbed. Drizzle the caramel topping evenly over the cake. Cover and chill for 2 hours or until cold. Spread the whipped topping over the cake and sprinkle with the toffee chips. Cover and chill until serving time. Serves 12.

Barbara Gaddes
Kingston Springs, Tennessee

TEXAS SHEET CAKE

2 cups all-purpose flour
2 cups sugar
1/2 teaspoon salt
1 cup (2 sticks) margarine
1 cup water
1/4 cup baking cocoa
2 eggs
1/2 cup sour cream
1 teaspoon baking soda
Icing (page 195)

Mix the flour, sugar and salt together. Combine the margarine, water and baking cocoa in a 3-quart saucepan. Bring to a boil. Remove from the heat and stir in the dry ingredients.

Beat in the eggs. Beat in the sour cream and baking soda. Pour into a greased 10x15-inch cake pan. Bake at 375 degrees for 22 to 25 minutes or until a wooden pick inserted in the center comes out clean. Pour the icing evenly over the hot or cooled cake. Serves 15.

Chocolate Nut Icing

1/2 cup (1 stick) margarine
1/4 cup baking cocoa
6 tablespoons milk
1 cup chopped nuts
1 teaspoon vanilla extract
1 (16-ounce) package confectioners' sugar

Combine the margarine, baking cocoa and milk in a saucepan. Bring to a boil. Remove from the heat and stir in the nuts, vanilla and confectioners' sugar. Let stand until slightly cool.

Myrtle Curtis
Lenoir City, Tennessee

CREAM OF COCONUT CAKE

1 (2-layer) package white cake mix
2/3 cup flaked coconut
1 (14-ounce) can sweetened condensed milk
1 (8 1/2-ounce) can cream of coconut
1 (8-ounce) container frozen whipped topping, thawed
1 3/4 cups flaked coconut

Prepare the cake batter using the package directions. Stir 2/3 cup coconut into the batter. Pour into a greased 9x13-inch cake pan. Bake using the package directions. Poke holes in the top of the cake. Drizzle the sweetened condensed milk evenly over the warm cake. Let stand until cool. Fold the cream of coconut into the whipped topping in a bowl. Spread over the cake. Sprinkle with 1 3/4 cups coconut. Chill, covered, until serving time. Serves 15.

Billie Carson
Lafollette, Tennessee

COCONUT CAKE

1 (24-ounce) package frozen flaked coconut
2 cups sugar
2 cups sour cream
1 (2-layer) package butter-recipe cake mix
1 (12-ounce) container frozen whipped topping, thawed

Reserve 3/4 cup coconut. Mix the remaining coconut, sugar and sour cream in a bowl. Chill in an airtight container for 8 to 10 hours. Prepare and bake the cake using the package directions for two 9-inch cake layers. Cool in the pans for 10 minutes. Remove to a wire rack to cool completely. Split each layer horizontally into halves. Spread the sour cream mixture between the layers and over the top and side of the cake. Cover and chill for 3 to 4 days. Spread the whipped topping over the cake and sprinkle with the reserved coconut. Chill, covered, for 8 to 10 hours. Refrigerate any leftovers.
Serves 16.

Charlene Cowan
Bartlett, Tennessee

DRINK CAKE

1 1/2 cups (3 sticks) butter, softened
3 cups sugar
6 eggs
3 cups all-purpose flour
3/4 cup lemon-lime or pineapple soda
1 tablespoon lemon extract

Beat the butter and sugar in a mixing bowl until light and fluffy. Beat in the eggs 1 at a time. Beat in the flour. Add the soda and lemon extract and mix well. Pour into a greased bundt pan. Bake at 325 degrees for 1 hour or until a wooden pick inserted in the center comes out clean. Cool in the pan for 10 to 15 minutes. Remove to a wire rack to cool completely.
Serves 16.

Angel Harris
Memphis, Tennessee

LEMON CAKE SUPREME

1 (2-layer) package lemon cake mix
3 eggs
1/2 cup vegetable oil
1/4 cup sugar
1 cup milk
1 cup lemon juice
2 (14-ounce) cans sweetened condensed milk
2 tablespoons lemon extract
1 large container frozen whipped topping, thawed

Combine the cake mix, eggs, oil, sugar and milk in a mixing bowl and beat for 3 minutes. Pour into a greased 9x13-inch cake pan. Bake at 350 degrees for 20 to 30 minutes or until a wooden pick inserted in the center comes out clean. Cool in the pan on a wire rack. Mix the next 3 ingredients in a bowl. Pour over the cake. Chill, covered, until serving time. Spread with the whipped topping just before serving. Serves 16.

Doris Jones
Lexington, Tennessee

KEY LIME CAKE

1 (2-layer) package lemon cake mix
1 (6-ounce) package lime gelatin
5 eggs
1 1/2 cups vegetable oil
3/4 cup orange juice
1/2 cup (1 stick) margarine, softened
1 cup sour cream
1 (16-ounce) package confectioners' sugar
1 cup chopped nuts

Mix the first 5 ingredients in a bowl. Pour into an oiled and floured tube or bundt pan. Bake using the package directions. Cool in the pan for 15 minutes. Invert onto a cake plate and let stand until cool. Beat the margarine and sour cream in a bowl. Add the confectioners' sugar and stir until smooth. Add additional confectioners' sugar if needed for desired consistency. Stir in the chopped nuts. Spread over the cake. Serves 16.

Martha Hammonds
Nashville, Tennessee

SWEDISH NUT CAKE

2 cups sugar
2 cups all-purpose flour
2 teaspoons baking soda
2 eggs
1/2 cup pecans
1 teaspoon vanilla extract
1 (20-ounce) can crushed pineapple
Icing (below)

Mix the sugar, flour and baking soda in a large bowl. Add the eggs, pecans, vanilla and pineapple and mix well. Pour into a greased and floured 9x13-inch cake pan or dish. Bake at 350 degrees for 35 to 45 minutes or until a wooden pick inserted in the center comes out clean. Cool in the pan on a wire rack. Spread the icing over the hot cake. Serves 15.

Cream Cheese Pecan Icing

8 ounces cream cheese, softened
1/2 cup (1 stick) butter or margarine, melted
1 3/4 cups confectioners' sugar
1 teaspoon vanilla extract
1/2 cup chopped pecans

Beat the cream cheese, butter, confectioners' sugar and vanilla in a mixing bowl until smooth. Stir in the pecans.

Vera Raines
Lake City, Tennessee

ORANGE JUICE CAKE

1/2 cup finely chopped nuts
1 (2-layer) package yellow cake mix
1 (3 1/2-ounce) package vanilla instant pudding mix
1 cup orange juice
4 eggs
1/2 cup vegetable oil
1 cup sugar
1/2 cup orange juice
1/2 cup (1 stick) butter

Sprinkle the nuts evenly over the bottom of a greased bundt pan. Combine the cake mix, pudding mix, 1 cup orange juice, eggs and oil in a large bowl and mix well. Pour into the prepared bundt pan.

Bake at 325 degrees for 50 to 60 minutes or until the cake tests done. Cool in the pan on a wire rack. Combine the sugar, 1/2 cup orange juice and butter in a saucepan. Bring to a boil, stirring occasionally. Boil for 2 minutes. Pour evenly over the hot cake. Let stand for 30 minutes. Invert the cake onto a serving plate. Serves 16.

Kaye Lewis
Joelton, Tennessee

DANISH PUDDING

1 cup (2 sticks) butter, softened
1 3/4 cups sugar
3 eggs
1 1/2 teaspoons baking soda
1 cup buttermilk
1 tablespoon grated orange zest
1 tablespoon orange juice
3 cups all-purpose flour
1 teaspoon baking powder
1 cup chopped dates
1 cup chopped nuts
Sauce (below)

Beat the butter and sugar in a mixing bowl until light and fluffy. Beat in the eggs. Dissolve the baking soda in the buttermilk in a small bowl. Add to the butter mixture and mix well. Stir in the remaining ingredients. Pour into a greased tube pan. Bake at 300 degrees for 1 1/2 hours or until a wooden pick inserted in the center comes out clean. Cool in the pan on a wire rack. Remove the cake from the pan and place on a large piece of foil. Pour the sauce over the cake. Wrap in the foil to seal. Refrigerate, covered, for 8 to 10 hours. Serves 16.

Orange Sauce

1 cup sugar
Grated zest of 1 orange
1/2 cup orange juice

Combine the sugar, orange zest and orange juice in a bowl and stir until the sugar is dissolved.

Jeana Pesch
Wartrace, Tennessee

HAWAIIAN SUNSET CAKE

1 (2-layer) package orange or white cake mix
1 ($3^1/_2$-ounce) package vanilla instant pudding mix
1 (3-ounce) package orange gelatin
4 eggs
$^1/_2$ cup vegetable oil
$1^1/_2$ cups milk
1 (20-ounce) can crushed pineapple, well drained
1 (10-ounce) package flaked coconut
1 cup sour cream
2 cups sugar
1 (8-ounce) container frozen whipped topping, thawed

Combine the cake mix, pudding mix, gelatin, eggs, oil and milk in a mixing bowl and beat for 3 minutes. Pour into 3 greased and floured 9-inch cake pans. Bake at 350 degrees for 30 minutes or until a wooden pick inserted in the center comes out clean. Let cool in the pans for 10 minutes. Remove to a wire rack to cool completely.

Combine the pineapple, coconut, sour cream and sugar in a bowl and mix well. Fold 1 cup of the pineapple mixture into the whipped topping in a bowl. Spread the remaining pineapple mixture between the cake layers. Spread the whipped topping mixture over the top and side of the cake. Chill, covered, until serving time. Serves 16.

Ruby Rigsby
Soddy-Daisy, Tennessee

PINEAPPLE CAKE

2 cups all-purpose flour
2 cups sugar
2 teaspoons baking soda
2 eggs
1 (20-ounce) can crushed pineapple
Icing (page 201)

Mix the flour, sugar and baking soda in a large bowl. Add the eggs and pineapple and mix well. Pour into a greased and floured 9x13-inch cake pan.

Bake at 350 degrees for 35 to 40 minutes or until a wooden pick inserted in the center comes out clean. Spread the icing over the warm cake. Serves 15.

Cream Cheese Icing

6 ounces cream cheese, softened
1/4 cup (1/2 stick) butter, softened
2 1/2 to 3 cups confectioners' sugar
1 teaspoon vanilla extract

Beat the cream cheese and butter until light and fluffy. Beat in the confectioners' sugar and vanilla and beat until smooth.

Bob and Barbara Burton
Clinton, Tennessee

PINEAPPLE ORANGE SUNSHINE CAKE

1 (2-layer) package yellow cake mix
4 eggs
1 (11-ounce) can mandarin oranges in light syrup
1 (15 1/2-ounce) can crushed pineapple in juice
1 (8-ounce) container frozen whipped topping, thawed
1 (3 1/2-ounce) package vanilla instant pudding mix

Stir the cake mix, eggs and oranges in a bowl until moistened. Beat by hand for 2 minutes. Pour into a 9x13-inch cake pan coated with nonstick cooking spray. Bake at 350 degrees for 30 to 40 minutes or until a wooden pick inserted in the center comes out clean. Let stand until completely cool. Combine the pineapple, whipped topping and pudding mix in a bowl and mix well. Spread over the cooled cake. Chill, covered, until serving time. Serves 15.

Edith Walker
Knoxville, Tennessee

PIÑA COLADA CAKE

1 (2-layer) package yellow cake mix
1 cup water
1 (8-ounce) can crushed pineapple
2 tablespoons vegetable oil
3 eggs
1 tablespoon coconut flavoring

Combine the cake mix, water, pineapple, oil, eggs and coconut flavoring in a mixing bowl and beat at low speed until moistened. Beat at medium speed for 2 minutes. Pour into a greased and floured bundt pan. Bake at 350 degrees for 40 to 45 minutes or until a wooden pick inserted in the center comes out clean. Cool in the pan for 10 to 15 minutes. Remove to a wire rack to cool completely. Serves 12.

Rubye Morrison
Shelbyville, Tennessee

PISTACHIO CAKE

1 (2-layer) package white cake mix
1 (3 1/2-ounce) package pistachio instant pudding mix
3 eggs
1 cup corn oil
1 cup club soda
1/2 cup chopped pecans
Icing (page 203)

Combine the cake mix, pudding mix, eggs, oil, club soda and pecans in a large bowl and stir until moistened. Beat with an electric mixer at high speed for 4 minutes. Pour into a greased and floured bundt pan. Bake at 350 degrees for 35 to 40 minutes or until a wooden pick inserted in the center comes out clean. Cool in the pan for 10 minutes. Remove to a wire rack to cool completely. Spread the icing over the cooled cake. Chill until serving time. Serves 16.

Pistachio Icing

1 (3 1/2-ounce) package pistachio instant pudding mix
1 cup cold milk
1 envelope Dream Whip topping mix

Combine the pudding mix, milk and topping mix in a mixing bowl and beat until thick.

Jeana Pesch
Wartrace, Tennessee

SUGAR PLUM PUDDING CAKE

1 cup pitted prunes
2 cups sifted self-rising flour
1 1/2 cups sugar
1 1/4 teaspoons baking soda
1 teaspoon nutmeg
1 teaspoon cinnamon
1 teaspoon ground allspice
3 eggs
3/4 cup vegetable oil
1 cup buttermilk
1 cup chopped nuts
Glaze (below)

Cook the prunes in a small amount of water until very soft; drain. Mash the prunes. Sift the flour, sugar, baking soda, nutmeg, cinnamon and allspice together. Beat the eggs and oil in a large bowl. Stir in the buttermilk, prunes, nuts and dry ingredients. Pour into a greased 9x13-inch cake pan. Bake at 350 degrees for 40 minutes or until a wooden pick inserted in the center comes out clean. Pour the glaze over the hot cake. Serves 24.

Buttermilk Glaze

1 cup sugar
1/2 cup (1 stick) margarine
1/2 cup buttermilk
1 tablespoon light corn syrup
1 teaspoon vanilla extract

Combine the sugar, margarine, buttermilk, corn syrup and vanilla in a saucepan. Bring to a boil, stirring frequently.

Paula Hartley
Franklin, Tennessee

FROSTED PUMPKIN CAKE

1 cup sugar
2 eggs
1 cup canned or mashed cooked pumpkin
1/2 cup vegetable oil
1 cup all-purpose flour
1 teaspoon ground cinnamon
1 teaspoon baking soda
1/2 teaspoon baking powder
1/2 teaspoon salt
Frosting (below)

Combine the sugar and eggs in a bowl. Beat with an electric mixer at medium speed for 2 minutes. Beat in the pumpkin and oil. Add the flour, cinnamon, baking soda, baking powder and salt and beat at low speed for 1 minute. Pour into a greased 9x9-inch cake pan. Bake at 350 degrees for 25 to 30 minutes or until a wooden pick inserted in the center comes out clean. Cool in the pan on a wire rack. Spread the frosting over the cake. Serves 9.

Cream Cheese Frosting

2 ounces cream cheese, softened
2 tablespoons butter, softened
3/4 cup confectioners' sugar
1/2 teaspoon vanilla extract

Combine the cream cheese, butter, confectioners' sugar and vanilla in a bowl. Beat with an electric mixer at low speed until light and fluffy.

Arizona Powell
Lafollette, Tennessee

RED VELVET CAKE

1 1/2 cups sugar
1 cup shortening
2 eggs
1 teaspoon baking cocoa
2 ounces red food color
2 1/2 cups flour, sifted
1 teaspoon salt
1 cup buttermilk
1 teaspoon baking soda
1 teaspoon vinegar
1 teaspoon vanilla extract
Frosting (below)

Beat the sugar, shortening and eggs in a bowl until light and fluffy. Mix the baking cocoa and food color in a small bowl and stir into the shortening mixture. Stir the flour and salt alternately with the buttermilk into the shortening mixture. Mix the baking soda, vinegar and vanilla in a small bowl. Stir into the shortening mixture. Pour into 3 greased and floured 9-inch cake pans. Bake 1 pan at a time at 350 degrees for 22 minutes or until a wooden pick inserted in the center comes out clean. Cool in the pans for 10 minutes. Remove to a wire rack to cool completely. Spread the frosting between the layers and over the top and side of the cake. Serves 16.

Cream Cheese Frosting

8 ounces cream cheese, softened
1/2 cup (1 stick) butter, softened
1 (16-ounce) package confectioners' sugar
1/4 cup milk

Beat the cream cheese, butter, confectioners' sugar and milk in a bowl until smooth.

Betty Ann Webb
Knoxville, Tennessee

STRAWBERRY CAKE

1 (2-layer) package white cake mix
1 (3-ounce) package strawberry gelatin
1 cup vegetable oil
1/2 cup water
4 eggs
1/2 cup fresh or frozen strawberries, thawed
Frosting (below)

Combine the cake mix, gelatin, oil, water, eggs and strawberries in a large bowl. Beat with an electric mixer for 5 minutes. Pour into a lightly greased 9x13-inch cake pan. Bake at 350 degrees for 40 to 45 minutes or until a wooden pick inserted in the center comes out clean. Let stand until completely cool. Spread the frosting over the cake. Serves 12 to 15.

Strawberry Frosting

1/2 cup (1 stick) margarine, melted
1 (16-ounce) package confectioners' sugar
1/2 cup fresh strawberries or frozen strawberries, thawed and drained

Beat the melted margarine and confectioners' sugar in a bowl until smooth. Stir in the strawberries.

Sandra McCord
Chattanooga, Tennessee

SWEET POTATO CAKE

1 1/2 cups vegetable oil
2 cups sugar
4 egg yolks
1/4 cup hot water
2 1/2 cups sifted cake flour
2 teaspoons baking powder
1/4 teaspoon salt
1 teaspoon ground cinnamon
1 teaspoon nutmeg
1 1/2 cups grated peeled fresh sweet potatoes
1 cup chopped pecans
1 teaspoon vanilla extract
4 eggs whites
1 (14-ounce) can evaporated milk
1 cup sugar
1/2 cup (1 stick) butter or margarine
3 tablespoons flour
1 teaspoon vanilla extract
1 1/2 cups flaked coconut

Beat the oil and 2 cups sugar in a large bowl. Beat in the egg yolks. Stir in the hot water. Mix the next 5 ingredients together. Stir into the egg mixture. Add the sweet potatoes, pecans and vanilla and mix well. Beat the egg whites in a bowl until stiff. Fold into the batter. Pour into 3 nonstick 8-inch cake pans. Bake at 350 degrees for 20 to 25 minutes or until the layers test done. Cool in the pans for 10 minutes. Remove to a wire rack to cool completely. Combine the next 4 ingredients in a saucepan. Cook over medium heat until thick, stirring constantly. Remove from the heat and add the coconut. Beat until cool. Spread between the layers and over the top of the cake. Serves 12.

Addie Downs
Antioch, Tennessee

MEXICAN FRUITCAKE

2 cups self-rising flour
2 cups sugar
2 teaspoons baking soda
2 eggs, beaten
1 (20-ounce) can crushed pineapple
1 cup pecans
Icing (below)

Mix the flour, sugar and baking soda in a large bowl. Add the eggs, pineapple and pecans and mix well. Pour into a 9x13-inch cake pan coated with nonstick cooking spray. Bake at 350 degrees for 45 minutes or until a wooden pick inserted in the center comes out clean. Spread the icing over the hot cake. Serves 15.

Cream Cheese Icing

8 ounces cream cheese, softened
1/2 cup (1 stick) butter, softened
2 cups confectioners' sugar
1 teaspoon vanilla extract

Beat the cream cheese and butter in a bowl. Beat in the confectioners' sugar and vanilla until smooth.

Vivian W. Chaffin
Powell, Tennessee

DELICIOUS FRUITCAKE

- 8 eggs
- 2 cups sugar
- 3/4 cup (1 1/2 sticks) margarine, melted
- 3 cups all-purpose flour
- 2 teaspoons baking powder
- 2 teaspoons salt
- 3 tablespoons vanilla extract
- 1 tablespoon almond extract
- 2 pounds dates, each date cut into 3 to 4 pieces
- 1 pound candied cherries, coarsely chopped
- 1 pound candied pineapple, coarsely chopped
- 8 cups pecans

Place a large pan of boiling water on the bottom shelf in a 250 degree oven. Beat the eggs, sugar and melted margarine in a large bowl. Add the flour, baking powder, salt, vanilla and almond extract and mix well. Add the dates, cherries, pineapple and pecans and mix well. Spoon into 3 greased and floured loaf pans. Bake on the middle rack at 250 degrees for 1 1/2 hours. Increase the temperature to 275 degrees and bake for 30 minutes longer or until a wooden pick inserted in the center comes out clean. Remove to a wire rack to cool. Wrap each cooled loaf in plastic wrap and then in foil. Chill until serving time. Serves 45.

Mackie Jernigan
Memphis, Tennessee

BOURBON POUND CAKE

- 1/3 cup bourbon
- 2 teaspoons vanilla extract
- 2 teaspoons almond extract
- 2 cups (4 sticks) butter, softened
- 3 cups sugar
- 8 egg yolks
- 3 cups sifted all-purpose flour
- 8 egg whites
- 1 cup sugar
- 1/2 cup chopped nuts

Combine the bourbon, vanilla and almond extract in a small bowl. Beat the butter and 3 cups sugar in a large bowl until light and fluffy. Add the egg yolks, 1 at a time, beating well after each addition. Add the bourbon mixture alternately with the flour, beating well after each addition. Beat the egg whites in a bowl until stiff but not dry. Beat in 1 cup sugar. Fold into the batter. Sprinkle the nuts in the bottom of a well buttered 10-inch tube pan or fold the nuts into the batter. Pour the batter gently into the prepared pan. Bake at 350 degrees for 1 1/2 hours or until a wooden pick inserted in the center comes out clean. Cool in the pan for 10 to 15 minutes. Remove to a wire rack to cool completely. Serves 16.

Shirley Brien
Jackson, Tennessee

ALL BUTTER POUND CAKE

1 1/2 cups (3 sticks) butter, softened
8 ounces cream cheese, softened
3 cups sugar
6 eggs
1 teaspoon vanilla extract
1 teaspoon lemon juice
2 cups all-purpose flour

Beat the butter, cream cheese and sugar in a large bowl until light and fluffy. Beat in the eggs, vanilla and lemon juice. Beat in the flour. Pour into a well greased bundt pan. Place in a cold oven and set the temperature to 300 degrees. Bake for 1 hour and 15 minutes or until a wooden pick inserted in the center comes out clean. Cool in the pan for 10 to 15 minutes. Remove to a wire rack to cool completely. Serves 12.

Betty Reddick
Knoxville, Tennessee

GERMAN CHOCOLATE POUND CAKE

3 cups sifted all-purpose flour
1 teaspoon salt
1/2 teaspoon baking soda
2 cups sugar
1 cup shortening
4 eggs
1 teaspoon vanilla extract
2 teaspoons butter flavoring
1 cup buttermilk
4 ounces German's sweet chocolate, melted in the top of a double boiler

Sift the flour, salt and baking soda together. Beat the sugar and shortening in a large bowl until light and fluffy. Beat in the next 4 ingredients and the dry ingredients. Beat in the melted chocolate. Pour into a greased and floured 9-inch tube pan. Bake at 300 degrees for 1 1/2 hours or until a wooden pick inserted in the center comes out clean. Cool in the pan for 10 to 15 minutes. Remove to a wire rack; cover. Let stand until cool. Spread with your favorite icing. Serves 20.

Peggy McCanless
Nashville, Tennessee

COCONUT POUND CAKE

5 eggs
2 cups sugar
1 cup vegetable oil
2 cups self-rising flour
1 tablespoon vanilla extract
2 tablespoons coconut flavoring
1 (3 1/2-ounce) can flaked coconut
1 cup sugar
1/2 cup (1 stick) margarine
1/2 cup water

Beat the eggs, 2 cups sugar and oil in a large bowl. Beat in the flour, vanilla, 1 tablespoon of the coconut flavoring and coconut. Pour into a greased and floured bundt pan. Bake at 350 degrees for 1 hour or until a wooden pick inserted in the center comes out clean. Combine the 1 cup sugar, margarine, water and remaining coconut flavoring in a saucepan. Bring to a boil, stirring frequently. Pour evenly over the hot cake. Let stand until cool. Serves 16.

Doris Rich

Huntingdon, Tennessee

LEMON POUND CAKE

1 1/2 cups (3 sticks) butter, softened
1 cup sugar
5 eggs
3 cups all-purpose flour
3/4 cup lemon-lime soda
3 tablespoons lemon extract

Beat the butter and sugar in a large bowl until light and fluffy. Beat in the eggs 1 at a time. Beat in the flour, soda and lemon extract. Pour into a nonstick bundt pan. Bake at 350 degrees for 1 hour and 10 minutes or until the cake tests done. Cool in the pan for 10 to 15 minutes. Remove to a wire rack to cool completely. Serves 20.

Peggy McCanless
Nashville, Tennessee

WHIPPED CREAM POUND CAKE

1 cup (2 sticks) butter, softened
3 cups sugar
6 eggs
3 cups all-purpose four
2 teaspoons vanilla extract
1 cup heavy whipping cream, whipped

Beat the butter and sugar in a large bowl until light and fluffy. Beat in the eggs alternately with the flour. Beat in the vanilla. Fold in the whipped cream. Pour into a greased and floured large tube pan. Bake at 325 degrees for 1 1/2 hours or until a wooden pick inserted in the center comes out clean. Cool in the pan for 10 to 15 minutes. Remove to a wire rack to cool completely. Serves 16.

Colleen Ferguson
Loudon, Tennessee

TIGER CAKE

1 (2-layer) package yellow or German chocolate cake mix
4 eggs
1/2 cup vegetable oil
1 cup water
1 can coconut pecan frosting
1/2 cup chopped nuts

Combine the cake mix, eggs, oil, water, frosting and nuts in a large bowl. Beat for 3 to 4 minutes. Pour into a greased 10-inch tube pan. Bake at 350 degrees for 35 to 45 minutes or until a wooden pick inserted in the center comes out clean. Cool in the pan for 10 to 15 minutes. Remove to a wire rack to cool completely. Serves 10 to 12.

Willie M. White
Germantown, Tennessee

PLAIN YELLOW CAKE AND CARAMEL FROSTING

3 cups sifted all-purpose flour
1 tablespoon baking powder
1/2 teaspoon salt
1 cup (2 sticks) butter, softened
1 cup milk
4 eggs
2 cups sugar
1 tablespoon vanilla extract
Frosting (page 213)

Sift the flour, baking powder and salt together. Beat the butter in a large bowl until smooth. Beat in the dry ingredients alternately with the milk. Beat the eggs, sugar and vanilla in a bowl. Stir into the butter mixture gradually and beat until smooth. Pour into 2 greased and floured 8-inch round cake pans or two 7-inch square cake pans. Bake at 350 degrees for 30 to 40 minutes or until a wooden pick inserted in the center comes out clean. Cool in the pans for 10 minutes. Remove to a wire rack to cool completely. Spread the frosting between the layers and over the top and side of the cake. Serves 10 to 12.

Caramel Frosting

1/2 cup (1 stick) butter
1 cup packed brown sugar
1 teaspoon vanilla extract
1 (16-ounce) package confectioners' sugar
2 tablespoons milk

Melt the butter in a saucepan. Stir in the brown sugar and vanilla. Stir in the confectioners' sugar alternately with the milk and stir until thick and smooth.

Evelyn Tyler
Memphis, Tennessee

POOR MAN'S CAKE

1/2 cup shortening
2 cups sugar
1 tablespoon ground cinnamon
1/2 teaspoon ground cloves
1/2 teaspoon nutmeg
1/2 teaspoon ground allspice
1/2 teaspoon vanilla extract
1/2 teaspoon lemon extract
2 scant teaspoons baking soda
2 cups buttermilk
3 cups all-purpose flour
8 ounces raisins
1/2 teaspoon salt

Blend the shortening, sugar, cinnamon, cloves, nutmeg, allspice, vanilla and lemon extract in a bowl. Mix the baking soda and buttermilk in a bowl. Stir into the shortening mixture. Stir in the flour, raisins and salt. Pour into 2 nonstick 8-inch cake pans. Bake at 350 degrees for 50 minutes or until layers test done. Cool in the pans for 10 minutes. Remove to a wire rack to cool completely. Spread with your favorite icing, if desired. Serves 6.

Ella Mae Hasty
Memphis, Tennessee

ELIZABETH'S CARAMEL ICING

1 (16-ounce) package brown sugar
6 tablespoons margarine
1/2 cup milk
16 to 32 ounces confectioners' sugar

Bring the brown sugar, margarine and milk to a boil in a saucepan, stirring until the sugar is dissolved. Remove from the heat and stir in enough confectioners' sugar to reach a spreading consistency. Makes 3 to 4 cups.

Vavial Jamison
Shelbyville, Tennessee

BAKERY DECORATOR CAKE FROSTING

1 cup shortening
1/4 teaspoon salt
2/3 cup water
1 teaspoon butter flavoring
1 teaspoon flavoring of your choice
1 (32-ounce) package confectioners' sugar

Beat the shortening, salt, water and flavorings in a bowl with an electric mixer. Beat in the confectioners' sugar. Beat for 4 minutes. Frost and decorate a large layer cake. Note: This can be covered and chilled for several days. Makes 3 to 4 cups.

Wilma Kelly
Knoxville, Tennessee

EASY FROSTING

3/4 cup sugar
1 egg white
1/4 teaspoon cream of tartar
1/4 cup boiling water
1 teaspoon vanilla extract

Beat the sugar, egg white and cream of tartar in a chilled bowl until stiff. Beat in the boiling water slowly and beat until stiff. Beat in the vanilla. Makes about 1 cup.

Linda Brumley
Oakfield, Tennessee

APPLE PIE

6 cups cubed sliced Granny Smith apples
3/4 cup sugar
1/4 cup all-purpose flour
1 teaspoon ground cinnamon
1 (2-crust) deep-dish pie pastry
2 tablespoons butter, cut into pieces
1/2 cup packed brown sugar
1/2 cup (1 stick) butter
2 tablespoons half-and-half
1 cup chopped pecans

Combine the apples, sugar, flour and cinnamon in a large bowl. Toss to coat. Fit 1 pie pastry into a 9-inch deep-dish pie plate. Spoon the apple mixture into the pie shell. Dot with 2 tablespoons butter. Top with the other pie pastry and crimp the edges to seal. Bake at 350 degrees for 50 to 55 minutes. Combine the brown sugar, 1/2 cup butter, half-and-half and pecans in a saucepan. Bring to a boil, stirring frequently. Pour over the baked pie and return to the oven. Bake for 5 minutes longer. Remove to a wire rack to cool. Serve with French vanilla ice cream. Serves 8.

Joanne Taylor
Jackson, Tennessee

BLUEBERRY BANANA PIE

8 ounces cream cheese, softened
1/3 cup sugar
1 baked (9-inch) pie shell
2 bananas, sliced
1 cup blueberry pie filling
1 cup heavy whipping cream, whipped

Combine the cream cheese and sugar in a bowl. Beat with an electric mixer at high speed until light and fluffy. Spread evenly in the cooled pie shell. Arrange the banana slices on top. Spread the pie filling over the bananas. Top with the whipped cream. Chill, covered, until serving time. Serves 6 to 8.

Peggy Burr
Nashville, Tennessee

BUTTERSCOTCH PIE

1 cup packed brown sugar
3 tablespoons all-purpose flour
2 egg yolks
1 cup milk
2 tablespoons butter
1 teaspoon vanilla extract
1 baked (9-inch) pie shell
2 egg whites
3 tablespoons sugar

Mix the brown sugar and flour in a saucepan. Stir in the egg yolks and milk. Cook over low heat or in the top of a double boiler until thickened, stirring constantly. Remove from the heat and stir in the butter and vanilla. Pour into the pie shell. Beat the egg whites and sugar in a bowl until stiff. Spread over the filling to the edge. Bake at 350 degrees for 15 to 20 minutes or until golden brown and the egg white is cooked through. Serves 6.

Edith Walker
Knoxville, Tennessee

BUTTERSCOTCH PECAN PIE

1/2 cup butterscotch chips
1 cup pecan pieces
1 unbaked (9-inch) pie shell
1/4 cup (1/2 stick) unsalted butter, melted
1/2 cup sugar
1/2 cup light corn syrup
2 eggs

Sprinkle the butterscotch chips and pecans in the pie shell. Beat the melted butter, sugar, corn syrup and eggs in a bowl. Pour into the pie shell. Bake at 350 degrees for 45 to 50 minutes or until golden brown. Serves 8.

Lewis Miller
Memphis, Tennessee

CARAMEL PIE

1/4 cup (1/2 stick) margarine
1 cup chopped pecans
7 ounces flaked coconut
8 ounces cream cheese, softened
1 (14-ounce) can sweetened condensed milk
1 (12-ounce) container frozen whipped topping, thawed
2 (9-inch) graham cracker pie shells
Caramel ice cream topping

Melt the margarine in a 10x15-inch baking pan in the oven. Add the pecans and coconut and stir to coat. Spread in the baking pan. Bake at 325 degrees until toasted, stirring frequently. Remove to a wire rack to cool. Beat the cream cheese, sweetened condensed milk and whipped topping in a bowl until creamy. Spread half the cream cheese mixture in the pie shells. Sprinkle with half the pecans and coconut and drizzle with caramel topping. Repeat the layers. Serves 16.

Billie Pruitt
Nashville, Tennessee

CHESS PIE

1 cup (2 sticks) margarine
2 2/3 cups sugar
2 tablespoons cornmeal
6 eggs, well beaten
2 tablespoons vinegar
2 teaspoons vanilla extract
2 unbaked (9-inch) pie shells

Melt the margarine in a microwave-safe bowl in the microwave oven. Stir the sugar and cornmeal into the warm margarine. Stir in the eggs. Stir in the vinegar and vanilla. Pour into the pie shells. Bake at 350 degrees for 30 minutes or until firm. Serves 12.

Margaret Bivens
Memphis, Tennessee

EASY CHERRY CHEESE PIE

8 ounces cream cheese, softened
1 (14-ounce) can sweetened condensed milk
1/3 cup lemon juice
1 teaspoon vanilla extract
1 (9-inch) graham cracker pie shell
1 (21-ounce) can cherry pie filling

Beat the cream cheese in a bowl until light and fluffy. Stir in the sweetened condensed milk. Stir in the lemon juice and vanilla. Pour into the pie shell. Chill, covered, for 2 hours or until set. Spread the pie filling over the chilled pie. Serves 6.

Kathy Rives
Clarksville, Tennessee

NUTTY CHOCOLATE OR BUTTERSCOTCH CHIP PIE

1/2 cup (1 stick) butter, melted and cooled
1/2 cup all-purpose flour
2 eggs, lightly beaten
1 cup sugar
1 teaspoon vanilla extract
1 teaspoon almond extract
1 cup chocolate or butterscotch chips
1 cup pecans or unsalted peanuts
1 unbaked (9-inch) pie shell or 1 (9-inch) graham cracker pie shell

Combine the melted butter, flour, eggs, sugar, vanilla and almond extract in a bowl and mix well. Stir in the chips and nuts. Pour into the pie shell. Bake at 325 degrees for 30 minutes or until set. Serve with whipped cream or ice cream. Serves 6 to 8.

Ora Van Cobble
Talbott, Tennessee

CHOCOLATE TURTLE PIE

3/4 cup all-purpose flour
3/4 cup quick-cooking oats
1/2 cup sucralose
Dash of salt
1/2 cup (1 stick) margarine, melted
Caramel ice cream topping
Coarsely chopped nuts
8 ounces cream cheese, softened
1/2 cup sour cream
1 1/4 cups 2% milk
1 small package sugar-free chocolate instant pudding mix
1 (8-ounce) container frozen whipped topping, thawed
1/4 cup semisweet chocolate chips

Mix the flour, oats, sucralose and salt in a bowl. Add the melted margarine and mix well. Press into the bottom of a 9-inch pie plate. Bake at 375 degrees for 12 minutes. Remove to a wire rack to cool. Spread a thin layer of caramel topping over the cooled crust and sprinkle with nuts. Combine the cream cheese, sour cream, milk and pudding mix in a bowl. Beat until smooth. Pour over the nuts in the pie plate. Freeze for 5 to 10 minutes. Spoon the whipped topping around the edges of the pie. Drizzle with caramel topping. Sprinkle with the chocolate chips and nuts. Serves 6 to 8.

Teresa Flach and James Parrish
Nashville, Tennessee

CHOCOLATE PECAN PIE

1 cup chocolate chips
1 cup pecans
1 unbaked (9-inch) pie shell
2 eggs
1 cup sugar
1 cup light corn syrup
1/2 cup (1 stick) margarine, melted
1 teaspoon vanilla extract

Sprinkle the chocolate chips and pecans in the bottom of the pie shell. Beat the eggs, sugar, corn syrup, melted margarine and vanilla in a bowl. Pour into the pie shell. Bake at 325 degrees for 1 hour. Serves 6 to 8.

Ann Hart
Trenton, Tennessee

CHOCOLATE PIE

3 egg yolks, beaten
$1^1/_2$ cups sugar
$^1/_3$ cup all-purpose flour
3 tablespoons baking cocoa
$1^1/_2$ cups boiling water
$^1/_4$ cup ($^1/_2$ stick) margarine
1 teaspoon vanilla extract
1 baked (9-inch) pie shell
3 egg whites

Stir the egg yolks and sugar in a saucepan. Add the flour and baking cocoa and mix well. Add the boiling water and mix well. Cook until thick, stirring constantly. Stir in the margarine and vanilla. Pour into the pie shell. Beat the egg whites in a bowl until stiff. Spread over the filling to the edge. Bake at 350 degrees for 15 to 20 minutes or until golden brown and cooked through. Serves 6.

Melba Cleek
Shelbyville, Tennessee

FUDGE PIE

$^1/_2$ cup self-rising flour
2 cups sugar
5 tablespoons baking cocoa
4 eggs
1 cup (2 sticks) margarine, melted
1 teaspoon vanilla extract
2 unbaked (8-inch) pie shells

Mix the flour, sugar and baking cocoa in a bowl. Beat the eggs in a large bowl. Stir in the melted margarine. Add the dry ingredients and mix well. Stir in the vanilla. Pour into the pie shells. Bake at 375 degrees for 30 minutes or until not quite set; do not overbake. Serves 12.

Joan Looney
Henry, Tennessee

COCONUT CHOCOLATE PIE

3 cups sugar
1/4 teaspoon salt
6 tablespoons baking cocoa
4 eggs, beaten
1/2 cup (1 stick) margarine, melted
1 teaspoon vanilla extract
1 (12-ounce) can evaporated milk
2 cups flaked coconut
Chopped nuts (optional)
2 unbaked (9-inch) pie shells

Combine the sugar, salt, baking cocoa, eggs, melted margarine, vanilla, evaporated milk, coconut and nuts in a large bowl and mix well. Pour into the pie shells. Bake at 350 degrees for 40 minutes. Serves 12 to 16.

Charlotte James
Beech Bluff, Tennessee

COCONUT CARAMEL PIE

1/4 cup (1/2 stick) margarine
1 (7-ounce) package flaked coconut
1/2 cup chopped pecans
8 ounces cream cheese, softened
1 (14-ounce) can sweetened condensed milk
1 (16-ounce) container frozen whipped topping, thawed
2 (9-inch) baked pie shells or graham cracker pie shells
1 (12-ounce) jar caramel ice cream topping

Melt the margarine in a large skillet. Add the coconut and pecans and sauté until golden brown. Remove from the heat and let cool. Beat the cream cheese and sweetened condensed milk in a bowl until smooth. Fold in the whipped topping. Spread half the cream cheese mixture in the pie shells. Sprinkle with half the coconut mixture and drizzle with half the caramel topping. Repeat the layers. Freeze until serving time. Serves 16.

Ruby Rigsby
Soddy-Daisy, Tennessee

BUTTERMILK COCONUT PIE

6 tablespoons margarine, melted
1 1/4 cups sugar
1 tablespoon all-purpose flour
3 eggs
1/2 teaspoon vanilla extract
1/2 cup buttermilk
1 cup flaked coconut
1 unbaked (9-inch) pie shell

Mix the melted margarine, sugar and flour in a bowl. Add the eggs 1 at a time, beating well after each addition. Stir in the vanilla, buttermilk and coconut. Pour into the pie shell. Bake at 350 degrees for 35 minutes or until set. Serves 6.

Bobbie Latta
Columbia, Tennessee

COCONUT CARAMEL PIE

1/4 cup (1/2 stick) margarine
1 (7-ounce) package flaked coconut
1 1/2 cup chopped pecans
8 ounces cream cheese, softened
1 (14-ounce) can sweetened condensed milk
1 (16-ounce) container frozen whipped topping, thawed
2 (9-inch) graham cracker pie shells
1 (12-ounce) jar caramel ice cream topping

Melt the margarine in a large skillet. Add the coconut and pecans and sauté until golden brown. Remove from the heat and let cool. Beat the cream cheese and sweetened condensed milk in a bowl until smooth. Fold in the whipped topping. Spread half the cream cheese mixture in the pie shells. Drizzle with half the caramel topping and sprinkle with half the coconut mixture. Repeat the layers. Cover and freeze until firm. Thaw slightly before serving. Serves 16.

Janis Barker
Chattanooga, Tennessee

AMAZING COCONUT PIE

3 cups milk
3/4 cup sugar
1/2 cup buttermilk baking mix
4 eggs
1/4 cup (1/2 stick) butter or margarine, melted
1 1/2 teaspoons vanilla extract
1 cup flaked coconut

Combine the milk, sugar, baking mix, eggs, melted butter and vanilla in a blender. Process on low speed for 3 minutes. Pour into a greased 9-inch pie plate. Sprinkle with the coconut. Bake at 350 degrees for 40 minutes. Serve warm or cold. Serves 6.

Margie McAlister
Cleveland, Tennessee

LEMON CREAM PIE

1 cup sugar or equivalent sucralose
3 tablespoons cornstarch
1/4 cup lemon juice
3 egg yolks, beaten
Grated zest of 1 lemon (optional)
1/4 cup (1/2 stick) margarine
1 cup milk
1 cup sour cream
1 baked (9-inch) pie shell
Frozen whipped topping, thawed

Mix the sugar and cornstarch in a heavy saucepan. Stir in a small amount of the lemon juice and the egg yolks. Stir in the remaining lemon juice, lemon zest, margarine and milk. Cook over medium heat until thick, stirring constantly. Remove from the heat and stir in the sour cream. Pour into the pie shell. Refrigerate, covered, until chilled. Spread with whipped topping. Serves 8.

Betty Gainous
Tullahoma, Tennessee

STORMY'S KEY LIME PIE

1 (14-ounce) can sweetened condensed milk
3 egg yolks, beaten
1/2 cup fresh lime juice
1 (9-inch) graham cracker pie shell
3 egg whites
6 tablespoons sugar

Combine the sweetened condensed milk, egg yolks and lime juice in a bowl. Beat until smooth. Pour into the pie shell. Bake at 350 degrees for 15 minutes. Cool on a wire rack for 10 minutes. Refrigerate, covered, until chilled. Beat the egg whites in a bowl until soft peaks form. Beat in the sugar, 1 tablespoon at a time and beat until stiff. Spread over the filling to the edge. Bake at 400 degrees for 5 minutes or until golden brown and the egg white is cooked through. Note: You may spread whipped topping over the pie just before serving instead of the meringue topping, if desired. Serves 6 to 8.

Glenda Buchanan
College Grove, Tennessee

ORANGE COCONUT CHESS PIE

1 cup sugar
1 1/2 teaspoons cornmeal
1 1/2 teaspoons all-purpose flour
3 eggs, beaten
1/4 cup (1/2 stick) butter or margarine, melted
1/4 cup frozen orange juice concentrate, thawed
2 tablespoons water
1/4 cup flaked coconut
1 unbaked (9-inch) pie shell

Mix the sugar, cornmeal and flour in a large bowl. Beat the eggs, melted margarine, orange juice concentrate and water in a bowl. Add to the dry ingredients and mix well. Stir in the coconut. Pour into the pie shell. Bake at 350 degrees for 35 minutes or until set. Serves 6.

Bob Jeffries
Southaven, Mississippi

ORANGE PIE

1 (8-ounce) container frozen whipped topping, thawed
1 (14-ounce) can sweetened condensed milk
1 envelope sweetened orange-flavor drink mix
2 tablespoons hot water
1 (9-inch) graham cracker pie shell
Mandarin oranges or other fruit

Mix the whipped topping, sweetened condensed milk, drink mix and hot water in a bowl. Pour into the pie shell. Arrange mandarin oranges on top. Serves 6.

Janis and Pam Barker
Chattanooga, Tennessee

PEANUT BUTTER PIE

1½ cups peanut butter
8 ounces cream cheese, softened
1 cup confectioners' sugar
½ teaspoon vanilla extract
1 (16-ounce) container frozen whipped topping, thawed
1 (9-inch) graham cracker pie shell

Combine the peanut butter, cream cheese, confectioners' sugar, vanilla and ½ the whipped topping in a bowl and mix well. Pour into the crust. Freeze until firm. Spread with the remaining whipped topping and serve. Serves 6 to 8.

Janis and Pam Barker
Chattanooga, Tennessee

PECAN PIE

1 cup sugar
1/4 cup (1/2 stick) butter, softened
1/4 teaspoon salt
5 eggs
3 tablespoons all-purpose flour
1 teaspoon vanilla extract
2 cups light corn syrup
1 cup pecans
2 unbaked (9-inch) pie shells

Beat the sugar, butter and salt in a large bowl in a large bowl until light and fluffy. Beat in the eggs, flour, vanilla and corn syrup. Stir in the pecans. Pour into the pie shells. Bake at 300 degrees for 1 hour. Serves 12.

Rebecca Wilson
Cleveland, Tennessee

PECAN PIE

1 cup sugar
1 cup light corn syrup
1/4 cup (1/2 stick) butter, melted
Dash of salt
3 eggs, lightly beaten
1 teaspoon vanilla extract
1 1/2 cups pecan pieces
1 unbaked (9-inch) deep-dish pie shell

Mix the sugar, corn syrup, melted butter and salt in a bowl. Stir in the eggs, vanilla and pecans. Pour into the pie shell. Bake at 350 degrees for 1 hour or until set. Serves 8.

Sue Estes
Lebanon, Tennessee

RITZ CRACKER PIE

3 egg whites
1 cup sugar
1/2 teaspoon baking powder
16 Ritz crackers, crumbled
1 teaspoon vanilla extract
2/3 cup pecan pieces
Whipped cream or frozen whipped topping, thawed
Flaked coconut, tinted pink or green (optional)

Beat the egg whites in a bowl. Beat in the sugar and baking powder gradually and beat until stiff. Fold in the crumbled crackers, vanilla and pecans. Pour into a well greased 9-inch pie plate. Bake at 350 degrees for 25 minutes. Cool on a wire rack. Chill, covered, for 4 hours or longer. Spread with whipped cream and sprinkle with coconut. Serves 8.

Emma Jean Tomlinson
Lebanon, Tennessee

PINEAPPLE COCONUT PIE

1/2 cup (1 stick) butter, melted
2 cups sugar
4 eggs
1 (8-ounce) can crushed pineapple
1 (3 1/2-ounce) can flaked coconut
2 unbaked (9-inch) pie shells

Mix the melted butter and sugar in a large bowl. Add the eggs, 1 at a time, beating well after each addition. Stir in the pineapple and coconut. Pour into the pie shells. Bake at 350 degrees for 45 minutes. Serves 12.

Lonnie Dawson
Oliver Springs, Tennessee

PINEAPPLE CREAM PIE

1 (14-ounce) can sweetened condensed milk
1 (8-ounce) container frozen whipped topping, thawed
1/4 cup lemon juice
1 (20-ounce) can crushed pineapple, drained
1 (10-inch) graham cracker pie shell

Whisk the sweetened condensed milk, whipped topping, lemon juice and pineapple in a large bowl. Pour into the pie shell. Chill, covered, for 4 hours. Serves 6.

Patsy Ellis
Carthage, Tennessee

PUMPKIN PIE

3/4 cup sugar
1/2 teaspoon salt
1 teaspoon ground cinnamon
1 teaspoon ground ginger
1/4 teaspoon ground cloves
1 1/2 cups canned or mashed cooked pumpkin
2 eggs, beaten
1 1/2 cups hot milk
1 unbaked (9-inch) pie shell

Mix the sugar, salt, cinnamon, ginger and cloves in a large bowl. Add the pumpkin and eggs and mix well. Stir in the hot milk. Pour into the pie shell. Bake at 450 degrees for 10 minutes. Reduce the heat to 350 degrees. Bake for 1 hour or until a knife inserted near the center comes out clean. Serves 8.

Judy Barton
Clarksville, Tennessee

SWEET POTATO PIE

1 large, or 2 medium sweet potatoes
1/2 cup (1 stick) butter, softened
1 cup sugar
3 eggs, beaten
Pinch of baking powder
1/4 cup milk
1 teaspoon vanilla extract
1 unbaked (9-inch) pie shell

Bake the potatoes at 350 degrees for 1 hour or until soft. Peel and mash in a bowl. Add the butter and stir until mixed. Stir in the sugar, eggs, baking powder, milk and vanilla and mix well. Pour into the pie shell. Bake at 350 degrees for 35 to 40 minutes. Serves 6.

Mildred Johnson
Memphis, Tennessee

SWEET POTATO PIE

2 cups hot mashed cooked sweet potatoes
1/2 cup (1 stick) margarine
1 1/2 cups sugar
3 eggs, well beaten
2 teaspoons vanilla extract
1/4 cup milk
1/4 teaspoon nutmeg
1 unbaked (9-inch) deep-dish pie shell

Stir the sweet potatoes and margarine in a bowl until the margarine melts. Beat in the sugar, eggs, vanilla, milk and nutmeg. Pour into the pie shell. Place foil strips over the crust edge to prevent the crust from becoming too brown. Bake at 350 degrees for 30 to 40 minutes, do not overbake. Serve with whipped cream or whipped topping and a dash of nutmeg. Serves 6 to 8.

Janice Garner
Medina, Tennessee

JAPANESE FRUIT PIE

1/2 cup (1 stick) butter, melted
1 cup sugar
2 eggs, beaten
1/2 cup pecans
1/2 cup flaked coconut
1/2 cup mixed candied fruit or raisins
1 tablespoon vinegar
1 unbaked (9-inch) pie shell

Combine the melted butter, sugar, eggs, pecans, coconut, candied fruit and vinegar in a bowl and mix well. Pour into the pie shell. Bake at 325 degrees for 35 to 40 minutes.
Serves 6 to 8.

Edna Lindsey
Maryville, Tennessee

CHERRY TARTS

9 ounces cream cheese, softened
1 1/2 cups (3 sticks) butter, softened
3 cups all-purpose flour
Filling (below)

Beat 1/3 of the cream cheese and 1/3 of the butter in a bowl. Beat in 1/3 of the flour. Cover and chill for at least 1 hour. Repeat with the remaining crust ingredients to make 3 total batches of dough. Divide each batch into 24 portions and shape into balls. Press into the bottom and sides of nonstick mini-muffin cups.

Bake at 400 degrees for 20 minutes or until golden brown. Let stand until cool. Fill the baked tart shells with the filling. Top each tart with 1 cherry from the pie filling.
Makes 6 dozen tarts.

Cherry Filling

8 ounces cream cheese, softened
1 (14-ounce) can sweetened condensed milk
1/3 cup lemon juice
1 teaspoon vanilla extract
1 (21-ounce) can cherry pie filling

Beat the cream cheese, sweetened condensed milk, lemon juice and vanilla in a bowl until smooth.

Jeana Pesch
Wartrace, Tennessee

SMALL PECAN TARTS

3 ounces cream cheese, softened
1/2 cup (1 stick) butter, softened
1 cup all-purpose flour
2/3 cup chopped pecans
1 egg, beaten
3/4 cup packed brown sugar
1 tablespoon butter, melted
1 tablespoon vanilla extract
Pinch of salt

Beat the cream cheese and 1/2 cup butter in a bowl. Beat in the flour. Cover and chill for at least 1 hour. Divide into 24 portions and shape into balls. Press into the bottom and sides of nonstick mini-muffin cups. Sprinkle the pecans in the tart shells. Beat the egg, brown sugar, 1 tablespoon melted butter, vanilla and salt in a bowl. Pour into the tart shells. Bake at 400 degrees for 20 minutes. Makes 2 dozen tarts.

Jeana Pesch
Wartrace, Tennessee

EASY PASTRY

3 cups all-purpose flour
1 teaspoon salt
1 cup shortening
1 egg, beaten
1 tablespoon vinegar
1/3 cup cold water

Sift the flour and sift again with the salt into a bowl. Cut in the shortening with a pastry blender or fork until the consistency of cornmeal. Stir in the egg. Mix the vinegar and cold water in a small bowl. Add to the flour mixture. Stir rapidly with a fork to form a dough. Shape into a ball. Cover and chill for 30 minutes. Cut the dough in half. Roll out each half on a floured work surface to a 10-inch circle.
Makes 1 (2-crust) pie pastry

Linda Brumley
Oakfield, Tennessee

DOT MCCREERY'S CHEESECAKE

1 1/3 cups graham cracker crumbs
1/4 cup sugar
1/4 cup (1/2 stick) butter, melted
24 ounces cream cheese, softened
1 cup sugar
1 teaspoon vanilla extract
4 eggs
2 cups sour cream
1/2 cup sugar
1 teaspoon vanilla extract

Combine the graham cracker crumbs, 1/4 cup sugar and butter in a bowl and mix well. Press over the bottom of a springform pan. Bake at 350 degrees for 5 minutes. Maintain the oven temperature. Beat the cream cheese, 1 cup sugar and 1 teaspoon vanilla in a mixing bowl until creamy. Add the eggs 1 at a time, beating until smooth after each addition. Pour into the prepared pan. Bake for 25 minutes. Turn off the oven. Let the cheesecake stand in the oven with the door ajar for 1 hour. Combine the sour cream, 1/2 cup sugar and 1 teaspoon vanilla in a bowl and mix with a spoon. Spread over the top. Bake at 450 degrees for 5 minutes. Chill, covered, for 8 to 10 hours before serving. Serves 16.

Pat Breeden
Rossville, Georgia

WHITE CHOCOLATE CHEESECAKE

2 cups crushed chocolate sandwich cookies
1/2 cup (1 stick) margarine, melted
1 envelope unflavored gelatin
2/3 cup water
16 ounces cream cheese, softened
6 ounces white chocolate, melted
1 (14-ounce) can sweetened condensed milk
1 teaspoon vanilla extract
1 cup heavy whipping cream, whipped (optional)

Mix the crushed cookies and melted margarine in a bowl. Press into the bottom of a 9-inch springform pan. Sprinkle the gelatin over the water in a small saucepan.

Let stand for 5 minutes. Cook over low heat until the gelatin is dissolved, stirring constantly. Remove from the heat.

Beat the cream cheese and melted chocolate in a bowl until light and fluffy. Beat in the sweetened condensed milk, vanilla and gelatin mixture. Beat until smooth. Pour into the prepared crust. Chill for 3 hours.

Loosen from the side of the pan with a sharp knife and remove the side. Garnish with the whipped cream. Serves 8.

Lonnie Dawson
Oliver Springs, Tennessee

APPLE WALNUT COBBLER

5 cups thinly sliced peeled apples
1/4 cup sugar or equivalent sucralose
1/2 teaspoon ground cinnamon
1/2 cup English or black walnuts
1 cup all-purpose flour
1 teaspoon baking powder
1/2 cup sugar or equivalent sucralose
1 egg, beaten
1/2 cup evaporated milk
5 1/3 tablespoons butter or margarine, melted
1/4 cup English or black walnuts

Spread the apples in a lightly greased 8x8-inch baking dish. Mix 1/4 cup sugar and the cinnamon in a small bowl. Sprinkle over the apples. Sprinkle with 1/2 cup walnuts.

Mix the flour, baking powder and 1/2 cup sugar in a bowl. Mix the egg, evaporated milk and melted butter in a small bowl. Add to the dry ingredients and stir until smooth. Pour over the apples. Sprinkle with 1/4 cup walnuts.

Bake at 325 degrees for 50 to 55 minutes or until a wooden pick inserted in the center comes out clean. Cut into squares and serve warm. Serves 6.

Bob Jeffries
Southaven, Mississippi

CHOCOLATE COBBLER

$^3/_4$ cup ($1^1/_2$ sticks) butter or margarine
$1^1/_2$ cups self-rising flour
$1^1/_4$ cups sugar
$5^1/_4$ teaspoons baking cocoa
2 teaspoons vanilla extract
$^3/_4$ cup milk
$1^1/_2$ cups sugar
$^1/_2$ cup baking cocoa
$2^1/_4$ cups boiling water

Melt the butter in a 9x13-inch baking pan in the oven. Combine the flour, $1^1/_4$ cups sugar, $5^1/_4$ teaspoons baking cocoa, vanilla and milk in a bowl and mix well. Pour evenly over the melted butter in the baking pan. Mix $1^1/_2$ cups sugar and $^1/_2$ cup baking cocoa together. Sprinkle over the batter in the pan. Pour the boiling water evenly over the top, do not stir. Bake at 350 degrees for 30 minutes. Serves 8 to 10.

Emily Taylor
Jackson, Tennessee

FRUIT COBBLER

1 cup chopped nuts
3 cups fruit, such as cherries, blueberries or blackberries
1 cup sucralose
2 eggs
1 cup sucralose
1 cup self-rising flour
$^1/_2$ cup (1 stick) margarine, softened
2 tablespoons milk

Combine the nuts, fruit and 1 cup sucralose in a bowl. Toss to mix. Spread in a 9x13-inch baking pan. Beat the eggs in a bowl with an electric mixer until thick and pale yellow. Beat in 1 cup sucralose, the flour, margarine and milk. Pour over the fruit mixture. Bake at 350 degrees for 45 minutes. Serves 12.

Janice Gibson
Trenton, Tennessee

PEACH COBBLER

1/2 cup (1 stick) butter or margarine
1 cup all-purpose flour
1 cup sugar
1 cup milk
1 can peaches in heavy syrup

Melt the butter in a 9x13-inch baking pan in the oven. Beat the flour, sugar and milk in a bowl. Pour evenly over the melted butter in the baking pan. Pour the peaches and syrup evenly over the batter. Bake at 350 degrees for 40 minutes or until golden brown. Serve with ice cream. Serves 8.

Mary Beth Etherton
Sevierville, Tennessee

PEACH COBBLER

8 peaches, peeled, pitted and sliced
1 cup sugar
1/4 cup (1/2 stick) butter
1/4 teaspoon ground cinnamon
1/4 teaspoon nutmeg
Grated zest of 1 lemon
1 (1-crust) pie pastry or 1 small package yellow cake mix
1/4 cup (1/2 stick) butter, cut into pieces
Sugar

Combine the peaches, 1 cup sugar, 1/4 cup butter, cinnamon, nutmeg and lemon zest in a saucepan. Cook for 20 minutes, stirring occasionally. Pour into 9-inch baking dish. Top with the pastry or sprinkle with the cake mix. Dot with 1/4 cup butter and sprinkle with sugar. Bake at 350 degrees for 35 minutes. Serves 6.

Alene White
Nashville, Tennessee

TUTTI-FRUTTI ICE CREAM

2 1/2 cups sugar
4 eggs
Dash of salt
1 tablespoon vanilla extract
2 (12-ounce) cans evaporated milk
1 (20-ounce) can crushed pineapple
2 ripe bananas, mashed
1/2 small jar maraschino cherries, drained and crushed
3 cups milk

Combine the sugar, eggs, salt, vanilla, evaporated milk, pineapple, bananas and cherries in a food processor and process for a few minutes. Pour into a bowl and stir in the milk. Pour into an ice cream freezer container. Freeze using manufacturer's directions. Note: To make a smaller batch, reduce the amount of milk. Serves 5.

Nancy Bassett
Nashville, Tennessee

HOMEMADE ICE CREAM

2 1/2 cups sugar
2 cups half-and-half
1 (12-ounce) can evaporated milk
1 (5-ounce) can evaporated milk
2 teaspoons vanilla extract
Strawberries, bananas or peaches, mashed
Milk

Mix the sugar, half-and-half, evaporated milk, vanilla and fruit in a bowl. Pour into a 1-gallon ice cream freezer container. Add milk to the fill line. Freeze using manufacturer's directions. Makes 1 gallon.

Emma Jean Tomlinson
Lebanon, Tennessee

ORANGE SHERBET

1 (2-liter) bottle orange soda
1 (14-ounce) can sweetened condensed milk
1 small can crushed pineapple, drained (optional)
1 can mandarin oranges, drained (optional)

Combine the orange soda, sweetened condensed milk, pineapple and mandarin oranges in a bowl and mix well. Pour into an ice cream freezer container. Freeze using the manufacturer's directions. Serves 5.

Nancy Bassett
Nashville, Tennessee

SPICED APPLE GLACÉ

2 cups sugar
3 cups water
6 thin lemon slices
3 whole cloves
1 tablespoon grated orange zest
1 (1-inch) cinnamon stick
6 large apples, peeled, cored and halved
6 maraschino cherries
1 tablespoon cornstarch
1/4 cup cold water
Red food color

Combine the sugar and 3 cups water in a large skillet. Bring to a boil. Stir in the lemon slices, cloves, orange zest and cinnamon stick. Add the apples. Simmer, uncovered, over medium heat for 15 minutes or until the apples are tender but still firm, turning once. Remove the apples and lemon slices with a slotted spoon to a serving dish. Top with the cherries. Bring the syrup to a rolling boil. Cook for 5 minutes or until a very thin syrup forms. Dissolve the cornstarch in 1/4 cup cold water in a small bowl. Stir into the syrup. Cook for 2 minutes. Remove from the heat and stir in food color. Remove the cloves and cinnamon stick. Let cool slightly and pour over the apples. Serves 6.

Helen Cole
Knoxville, Tennessee

BAKED APPLES

1 (8-count) can refrigerator crescent rolls
2 Granny Smith apples, cored and quartered
1 cup sugar
1 cup orange juice
1/2 cup (1 stick) butter
1 teaspoon vanilla extract
1 teaspoon ground cinnamon

Separate the crescent rolls on a work surface. Wrap each apple quarter in a crescent roll and arrange in a 9-inch baking dish. Combine the sugar, orange juice and butter in a saucepan. Bring to a boil and cook until beginning to thicken, stirring frequently. Stir in the vanilla. Pour over the wrapped apples. Sprinkle with the cinnamon. Bake at 350 degrees until golden brown and the apples are tender. Serves 8.

Rubye Morrison
Shelbyville, Tennessee

APPLE DESSERT

2 (8-count) cans refrigerator crescent rolls
16 ounces cream cheese, softened
1 cup sugar
2 (21-ounce) cans apple pie filling
1/2 cup pecans, chopped
1/2 cup (1 stick) butter, melted
1/2 cup sugar
2 tablespoons ground cinnamon

Unroll 1 can of crescent dough and fit in the bottom of a buttered 9x13-inch baking dish. Press the seams to seal. Beat the cream cheese and 1 cup sugar in a bowl until light and fluffy. Spread over the dough. Spread the pie filling over the cream cheese mixture. Unroll the remaining can of crescent dough and press the seams to seal. Place on top of the apples. Sprinkle with the pecans. Pour the melted butter evenly over the pecans. Mix 1/2 cup sugar and the cinnamon in a small bowl. Sprinkle over the top. Bake at 350 degrees for 30 minutes. Serves 10 to 12.

Jean Mayo
Ashland City, Tennessee

EASY APPLE DESSERT

1 can refrigerator jumbo biscuits
1/2 cup (1 stick) butter or margarine
1/2 cup packed brown sugar
1 (21-ounce) can apple pie filling
1/2 cup chopped pecans
Ground cinnamon to taste
8 ounces cream cheese, softened
1/4 cup (1/2 stick) butter, softened
2 cups confectioners' sugar

Separate the biscuits and cut into quarters. Arrange in a greased 9x13-inch baking pan. Melt 1/2 cup butter in a saucepan. Stir in the brown sugar. Pour evenly over the biscuits. Spread the pie filling over the brown sugar mixture. Sprinkle with the pecans and cinnamon. Bake at 350 degrees for 30 minutes. Beat the cream cheese, 1/4 cup butter and confectioners' sugar in a bowl. Pour over the hot dessert. Serve with ice cream or whipped topping. Serves 12.

Florence Stubblefield
Morristown, Tennessee

APPLE DUMPLINGS

2 cups sugar
1 teaspoon ground cinnamon
1 teaspoon nutmeg
3 cups orange juice
1 teaspoon vanilla extract
2 (8-count) cans refrigerator crescent rolls
4 Granny Smith apples, peeled, cored and quartered
2 tablespoons butter

Mix the sugar, cinnamon and nutmeg in a saucepan. Stir in the orange juice. Bring to a boil. Remove from the heat and stir in the vanilla. Separate the crescent rolls on a work surface. Wrap each apple quarter in a crescent roll. Arrange in a 10x13-inch baking pan greased with the butter. Pour the orange juice mixture evenly over the apples. Bake at 350 degrees for 30 minutes. Serves 16.

Jeri and Fred Brockette
Lebanon, Tennessee

BANANA PUDDING

2 packages Pepperidge Farm Chessman cookies
6 to 8 bananas, sliced
8 ounces cream cheese, softened
1 (14-ounce) can sweetened condensed milk
1 (12-ounce) container frozen whipped topping, thawed
2 cups milk
1 (5-ounce) package French vanilla instant pudding mix

Line the bottom of 9x13-inch baking dish with 1 package of cookies. Arrange the banana slices on top.

Beat the cream cheese and sweetened condensed milk in a large bowl until smooth. Fold in the whipped topping. Beat the milk and pudding mix in a bowl with an electric mixer. Stir into the cream cheese mixture. Pour over the bananas. Top with the remaining package of cookies. Cover and chill until serving time. Serves 12.

Ann Howell Tickle
Morristown, Tennessee

JIFFY BANANA PUDDING

2 (6-ounce) packages vanilla instant pudding mix
3 cups milk
1 cup sour cream
1 large container frozen whipped topping, thawed
1 box vanilla wafers
6 large bananas, sliced

Whisk the pudding mix and milk in a large bowl until mixed. Fold in the sour cream and whipped topping. Arrange the wafers in a 3-quart baking dish. Top with the banana slices. Pour the pudding mixture over the bananas. Serves 12.

Shirley Clary
Nashville, Tennessee

BLUEBERRY CRUNCH

1 (20-ounce) can crushed pineapple
4 cups blueberries
3/4 cup sugar
1 (2-layer) package yellow cake mix
1 3/4 sticks margarine, melted
1 cup pecans

Spread the pineapple in a 9x13-inch baking dish. Top with the blueberries. Sprinkle with the sugar. Spread the cake mix on top. Pour the melted margarine evenly over the cake mix and sprinkle with the pecans. Bake at 350 degrees for 55 minutes. Let stand until cool. Serves 12.

Kathy Rives
Clarksville, Tennessee

BLUEBERRY CRUNCH

2 cups all-purpose flour
1 cup (2 sticks) margarine, softened
1 cup chopped pecans
8 ounces cream cheese, softened
1 (16-ounce) package confectioners' sugar
1 (12-ounce) container frozen whipped topping, thawed
1 (21-ounce) can blueberry pie filling (or strawberry or cherry pie filling)

Mix the flour, margarine and pecans in a bowl. Press or spread in a 9x13-inch baking dish. Bake at 350 degrees until golden brown. Let stand until cool. Stir the cream cheese, confectioners' sugar and whipped topping in a bowl until well blended. Spread over the crust. Top with the pie filling. Cut into squares. Serves 12 to 15.

Joyce Neely
Jackson, Tennessee

CHERRY CRUNCH

1 (21-ounce) can cherry pie filling
1 (2-layer) package white cake mix
1/2 cup (1 stick) margarine, melted
1/2 cup chopped nuts

Spread the pie filling in a 9x13-inch baking dish. Stir the cake mix, melted margarine and nuts in a bowl until crumbly. Spread over the pie filling. Bake at 350 degrees for 35 to 40 minutes. Serve with ice cream. Serves 12.

Louise Spahr
Knoxville, Tennessee

PINEAPPLE CHERRY DUMP CAKE

1 (20-ounce) can crushed pineapple
1 (21-ounce) can cherry pie filling
1 (2-layer) package yellow cake mix
1/2 cup (1 stick) butter, cut into thin slices
1/2 cup chopped pecans

Spread the pineapple in an oiled 9x13-inch cake pan. Spread the pie filling evenly over the pineapple. Spread the cake mix evenly over the pie filling. Dot with the butter and sprinkle with the pecans. Bake at 350 degrees for 1 hour. Serves 12.

Betty Ann Webb
Knoxville, Tennessee

ICE CREAM BARS

Ice cream sandwich bars
Caramel or chocolate ice cream topping
Crushed chocolate-covered toffee candy bars
1 large container frozen whipped topping, thawed or whipped cream

Fit ice cream sandwich bars in a square baking dish. Drizzle with caramel topping and sprinkle with candy pieces. Spread with whipped topping. Cover and freeze until firm. Let stand at room temperature for 20 minutes before serving. Serves 9.

Addie Downs
Nashville, Tennessee

DIRT CAKE

20 ounces chocolate sandwich cookies
8 ounces cream cheese, softened
1/2 cup (1 stick) butter
1 cup confectioners' sugar
3 small packages vanilla instant pudding mix
3 1/2 cups milk
1 (12-ounce) container whipped topping

Place the cookies in a blender and process until crumbly. Combine the cream cheese, butter and confectioners' sugar in a large mixing bowl and beat until blended. Combine the pudding mix, milk and whipped topping in a mixing bowl and beat until blended. Add to the cream cheese mixture and mix well. Layer the cookie crumbs and pudding mixture 1/2 at a time in a clean unused flowerpot. Chill, covered, until serving time. Serves 15.

Juli Simms
Knoxville, Tennessee

CHOCOLATE BROWNIE VOLCANO

- **1 family-size package brownie mix**
- **1 (6-ounce) package chocolate fudge instant pudding mix**
- **1 cup pecan pieces**
- **4 chocolate-covered toffee candy bars, broken into pieces**
- **1 (8-ounce) container frozen whipped topping, thawed**

Prepare and bake the brownies using the package directions. Let stand until cool. Break the cooled brownies into bite-size pieces and place 1/2 in a trifle bowl. Prepare the pudding using the package directions. Layer half the pudding, pecans and candy pieces over the brownies. Top with the remaining brownies and then the remaining pudding. Spread the whipped topping over the pudding. Sprinkle with the remaining pecans and candy pieces. Garnish with a maraschino cherry. Chill for at least 2 hours. Serves 16.

Deborah Horton
Nashville, Tennessee

CHOCOLATE DEATH

- **1 package brownie mix**
- **1 package toffee bits**
- **1 cup broken pecans**
- **1/3 cup amaretto liqueur**
- **1 (6-ounce) package chocolate instant pudding mix**
- **1 (8-ounce) container frozen whipped topping, thawed**

Prepare and bake the brownies using the package directions. Let stand until cool. Break the cooled brownies into bite-size pieces and place 1/2 in a trifle bowl. Prepare the pudding using the package directions. Sprinkle with 1/2 the toffee bits and 1/2 the pecans. Drizzle 1/2 the liqueur over the top. Spread with 1/2 the pudding and then 1/2 the whipped topping. Repeat the layers. Serves 16.

Ann Harville
Talbott, Tennessee

CHOCOLATE SAUCE

1 tablespoon cornstarch
3 tablespoons baking cocoa
1/2 cup sugar
1/2 cup water
1/2 cup (1 stick) butter or margarine
3/4 cup marshmallow creme
1 teaspoon vanilla extract

Mix the cornstarch, baking cocoa and sugar in a heavy saucepan. Stir in the water and butter. Bring to a boil, stirring constantly. Remove from the heat and add the marshmallow creme and vanilla and stir until smooth. Serve warm over ice cream or cake or use as a dip for fresh fruit. Makes 2 cups.

Wanda (Susie) Ladd
Williamsport, Tennessee

LAYER DESSERT

1 cup all-purpose flour
2 tablespoons sugar
1/2 cup (1 stick) butter, melted
1/4 cup chopped pecans
8 ounces cream cheese, softened
2/3 cup sugar
1 (8-ounce) container frozen whipped topping, thawed
2 1/2 cups milk
2 (3 1/2-ounce) packages instant pudding mix, flavor of choice
Chopped pecans

Stir the flour, 2 tablespoons sugar, butter and 1/4 cup pecans in a bowl until crumbly. Press in a 9x13-inch baking pan. Bake at 350 degrees for 15 minutes. Let stand until cool. Beat the cream cheese and 2/3 cup sugar in a bowl until smooth. Fold in 1/2 the whipped topping. Spread over the cooled crust. Combine the milk and pudding mix in a bowl. Beat for 2 minutes or until thick. Spread over the cream cheese mixture. Top with the remaining whipped topping and sprinkle with pecans. Cover and chill. Serves 12.

Kathy Duncan
Memphis, Tennessee

LEMON DESSERT DELIGHT

2 sleeves (about 72) butter crackers, finely crushed
1/2 cup confectioners' sugar
1/2 cup (1 stick) butter or margarine, melted
1 (14-ounce) can sweetened condensed milk
1 (6-ounce) can frozen lemonade concentrate, thawed
1 (8-ounce) container frozen whipped topping, thawed

Mix the crushed crackers, confectioners' sugar and melted butter in a bowl. Remove 1 cup and set aside. Press the remaining mixture in a 9-inch pie plate. Combine the remaining ingredients in a bowl and mix well. Pour into the prepared crust. Sprinkle with the reserved crumb mixture. Serves 4 to 6.

Glenda Buchanan
College Grove, Tennessee

LEMON LUST

1 1/2 cups all-purpose flour
3/4 cup (1 1/2 sticks) margarine, softened
1/2 cup broken walnuts
8 ounces cream cheese
1 cup confectioners' sugar
1/2 cup frozen whipped topping, thawed
3 cups milk
3 (3 1/2-ounce) packages lemon instant pudding mix
1/2 cup frozen whipped topping, thawed
Broken walnuts

Mix the flour, margarine and 1/2 cup nuts in a bowl. Press in a 9x13-inch baking pan. Bake at 350 degrees for 20 minutes. Let stand until cool. Beat the cream cheese and confectioners' sugar in a bowl until light and fluffy. Fold in 1/2 cup whipped topping. Spread over the crust. Combine the milk and pudding mix in a bowl. Beat until thick. Spread over the cream cheese mixture. Top with 1/2 cup whipped topping and sprinkle with nuts. Cover and chill for 8 to 10 hours. Serves 12.

Carolyn Payne
Jackson, Tennessee

PEACH DESSERT

1 (6-ounce) package peach gelatin
2 tablespoons sugar
1 cup water
2 cups sliced peeled fresh peaches
1 cup buttermilk
1 (15-ounce) can crushed pineapple
2 tablespoons sugar
1 (12-ounce) container frozen whipped topping, thawed

Bring the gelatin, 2 tablespoons sugar and water to a boil in a small saucepan. Pour into a 9x13-inch baking dish. Chill until beginning to set. Mix the peaches, buttermilk, pineapple and 2 tablespoons sugar in a bowl. Stir the peach mixture into the gelatin. Fold in the whipped topping. Cover and chill for several hours or overnight. Serves 12.

Kathleen Price
Rockwood, Tennessee

BRANDY PEACHES

16 canned peach halves
1 cup maple syrup
1 cup firmly packed brown sugar
5 1/3 tablespoons butter, melted
Ground cinnamon to taste
1/3 cup brandy
Vanilla ice cream

Place the peaches, cavity side up, in a greased 9x13-inch baking dish. Spoon 1 tablespoon maple syrup, 1 tablespoon brown sugar and 1 teaspoon melted butter into each cavity. Sprinkle lightly with cinnamon. Bake at 325 degrees for 20 minutes. Pour the brandy over the peaches. Remove the peach halves to individual serving dishes and top with a scoop of ice cream. Serves 16.

Peggy Burr
Nashville, Tennessee

PEACH FLUFF

1 cup all-purpose flour
1/4 cup packed brown sugar
1 cup (2 sticks) margarine, melted
1 large container frozen whipped topping, thawed
8 ounces cream cheese, softened
1 cup confectioners' sugar
1 cup water
1 cup sugar
2 tablespoons cornstarch
1 (6-ounce) package peach gelatin
5 peaches, peeled, pitted and sliced (about 6 cups)

Mix the flour, brown sugar and melted margarine in a bowl. Press in a 9x13-inch baking dish. Bake at 350 degrees for 15 minutes. Cool on a wire rack. Beat the whipped topping, cream cheese and confectioners' sugar in a bowl until smooth. Spread over the crust and chill. Combine the water, sugar and cornstarch in a saucepan. Bring to a boil, stirring frequently. Remove from the heat and stir in the gelatin. Let cool to room temperature. Stir in the peaches. Pour over the cream cheese mixture. Chill, covered, overnight or for 45 minutes in the freezer. Serves 12.

Kaye Lewis
Joelton, Tennessee

SUMMER SURPRISE DESSERT

1 cup seedless grapes, halved
1 cup fresh blueberries
1 cup fresh strawberries, halved
1 cup peeled fresh peaches, cut into bite-size pieces
1 cup packed brown sugar
2 cups sour cream

Combine the grapes, blueberries, strawberries and peaches in a 9x12-inch baking dish. Toss to mix well. Sprinkle the brown sugar over the fruit. Spread the sour cream over the brown sugar. Cover and chill overnight and mix gently. Spoon into sherbet glasses. Note: Any combination of fresh fruits will work, but be sure to include grapes, blueberries and peaches. Do not use canned or frozen fruit. Serves 8.

Sandy Walker
Clarksville, Tennessee

FRENCH PINEAPPLE PUDDING

1 small box vanilla wafers, crushed
2 medium cans crushed pineapple, drained, 2 cups juice reserved
2 (3½-ounce) packages French instant vanilla pudding mix
2 cups milk
1 large container frozen whipped topping, thawed

Spread ½ the crushed wafers in a 9x13-inch pan. Beat the reserved pineapple juice, pudding mix and milk in a bowl. Stir in the drained pineapple. Pour ½ over the crushed wafers in the baking pan. Sprinkle the remaining crushed wafers over the pineapple layer. Fold ½ of the whipped topping into the remaining pineapple mixture. Pour over the crushed wafer layer. Top with the remaining whipped topping. Serves 12.

Dianne Anderson
Nashville, Tennessee

DEBBIE'S MOM'S STRAWBERRY DELIGHT

1 (3½-ounce) package vanilla instant pudding mix
1 cup sour cream
1 (8-ounce) container frozen whipped topping, thawed
1 baked angel food cake, torn into bite-size pieces
1 quart fresh strawberries, hulled and sliced
1 container strawberry pie jell

Prepare the pudding using the package directions. Add the sour cream and mix well. Add the whipped topping and mix well. Spread some of the cake pieces in a serving bowl. Top with some of the pudding mixture and a few sliced strawberries. Continue layering to use all the cake, pudding mixture and most of the strawberries. Spread about ¼ inch of pie jell evenly over the top and sprinkle with the remaining strawberries. Chill until cold. Serves 8 to 10.

Bonnie Chadwell
Nashville, Tennessee

PIRATES' HOUSE TRIFLE

1 large package sugar-free vanilla instant pudding mix
3 cups 2% milk
1/2 cup sucralose
1 teaspoon vanilla extract
2 cups 2% milk
Nutmeg to taste (optional)
1 (10-ounce) baked sugar-free angel food cake, torn into bite-size pieces
1 large container light frozen whipped topping, thawed

Beat the pudding mix and 3 cups milk in a bowl using the package directions. Add the sucralose, vanilla and 2 cups milk. Season with nutmeg and beat well.

Place 1/3 of the cake into a 3-quart serving bowl. Top with 1/3 of the pudding mixture and spread with 1/3 of the whipped topping. Repeat the layers twice to use the remaining cake, pudding mixture and whipped topping. Cover and chill for 1 hour.

Note: This recipe is from a 2003 holiday supplement to the *Columbia Herald*. It was adapted from a Savannah Junior League cookbook. Serves 6 to 8.

Teresa Flach and James Parrish
Nashville, Tennessee

CANDY AND COOKIES

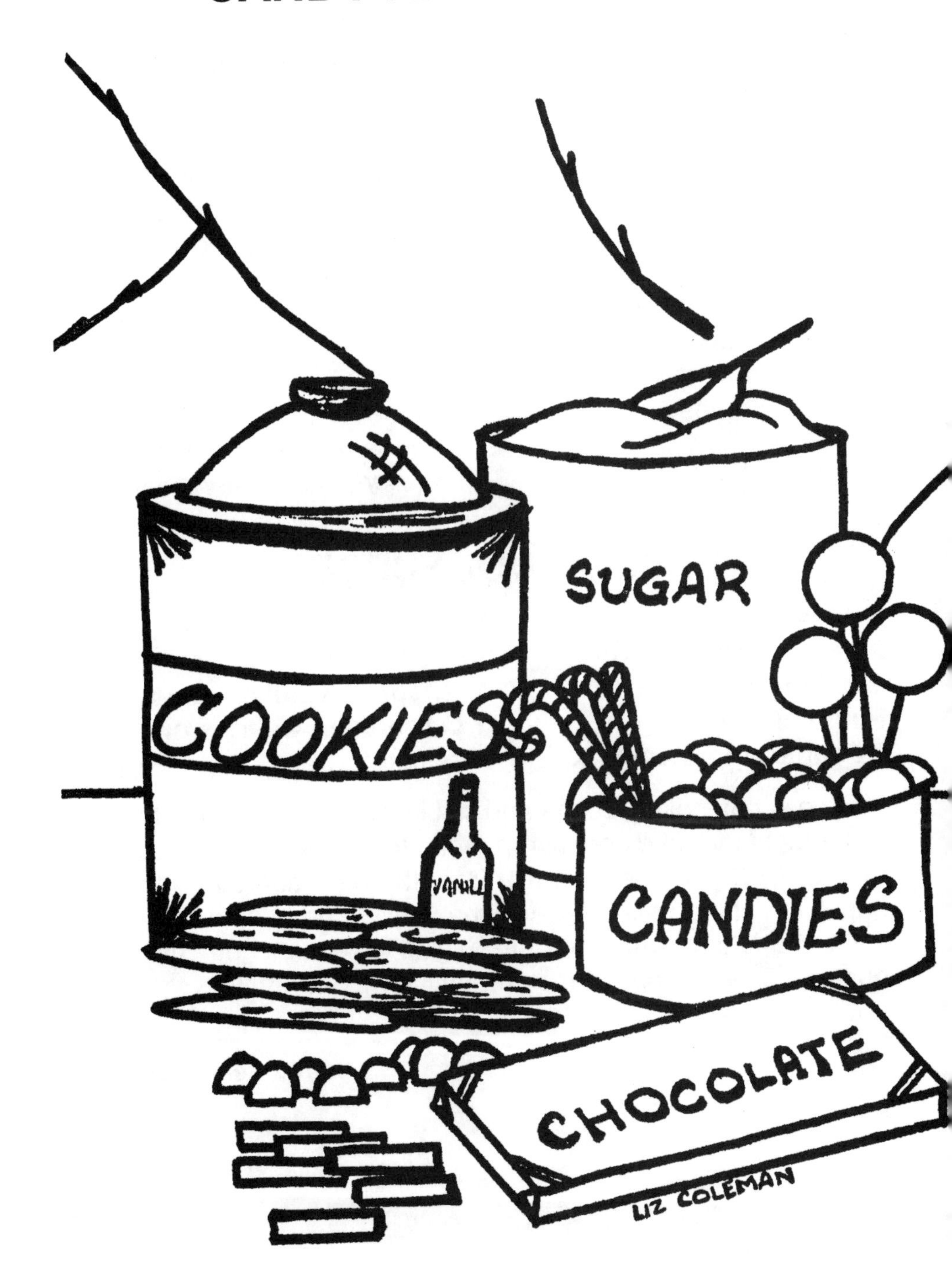

DONETTA'S FUDGE

1/4 cup baking cocoa
4 cups sugar
1 cup evaporated milk
1 cup milk
2/3 cup butter
1 teaspoon vanilla extract
1/2 to 1 cup chopped nuts

Combine the cocoa, sugar, evaporated milk and milk in a saucepan and mix well. Add the butter and bring to a boil over medium heat. Boil, covered, for 3 minutes. Cook, uncovered, to 234 to 240 degrees on a candy thermometer, soft-ball stage. Remove from the heat. Let stand for 15 minutes. Add the vanilla and nuts and beat until thickened. Pour into a buttered pan. Let stand until completely cool. Cut into squares. Serves 48.

Jan Moore
Henderson, Tennessee

FOOLPROOF FUDGE

2 cups sugar
2 heaping tablespoons baking cocoa
Pinch of salt
1/2 cup evaporated milk
1/4 cup light corn syrup
1/4 cup (1/2 stick) butter
1 teaspoon vanilla extract
1 cup broken walnuts or pecans

Mix the sugar, baking cocoa and salt in a saucepan. Stir in the evaporated milk and corn syrup. Bring to a rolling boil and boil for exactly 2 minutes. Remove from the heat and stir in the butter. Let stand until cool. Add the vanilla and beat well. Stir in the walnuts when the mixture begins to thicken. Pour into a buttered 8x8-inch pan. Let stand until firm. Serves 24.

Myra Pryor
Troy, Tennessee

CHOCOLATE FUDGE

$2/3$ cup milk
3 to 4 tablespoons baking cocoa
2 cups sugar
1 teaspoon light corn syrup
$1/4$ teaspoon salt
2 tablespoons butter
1 teaspoon vanilla extract
1 to $1\frac{1}{2}$ cups chopped nuts (optional)

Stir the milk, baking cocoa, sugar, corn syrup and salt in a saucepan. Cook over medium heat to 234 to 240 degrees on a candy thermometer, soft-ball stage, stirring gently. Remove from the heat and add the butter and vanilla. Beat until thick and no longer glossy. Stir in the nuts. Spread on waxed paper or a buttered plate. Let stand until firm. Serves 24.

JoAnn Gunn
Lake City, Tennessee

MARSHMALLOW CREME FUDGE

$1/2$ cup (1 stick) margarine
3 cups sugar
$2/3$ cup evaporated milk
1 teaspoon vanilla extract
2 cups chocolate chips
1 (7-ounce) jar marshmallow creme
1 (2-ounce) package black walnuts (optional)

Combine the margarine, sugar, evaporated milk and vanilla in a saucepan. Bring to a rolling boil over medium heat, stirring constantly. Reduce the heat to medium-low and cook for exactly 5 minutes, stirring constantly. Remove from the heat and stir in the chocolate chips, marshmallow creme and walnuts. Pour into a greased 9x13-inch pan. Let stand until cool. Note: To make peanut butter fudge, use peanut butter chips instead of chocolate chips and add 1 to 2 tablespoons creamy peanut butter. Serves 24.

Helen Wynegar
Powell, Tennessee

RIBBON FANTASY FUDGE

1 1/2 cups sugar
6 tablespoons margarine
1/3 cup evaporated milk
1 cup chocolate chips
1 cup marshmallow creme
1/2 teaspoon vanilla extract
1 1/2 cups sugar
6 tablespoons margarine
1/3 cup evaporated milk
1/2 cup creamy or chunky peanut butter
1 cup marshmallow creme
1/2 teaspoon vanilla extract

Combine 1 1/2 cups sugar, 6 tablespoons margarine and 1/3 cup evaporated milk in a heavy 1 1/2-quart saucepan. Bring to a rolling boil over medium heat, stirring constantly. Boil for 4 minutes, stirring constantly. Remove from the heat and add the chocolate chips. Stir until the chocolate melts. Beat in 1 cup marshmallow creme and 1/2 teaspoon vanilla. Pour into a greased 9x13-inch baking pan. Combine 1 1/2 cups sugar, 6 tablespoons margarine and 1/3 cup evaporated milk in a heavy 1 1/2-quart saucepan. Bring to a rolling boil over medium heat, stirring constantly. Boil for 4 minutes, stirring constantly. Remove from the heat and add the peanut butter. Stir until the peanut butter melts. Beat in 1 cup marshmallow creme and 1/2 teaspoon vanilla. Spread over the chocolate layer. Let stand until cool. Cut into squares. Serves 48.

Jimmie Ruth Humberd
Cleveland, Tennessee

TWO-FLAVOR FUDGE

2 cups firmly packed brown sugar
1 cup granulated sugar
1 cup evaporated milk
1/2 cup (1 stick) butter
1 jar marshmallow creme
1 cup semisweet chocolate chips
1 cup butterscotch chips
1 cup nuts, chopped
1 teaspoon vanilla extract

Combine the brown sugar, granulated sugar, evaporated milk and butter in a saucepan. Bring to a rolling boil over medium heat, stirring occasionally. Remove from the heat.

Add the marshmallow creme, chocolate chips and butterscotch chips. Stir until melted and smooth. Stir in the nuts and vanilla. Pour into a greased 9x9-inch pan. Chill, covered, until firm. Serves 36.

Colleen Ferguson
Loudon, Tennessee

BROWN SUGAR PEANUT BUTTER FUDGE

2 (16-ounce) packages brown sugar
2 cups granulated sugar
1 tablespoons baking cocoa
1 cup milk, or 1½ cans evaporated milk
1 cup peanut butter
1 tablespoon vanilla extract

Mix the brown sugar, granulated sugar, baking cocoa and milk in a heavy saucepan. Cook over medium heat to 234 to 240 degrees on a candy thermometer, soft-ball stage. Remove from the heat and beat in the peanut butter and vanilla. Pour into a greased 9x13-inch pan. Let stand until firm. Serves 80.

Rosalie Williams
Chattanooga, Tennessee

PEANUT BUTTER FUDGE

⅔ cup evaporated milk
2 cups granulated sugar
1 cup peanut butter
1 (7-ounce) jar marshmallow creme

Mix the evaporated milk and granulated sugar in a saucepan. Cook to 240 degrees on a candy thermometer, soft-ball stage. Remove from the heat and add the peanut butter and marshmallow creme. Beat until the mixture begins to thicken. Pour into an oiled or foil-lined pan. Let stand until cool. Cut into squares. Serves 48.

Wilma Kelly
Knoxville, Tennessee

PEANUT BUTTER FUDGE

6 cups sugar
$1\frac{1}{2}$ cups evaporated milk
$\frac{3}{4}$ cup milk
1 tablespoon light corn syrup
$\frac{1}{4}$ teaspoon salt
1 (18-ounce) jar peanut butter
$\frac{1}{2}$ cup (1 stick) margarine
2 teaspoons vanilla extract

Combine the sugar, evaporated milk, milk, corn syrup and salt in a saucepan. Cook over medium heat to 234 to 240 degrees on a candy thermometer, soft-ball stage, stirring constantly. Remove from the heat and add the peanut butter, margarine and vanilla. Beat just until thickened. Pour into a buttered 9x13-inch pan. Let cool and cut into squares. Note: To make chocolate fudge, add $\frac{1}{4}$ cup baking cocoa to the sugar mixture and omit the peanut butter. Serves 50.

Wilma Quarles
Harrison, Tennessee

PEANUT BUTTER BALLS

1 (16-ounce) package confectioners' sugar
1 cup (2 sticks) margarine, softened
1 cup peanut butter
$1\frac{1}{2}$ cups butterscotch chips
2 ounces paraffin

Mix the confectioners' sugar, margarine and peanut butter in a bowl. Shape into marble-size balls. Combine the butterscotch chips and paraffin in the top of a double boiler. Cook over simmering water until melted, stirring occasionally. Dip the balls in the butterscotch mixture to coat and remove to waxed paper. Let stand until firm. Store in an airtight container. Serves 72.

JoAnn & Anthony Gunn
Lake City, Tennessee

PEANUT BRITTLE

2 cups sugar
1 cup light corn syrup
1/2 cup water
1 bag unsalted raw peanuts
1 tablespoon butter or margarine
2 teaspoons baking soda

Mix the sugar, corn syrup and water in a saucepan. Bring to a boil and cook to 230 degrees on a candy thermometer. Remove from the heat and stir in the peanuts. Return to a boil and cook to 300 degrees on a candy thermometer. Remove from the heat and stir in the butter and baking soda. Pour immediately onto a buttered foil-lined baking sheet and spread thinly. Let stand until set. Break into pieces. Serves 32.

Wilma Kelly
Knoxville, Tennessee

DIVINITY

4 cups sugar
1 cup light corn syrup
3/4 cup water
3 egg whites
1 teaspoon vanilla extract
1 cup nut pieces

Combine the sugar, corn syrup and water in a saucepan and mix well. Cook over low heat until the sugar dissolves, stirring constantly. Continue to cook over low heat to 255 degrees on a candy thermometer, hard-ball stage; do not stir. Remove from the heat. Beat the egg whites in a mixing bowl until stiff peaks form. Add the hot syrup gradually, beating constantly. Beat at high speed until the mixture holds its shape and loses its gloss. Stir in the vanilla and nuts. Drop by spoonfuls onto waxed paper. Let stand until cool. May spread in a buttered dish, let stand until completely cool and cut into 1-inch squares. Makes 8 dozen pieces.

Pat Breeden
Rossville, Georgia

MOLASSES TAFFY

1/2 cup dark molasses
1 1/2 cups sugar
1/2 cup water
1 1/2 tablespoons cider vinegar
1/4 teaspoon cream of tartar
1/4 cup (1/2 stick) butter, melted
1/8 teaspoon baking soda

Mix the molasses, sugar, water and cider vinegar in a heavy 3-quart saucepan. Bring to a boil over medium heat, stirring constantly. Stir in the cream of tartar. Boil, covered, for 2 to 3 minutes. Wash down the inside of the pan with a pastry brush dipped in water. Cook, uncovered, to 256 degrees on a candy thermometer; do not stir. Stir in the melted butter and baking soda. Pour immediately onto an oiled marble slab or baking sheet. Pull the edges of the taffy with well-oiled hands as it begins to cool, pulling the outside to overlap the center. Continue until porous and difficult to pull. Break into small pieces and store in an airtight container in a cool place. Serves 16.

Rubye C. Morrison
Shelbyville, Tennessee

HOMEMADE HEATH BARS

2 cups (4 sticks) butter
2 cups sugar
3/4 cup chopped almonds
2 cups semisweet chocolate chips
3/4 cup chopped almonds

Combine the butter and sugar in a saucepan. Cook over medium heat to 325 degrees on a candy thermometer, stirring constantly. Remove from the heat and stir in 3/4 cup almonds. Spread evenly in a 10x15-inch pan. Sprinkle the chocolate chips over the top and let stand for 5 minutes. Spread the melted chocolate evenly over the toffee layer. Sprinkle 3/4 cup almonds over the chocolate. Chill, covered, until firm. Break into bite-size pieces. Serves 48.

Cathy Hurdle
Collierville, Tennessee

PEANUT BUTTER CHEWIES

1 cup sugar
1 cup light corn syrup
1 cup peanut butter
5 to 6 cups cornflakes

Cook the sugar and corn syrup in a saucepan over medium heat until the sugar is dissolved, stirring constantly until well blended. Add the peanut butter and cook until incorporated, stirring constantly until blended.

Place the cornflakes in a bowl. Add the peanut butter mixture and stir until the cornflakes are coated. Drop by large spoonfuls or ice cream scoopfuls onto waxed paper. Let stand until completely cool.

Angel Harris
Memphis, Tennessee

VERY EASY PEANUT BUTTER ROLL

3 ounces cream cheese, softened
$^1/_3$ cup ($^2/_3$ stick) margarine
1 teaspoon vanilla extract
1 to $1^1/_2$ (16-ounce) packages confectioners' sugar
Creamy peanut butter

Cream the cream cheese, margarine and vanilla in a large mixing bowl. Beat in enough of the confectioners' sugar to form a dough.

Sprinkle a large piece of waxed paper with a small amount of confectioners' sugar. Roll out the dough into a rectangle on top of the confectioners' sugar. Spread with peanut butter. Roll as for a jelly roll from the short side. Chill, covered, until serving time. Cut into slices.

Trilby Williams
Morristown, Tennessee

APRICOT CREAM CHEESE PINWHEELS

1 cup (2 sticks) unsalted butter, softened
8 ounces cream cheese, softened
1/4 teaspoon salt
2 cups all-purpose flour
2/3 cup apricot preserves
1 cup walnuts, finely chopped

Beat the butter, cream cheese and salt in a mixing bowl until smooth. Add the flour gradually, beating constantly. Roll into a 6x8-inch rectangle on a work surface. Wrap in plastic wrap. Chill for 12 hours. Combine the preserves and walnuts in a bowl and mix well. Roll the chilled dough into a 12x14-inch rectangle on a floured surface. Spread the preserve mixture over the dough, leaving a 1/2-inch border. Roll as for a jelly roll from the long side, pressing the seams to seal. Cut the roll in half. Chill, wrapped in plastic wrap, until very firm, or place in the freezer for 30 minutes. Cut each roll with a serrated knife into 28 slices. Arrange 1 inch apart on a greased cookie sheet. Bake 1 sheet at a time at 350 degrees for 15 minutes or until the edges are golden brown. Remove to a wire rack to cool. Store, tightly covered, in the refrigerator for up to 1 week. May freeze for up to 1 month. Makes 56 pinwheels.

Claudette Quinn
Jackson, Tennessee

TOFFEE BARS

Graham crackers
1 cup (2 sticks) butter
1 cup packed brown sugar
1 cup chopped nuts

Arrange graham crackers in a single layer in a 10x15-inch baking pan. Melt the butter in a saucepan. Stir in the brown sugar. Bring to a rolling boil and boil for 2 minutes. Remove from the heat and stir in the nuts. Pour evenly over the crackers. Bake at 350 degrees for 10 minutes. Remove to a wire rack and let stand to cool for 2 minutes. Remove to waxed paper. Let stand until completely cool. Serves 12 to 15.

Linda Brumley
Oakfield, Tennessee

GRAHAM CRACKER BARS

Graham crackers
1 cup (2 sticks) margarine
1 cup sugar
1/2 cup milk
1 egg
1 cup nuts
1 cup flaked coconut
1 3/4 cups graham cracker crumbs
8 ounces cream cheese, softened
1 (16-ounce) package confectioners' sugar

Arrange graham crackers in a single layer in a 9x13-inch pan or dish. Mix the margarine, sugar, milk and egg in a saucepan. Bring to a boil, stirring constantly. Boil for 6 minutes, stirring constantly. Remove from the heat and stir in the nuts, coconut and graham cracker crumbs. Spread over the graham crackers in the pan. Top with a single layer of graham crackers. Beat the cream cheese and confectioners' sugar in a bowl until smooth. Spread over the graham cracker layer. Cover and freeze overnight or for up to 6 months. Let stand at room temperature for 1 hour before serving. Serves 24.

Elaine Huff
Harrison, Tennessee

JOE'S NO-BAKE COOKIES

1/2 cup (1 stick) butter
2 cups sugar
1/2 cup milk
1 teaspoon vanilla extract
3/4 teaspoon salt
3 tablespoons baking cocoa
1 heaping tablespoon peanut butter
3 cups rolled oats

Melt the butter in a saucepan over medium heat. Add the sugar, milk, vanilla, salt and baking cocoa and stir to mix well. Increase the heat to high and bring to a rolling boil. Boil for 1 1/2 minutes, stirring frequently. Remove from the heat and stir in the peanut butter and oats quickly. Drop by spoonfuls onto waxed paper. Makes 4 dozen cookies.

Joe Huffman
Nashville, Tennessee

SPANISH COOKIES

1 package white chocolate or almond bark
2 tablespoons peanut butter
2 cups Spanish peanuts
2 cups chow mein noodles
2 cups Cap'n Crunch cereal

Combine the white chocolate and peanut butter in a large microwave-safe bowl. Microwave until melted, stirring occasionally. Add the peanuts, chow mein noodles and cereal and mix well. Drop by tablespoonfuls onto waxed paper. Let stand until cool. Store in an airtight container.
Makes 4 dozen cookies.

Ina Burkhalter
Springfield, Tennessee

PEANUT BUTTER BALLS

$1^1/_2$ cups graham cracker crumbs
$1^1/_2$ cups chunky peanut butter
1 cup (2 sticks) margarine, softened
1 (16-ounce) package confectioners' sugar
1 teaspoon vanilla extract
1 (16-ounce) package chocolate Candy Quick

Combine the graham cracker crumbs, peanut butter, margarine, confectioners' sugar and vanilla in a bowl and mix well. Shape into 1-inch balls and arrange on a baking sheet. Chill, covered, for 1 hour. Melt the chocolate using the package directions. Dip the peanut butter balls into the melted chocolate to coat and remove to waxed paper. Let stand until firm. Makes 30 peanut butter balls.

Carolyn Carter
Antioch, Tennessee

CRUNCH CLUSTERS

2 cups milk chocolate chips
$^1/_2$ cup peanut butter
2 cups dry-roasted peanuts, coarsely chopped

Combine the chocolate chips and peanut butter in a double boiler. Cook over simmering water until melted, stirring occasionally. Stir in the peanuts. Drop by teaspoonfuls onto 2-inch squares of foil or into paper muffin cups. Chill, covered, until serving time. Makes 40 clusters.

Theda Dranes
Mt. Juliet, Tennessee

PECAN LOG ROLLS

1 (12-ounce) box vanilla wafers, crushed
1 (14-ounce) can sweetened condensed milk
1 pound pecan pieces
1 pound (or more) candied cherries, chopped
Chopped candied pineapple (optional)

Mix the vanilla wafers and sweetened condensed milk in a large bowl. Stir in the pecans, cherries and pineapple. Shape into nine 6-inch logs. Chill, wrapped in waxed paper or plastic wrap, for several hours. Serves 50.

Lauraette Cheatham
Nashville, Tennessee

OLD-FASHIONED TEA CAKES

1 cup (2 sticks) butter, softened
1 cup sugar
1 egg, lightly beaten
2 teaspoons baking soda
1/4 cup buttermilk
1 teaspoon vanilla or lemon extract
3 1/2 to 4 cups all-purpose flour

Beat the butter and sugar in a mixing bowl until light and fluffy. Beat in the next 4 ingredients. Stir in the flour until a dough forms. Cover and chill slightly. Roll the dough 1/8 inch thick on a well-floured work surface. Cut into desired shapes. Arrange on a greased cookie sheet using a metal spatula. Bake at 350 degrees for 8 minutes. Remove the cookies to a wire rack to cool. Makes 3 to 4 dozen cookies.

Martha Hammonds
Nashville, Tennessee

BLACK PEPPER COOKIES

1 cup (2 sticks) butter or margarine, softened
3/4 cup packed brown sugar
3/4 cup granulated sugar or equivalent sucralose
1 egg
2 tablespoons molasses or dark corn syrup
3 cups all-purpose flour
2 teaspoons baking soda
2 teaspoons pepper
1 teaspoon ground cinnamon
Tinted sugar (optional)

Beat the butter, brown sugar and granulated sugar in a large bowl until light and fluffy. Beat in the egg and molasses. Mix the flour, baking soda, pepper and cinnamon together. Add to the butter mixture and stir to mix well. Divide the dough into three 1-inch-thick patties. Wrap each pattie in waxed paper and chill for 30 minutes. Roll 1 patty 1/8 inch thick between waxed paper on a work surface. Cut into desired shapes and space widely on an ungreased cookie sheet. Repeat with the remaining dough. Sprinkle with tinted sugar, if desired. Bake at 400 degrees for 7 to 10 minutes. Remove the cookies to a wire rack to cool. Makes 30 cookies.

Bob Jeffries
Southaven, Mississippi

WHOOPIE PIES

2 cups all-purpose flour
2 teaspoons baking powder
2 teaspoons baking soda
1/2 teaspoon salt
1/2 cup (1 stick) unsalted butter, softened
1 cup packed brown sugar
1 teaspoon vanilla extract
2 eggs
1/3 cup baking cocoa
3/4 cup milk
3/4 cup (1 1/2 sticks) butter, softened
3 ounces cream cheese, softened
6 cups confectioners' sugar
2 tablespoons vanilla extract

Mix the first 4 ingredients together. Combine 1/2 cup butter and the brown sugar in a mixing bowl. Beat at medium speed until creamy. Beat in 1 teaspoon vanilla and the eggs.

Add the baking cocoa and beat at low speed until well mixed. Beat in the dry ingredients alternately with the milk in 3 additions. Place a 2 1/2-inch biscuit cutter on a cookie sheet coated with nonstick cooking spray. Spoon 2 tablespoons of the dough into the cutter and spread to smooth. Lift the cutter and move 3 inches. Fill with 2 tablespoons of dough and spread to smooth. Continue filling the cutter to make 30 cookies. Bake at 375 degrees for 11 to 14 minutes. Cool on the cookie sheet for 5 minutes. Remove the cookies to a wire rack to cool completely. Combine 3/4 cup butter, the cream cheese, confectioners' sugar and 2 tablespoons vanilla in a mixing bowl and beat for 5 minutes. Spread 1/4 cup filling over the flat side of 15 cookies. Top with the remaining cookies flat sides down. Store between sheets of waxed paper in an airtight container in the refrigerator. Makes 15 pies.

Donna Burns
Dickson, Tennessee

BANANA CRISPY COOKIES

1/2 cup (1 stick) butter, softened
1 cup packed brown sugar
1/2 cup granulated sugar
2 large ripe bananas, mashed
1 egg
1 teaspoon vanilla extract
1 cup all-purpose flour
1 teaspoon baking powder
1/2 teaspoon salt
1/2 teaspoon ground cinnamon
2 1/2 cups rolled oats
1 cup raisins

Beat the butter, brown sugar and granulated sugar in a mixing bowl until light and fluffy. Stir in the bananas, egg and vanilla. Mix the flour, baking powder, salt and cinnamon together. Add to the butter mixture and mix well. Fold in the oats and raisins. Drop by spoonfuls about 3 inches apart onto a greased cookie sheet. Bake at 350 degrees for 15 to 18 minutes. Remove the cookies to a wire rack to cool. Makes 5 dozen cookies.

Rosalie Williams
Chattanooga, Tennessee

BITS-'O-BRICKLE COOKIES

1 (2-layer) package yellow cake mix
1/2 cup vegetable oil
2 eggs
1 (7 1/2-ounce) package Bits 'O Brickle toffee chips
1/2 cup chopped nuts

Beat the cake mix, oil, eggs, brickle chips and nuts in a mixing bowl. Drop by spoonfuls onto a greased cookie sheet. Bake at 350 degrees for 8 to 10 minutes; do not overbake. Remove the cookies to a wire rack to cool completely.
Makes 3 to 4 dozen cookies.

Faye Richardson
Memphis, Tennessee

MONSTER COOKIES

12 eggs
2 pounds light brown sugar
2 pounds granulated sugar
2 tablespoons vanilla extract
1 tablespoon light corn syrup
2 cups (4 sticks) margarine, softened
5 1/3 cups peanut butter
1 cup all-purpose flour
2 tablespoons plus 1 teaspoon baking soda
1 (16-ounce) package semisweet chocolate chips
1 (16-ounce) package candy-coated chocolate pieces
1 (16-ounce) package butterscotch chips
11 cups quick-cooking oats

Beat the eggs in a large bowl. Add the brown sugar and stir to mix well. Stir in the granulated sugar. Stir in the vanilla and corn syrup. Add the remaining ingredients 1 at a time, stirring after each addition. Drop by tablespoonfuls onto a greased cookie sheet. Bake at 350 degrees for 10 to 12 minutes or until the edges are golden brown. Cool on a wire rack. Makes 15 dozen cookies.

Kathy Duncan
Memphis, Tennessee

DISH PAN COOKIES

2 cups packed dark brown sugar
2 cups granulated sugar
2 cups vegetable oil
4 eggs
2 teaspoons vanilla extract
4 cups all-purpose flour
1 teaspoon salt
1 1/2 teaspoons baking soda
1 1/2 cups rolled oats
2 cups flaked coconut
4 cups whole grain wheat and brown rice flakes cereal
1 1/2 cups pecans

Beat the brown sugar, granulated sugar and oil in a mixing bowl. Beat in the eggs and vanilla. Mix the flour, salt and baking soda together. Add to the brown sugar mixture and stir to mix well. Mix the oats, coconut, cereal and pecans in a large pan. Add the batter and stir to mix well. Drop by teaspoonfuls onto an ungreased cookie sheet. Bake at 325 degrees for 8 to 10 minutes. Note: You may use coconut extract instead of vanilla extract and omit the flaked coconut, if desired. Makes 8 dozen cookies.

Ann Wooten
Cordova, Tennessee

MOTHER'S MACAROONS

4 egg whites
1/4 cup all-purpose flour
2 cups sugar
1 teaspoon vanilla extract
4 cups cornflakes
2 cups flaked coconut

Beat the egg whites in a mixing bowl until stiff peaks form. Stir in the flour, sugar and vanilla. Stir in the cornflakes and coconut. Drop by tablespoonfuls onto a greased cookie sheet. Bake at 400 degrees for 10 minutes or until golden brown. Remove the cookies to a wire rack to cool.
Makes 5 to 6 dozen cookies.

Nancy Bassett
Nashville, Tennessee

BILLY GOAT COOKIES

1 cup (2 sticks) margarine
$1^1/_2$ cups sugar
3 egg yolks
1 teaspoon vanilla extract
$^1/_2$ teaspoon salt
1 teaspoon baking soda
1 teaspoon ground cinnamon
$^1/_2$ teaspoon ground cloves
2 tablespoons buttermilk
2 cups self-rising flour
4 cups chopped pecans
1 pound chopped dates
1 pound raisins
$^1/_2$ cup self-rising flour

Cream the margarine and sugar in a large mixing bowl. Add the egg yolks, vanilla, salt, baking soda, cinnamon, cloves and buttermilk and mix well. Stir in 2 cups flour. Combine the pecans, dates, raisins and $^1/_2$ cup flour in a bowl and mix well. Add to the egg mixture and mix well; the mixture will be stiff. Chill, covered, for 1 hour. Shape into 1-inch balls and arrange on a nonstick cookie sheet. Press lightly with a fork. Bake at 325 degrees for 8 to 10 minutes or until light brown. Cool on the cookie sheet for 2 minutes. Remove to a wire rack to cool completely. Makes 6 to 8 dozen cookies.

Martha Stiles
Knoxville, Tennessee

FRUITCAKE COOKIES

1 pound mixed candied fruit
$^1/_2$ cup all-purpose or self-rising flour
Pinch of salt
2 cups chopped pecans
1 ($3^1/_2$-ounce) can flaked coconut
1 (14-ounce) can sweetened condensed milk

Combine the candied fruit and flour in a bowl and toss to coat. Stir in the salt, pecans and coconut. Add the sweetened condensed milk and stir to mix well. Drop by spoonfuls onto a greased cookie sheet. Bake at 275 degrees for 25 to 30 minutes. Remove the cookies to a wire rack to cool. Store in an airtight container for 5 days before serving.
Makes 3 to 4 dozen cookies.

Edna Lindsey
Maryville, Tennessee

FORGOTTEN COOKIES

2 egg whites
$^{1}/_{4}$ teaspoon cream of tartar
Dash of salt
$^{2}/_{3}$ cup sugar
1 cup chocolate chips
1 cup pecans, chopped
1 teaspoon vanilla extract

Beat the egg whites in a mixing bowl until soft peaks form. Add the cream of tartar, salt and sugar and beat until stiff. Fold in the chocolate chips, pecans and vanilla. Drop by spoonfuls onto a greased cookie sheet. Place in a 350-degree oven and turn off the heat. Leave in the oven for 8 hours without opening the oven door. Makes 3 dozen cookies.

Kaye Lewis
Joelton, Tennessee

LEMON WHIPPERSNAPPER COOKIES

1 (2-layer) package lemon cake mix
2 eggs, beaten
1 (8-ounce) tub frozen whipped topping, thawed
Confectioners' sugar

Combine the cake mix, eggs and whipped topping in a bowl and stir or whisk to mix well. Drop by teaspoonfuls onto a greased cookie sheet dusted with confectioners' sugar. Bake at 350 degrees for 15 minutes. Remove the cookies to a wire rack to cool. Makes 4 dozen cookies.

Ella Mae Hasty
Memphis, Tennessee

OATMEAL COOKIES

3/4 cup shortening
1 cup packed brown sugar
1/2 cup granulated sugar
1 egg
1/4 cup water or milk
1 teaspoon vanilla extract
1 cup all-purpose flour
1 teaspoon salt
1/2 teaspoon baking soda
3 cups rolled oats

Beat the shortening, brown sugar, granulated sugar, egg, water and vanilla in a mixing bowl. Mix the flour, salt and baking soda together. Add to the shortening mixture and stir to mix well. Stir in the oats. Drop by rounded teaspoonfuls onto a nonstick cookie sheet. Bake at 350 degrees for 12 to 15 minutes. Remove the cookies to a wire rack to cool. Note: Use water for a crisp cookie and milk for a soft cookie. Makes 3 dozen cookies.

Ina Burkhalter
Springfield, Tennessee

TOFFEE COOKIES

1 (2-layer) package butter-recipe cake mix
1/2 cup vegetable oil
2 eggs
1/2 cup chopped nuts
1/2 package toffee bits or miniature chocolate chips

Beat the cake mix, oil, eggs, nuts and toffee bits in a bowl. Drop by teaspoonfuls onto an ungreased cookie sheet. Bake at 350 degrees for 12 to 15 minutes; do not overbake. Remove the cookies to a wire rack to cool completely. Makes 2 dozen cookies.

Janice Gibson
Trenton, Tennessee

BROWNIES

1/2 cup (1 stick) margarine
1 cup sugar
1 (16-ounce) can chocolate syrup
4 eggs
1 cup all-purpose flour
1 teaspoon vanilla extract
Frosting

Cream the margarine and sugar in a mixing bowl. Add the chocolate syrup and mix well. Beat in the eggs 1 at a time. Add the flour and vanilla and mix well. Spread evenly in a 10x15-inch baking pan. Bake at 350 degrees for 25 minutes or until the brownies pull away from the sides of the pan. Let stand until cool. Spread the warm frosting over the top. Makes 4 to 5 dozen brownies.

Chocolate Frosting

1/2 cup (1 stick) margarine
1 1/2 cups sugar
1/3 cup evaporated milk
1/2 cup milk chocolate chips
1/2 teaspoon vanilla extract

Combine the margarine, sugar and evaporated milk in a saucepan. Bring to a boil over medium heat. Boil for 1 minute, stirring constantly. Remove from the heat. Add the chocolate chips and stir until melted. Stir in the vanilla.

Judy Knowles
Talbott, Tennessee

BLONDE BROWNIES WITH CHOCOLATE CHIPS

1 cup (2 sticks) margarine
1 (16-ounce) package light brown sugar
2 eggs, lightly beaten
2 cups all-purpose flour
1 cup milk chocolate chips
1 cup chopped pecans (optional)

Melt the margarine in a 9x13-inch baking pan in the oven. Combine the brown sugar and melted margarine in a large bowl and stir to mix well. Add the eggs and stir to mix well. Add the flour 1 cup at a time, mixing well after each addition.

Stir in the chocolate chips and pecans. Pour into the prepared baking pan. Bake at 350 degrees for 30 minutes. Remove to a wire rack to cool. Makes 2 to 3 dozen brownies.

Margaret (Bernie) Wright
Nashville, Tennessee

SOUTHERN BROWNIES

1 cup (2 sticks) margarine, melted
1 1/2 cups self-rising flour
2 cups sugar
6 tablespoons baking cocoa
4 eggs
2 teaspoons vanilla extract
1 cup nuts
Chocolate Frosting

Melt the margarine in a 9x13-inch baking pan in the oven. Mix the flour, sugar, baking cocoa, eggs and vanilla in a bowl. Add the melted margarine and nuts and stir to mix well. Pour into the prepared baking pan. Bake at 375 degrees for 30 minutes. Remove to a wire rack to cool. Spread the Chocolate Frosting over the cooled brownies. Makes 2 to 3 dozen brownies.

Chocolate Frosting

1/4 cup (1/2 stick) margarine
1 cup sugar
1/4 cup baking cocoa
1/3 cup milk
1/4 teaspoon salt
1 teaspoon vanilla extract

Mix the margarine, sugar, baking cocoa, milk, salt and vanilla in a saucepan. Bring to a boil and cook for 1 minute or longer. Remove from the heat and beat to desired consistency.

Elsie Beasley
Lebanon, Tennessee

PUMPKIN BROWNIES

4 eggs
1 cup vegetable oil
2 cups sugar
1 (15-ounce) can pumpkin
2 cups all-purpose flour
1 teaspoon baking powder
1 teaspoon baking soda
1 teaspoon ground cinnamon
1/2 teaspoon salt
Favorite cream cheese frosting or whipped topping
Chopped nuts or candy corn (optional)

Beat the eggs, oil, sugar and pumpkin in a large bowl. Mix the flour, baking powder, baking soda, cinnamon and salt together. Add to the pumpkin mixture and stir to blend. Pour into a greased and floured 9x13-inch baking dish.

Bake at 350 degrees for 30 minutes or until the center springs back when pressed lightly. Remove to a wire rack to cool. Frost with cream cheese frosting and sprinkle with chopped nuts. Makes 2 to 3 dozen brownies.

Deborah Surratt
Bethel Springs, Tennessee

PUMPKIN CHEESECAKE BARS

1 (16-ounce) package pound cake mix
1 egg
2 tablespoons butter, melted
2 teaspoons pumpkin pie spice
8 ounces cream cheese, softened
2 eggs
1 (14-ounce) can sweetened condensed milk
1 (16-ounce) can pumpkin
2 teaspoons pumpkin pie spice
1/2 teaspoon salt
1 cup chopped nuts

Beat the cake mix, 1 egg, the butter and 2 teaspoons pumpkin pie spice in a mixing bowl at low speed until crumbly. Press over the bottom of a nonstick 10x15-inch baking pan. Beat the cream cheese, 2 eggs, sweetened condensed milk, pumpkin, 2 teaspoons pumpkin pie spice and salt in a bowl until well blended. Pour over the prepared layer. Sprinkle with the nuts. Bake at 350 degrees for 30 to 35 minutes. Cool on a wire rack. Makes 5 to 6 dozen bars.

Jeana Pesch
Wartrace, Tennessee

CHESS SQUARES

1 (2-layer) package butter-recipe cake mix
1 egg
$1/2$ cup (1 stick) butter, softened
2 cups chopped pecans
8 ounces cream cheese, softened
$3\,2/3$ cups confectioners' sugar
2 eggs

Stir the cake mix, 1 egg and butter in a bowl. Add the pecans and stir to mix well. Press over the bottom of a greased 9x13-inch baking pan. Beat the cream cheese, confectioners' sugar and 2 eggs in a bowl until smooth. Pour evenly over the prepared layer. Bake at 350 degrees for 45 to 55 minutes or until golden brown. Cool in the pan on a wire rack. Cut into squares. Store, covered, in the refrigerator. Makes 3 dozen squares.

Doris Hight
Bolivar, Tennessee

CHEWY ENGLISH WALNUT BARS

1 cup firmly packed dark brown sugar
$1/4$ cup ($1/2$ stick) butter or margarine, softened
1 egg
1 teaspoon vanilla extract
$1\,1/4$ cups all-purpose flour
$1/4$ teaspoon baking soda
$1/4$ teaspoon salt
1 cup English walnuts, chopped

Combine the brown sugar, butter, egg and vanilla in a mixing bowl. Beat at medium speed until creamy. Mix the flour, baking soda and salt together. Beat into the brown sugar mixture. Stir in the walnuts. Press over the bottom of a greased 8x8-inch baking pan. Bake at 350 degrees for 19 to 20 minutes. Remove to a wire rack to cool completely. Cut into 1x2-inch bars and store in an airtight container. Makes 32 bars.

Nancy Bassett
Nashville, Tennessee

CHOCOLATE TOFFEE BARS

1/2 cup (1 stick) margarine, melted
1 3/4 cups crushed chocolate graham crackers
1 1/4 cups almond brickle chips
6 (1 1/2-ounce) chocolate-covered toffee candy bars
1 cup semisweet chocolate chips
1 cup pecans
1/2 cup walnuts
1 (14-ounce) can sweetened condensed milk

Line a 9x13-inch baking pan with a piece of foil large enough to hang over the edges. Pour the melted margarine evenly in the pan. Sprinkle with the crushed graham crackers and press into the margarine. Bake at 325 degrees for 5 minutes.

Sprinkle with the almond brickle chips and press into the baked layer. Arrange the candy bars in a single layer on top and press into the brickle chips. Sprinkle with the chocolate chips, pecans and walnuts, pressing each layer as added. Drizzle the sweetened condensed milk evenly over the top.

Bake at 325 degrees for 30 minutes or until light brown. Cool in the pan on a wire rack. Lift the foil out of the pan and place on a work surface. Cut into bars. Makes 2 dozen bars.

Wanda (Susie) Ladd
Williamsport, Tennessee

PARTY RAISIN BARS

2 1/4 cups all-purpose flour
1 teaspoon baking powder
1 teaspoon baking soda
1 teaspoon ground cinnamon
1/2 teaspoon ground cloves
1/2 teaspoon ground allspice
1 egg
1 teaspoon vanilla extract
Artificial sweetener equivalent to 6 tablespoons sugar
2 cups unsweetened applesauce
1/4 cup (1/2 stick) margarine, melted
2 tablespoons frozen unsweetened orange juice concentrate, thawed
3/4 cup plus 2 tablespoons raisins
Cream Cheese Frosting

Sift the flour, baking powder, baking soda, cinnamon, cloves and allspice together. Combine the egg, vanilla, artificial sweetener, applesauce, margarine and orange juice concentrate in a mixing bowl. Beat at low speed until smooth. Add the dry ingredients and beat at low speed until moistened. Beat at medium speed for 2 minutes. Stir in the raisins. Spread evenly in a 10x15-inch baking pan coated with nonstick cooking spray. Bake at 350 degrees for 15 minutes. Remove to a wire rack to cool. Spread the Cream Cheese Frosting over the cooled bars. Chill, covered, until serving time. Cut into bars and serve. Makes 5 to 6 dozen bars.

Cream Cheese Frosting

8 ounces low-fat cream cheese, softened
1 tablespoon vanilla extract
Artificial sweetener equivalent to 1/2 cup sugar

Beat the cream cheese, vanilla and sweetener in a bowl until smooth.

Betty Shields
Morristown, Tennessee

INDEX

This Cookbook is a perfect gift for Holidays, Weddings, Anniversaries, and Birthdays.

To order, mail a check to: Tennessee Chapter No. 21
TelecomPioneers
333 Commerce Street, Suite 2107
Nashville, Tennessee 37201-3300

Or you may order by credit card from our website at:
www.bellsouthtnpioneers.org

Cookbooks	Qty.	Price*	Total
Dining With Pioneers, Vol. I		$12.00	$
~~Dining With Pioneers, Vol. II~~		~~$10.00~~	**out of print**
Dining With Pioneers, Vol III		$12.00	$
Answering the Call of Those in Need (limited quantities available)		$ 3.00	$
Add $2.75 postage, handling, and tax per book			$
Grand Total			$

*Prices subject to change.

Please Print:

Name ____________________

Address ____________________

Work Address ____________________

Floor or Room No. ____________________

City ____________ State ______ Zip ______

Please make check payable to TelecomPioneers Chapter No. 21.

Photocopies will be accepted.